CHANGE AGENTS

Manuel London

CHANGE AGENTS

New Roles and Innovation Strategies for Human Resource Professionals

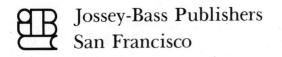

Jossey-Bass Publishers
San Francisco

CHANGE AGENTS
New Roles and Innovation Strategies for Human Resource Professionals
   by Manuel London

Copyright © 1988 by: Jossey-Bass Inc., Publishers
                     350 Sansome Street
                     San Francisco, California 94104

Library of Congress Cataloging-in-Publication Data

London, Manuel.
   Change agents.

   (Jossey-Bass management series)
   Bibliography: p.
   Includes index.
   1. Organizational change. 2. Personnel management.
I. Title. II. Series.
HD58.8.L66   1988   658.3   88-42793
ISBN 1-55542-107-5

Manufactured in the United States of America. Nearly all Jossey-Bass
books and jackets are printed on recycled paper that contains at least
50 percent recycled waste, including 10 percent postconsumer waste.
Many of our materials are also printed with vegetable-based ink; during
the printing process these inks emit fewer volatile organic compounds
(VOCs) than petroleum-based inks. VOCs contribute to the formation of
smog.

JACKET DESIGN BY WILLI BAUM

FIRST EDITION

HB Printing   10 9 8 7 6 5 4 3

Code 8837

The Jossey-Bass Management Series

For Harold and Estelle Mitnick

CONTENTS

Part Three: Human Resource Interventions
to Enhance Change

PREFACE

The challenges for management in today's business environment arise from deregulation, economic shifts, foreign competition, technological advancements, and attitudinal changes about work. Organizational responses have included force downsizing, flatter organizational structures, increased managerial responsibilities, and greater attention to improving productivity and quality while simultaneously reducing costs.

Human resource professionals must understand the roles of leaders and managers as change agents and how human resource policies and programs can contribute to organizational change. In general, leaders formulate change strategies and direct implementation. Mid- and lower-level managers refine and carry out the plans. Human resource professionals create and support change efforts to enhance the growth and productivity of employees. All three—leaders, managers, and human resource professionals—must be able to envision organizational trends, create responses that fit their units, and meet both organizational and customer needs. To do this, they must be change agents. This book will help them to understand what change is needed and then bring it about. In this book I describe the roles of change agents and how they can prepare themselves and others to handle change. I demonstrate ways to implement and track change efforts inside the organization and to involve employees in the process in order to ensure their commitment to the change.

In *Change Agents,* I use examples of several major organizational changes. For instance, I describe one organization's transformation from a bureaucratic stock and bond department to a flexible organization with a semiautonomous workgroup structure. Another example is of the movement of a stodgy, tradition-bound institution to a client-sensitive, market-driven organization. I give several examples of the effects of technological change on employees. One case, involving the introduction of a computerized central monitoring system, demonstrates the impact of new technology on workers' interpersonal relationships, status, and skill use. This example also illustrates the value of worker participation in the acceptance of a cost-saving, leading-edge technology. In another case I examine the adoption of an electronic mail system at a nationwide corporation to understand how the new technology affects the process of work. In addition to technological change, I consider organizational system changes, specifically, the introduction of participative management and quality of worklife programs, which involve workers in important decisions affecting them.

To be effective, human resource professionals need to understand change from the perspectives of the leaders and managers they support as well as from their own perspective. Human resource professionals have multiple roles in organizations: they are educators, innovators, evaluators, leaders, change agents, consultants, and futurists. Organizations accomplish their goals through people. In many cases today, the quality of employees—not new technology—is the differentiating factor in giving businesses a competitive advantage in the marketplace. Consequently, personnel managers must ensure that human resource strategies contribute to the organization's success.

Human resource programs and interventions are a powerful way for organizations not only to do what they do better but also to transform themselves and thereby find new ways of being successful. Organizational transformation is needed to keep pace with the many forces for change in today's environment. Human resource professionals can help by interpreting these forces for change, preparing managers to be agents for change, and acting as change agents themselves, for example, by designing and initiating employee involvement programs to enhance productivity and employee morale.

The tools of the personnel manager are effective when they are used by organizational leaders and managers to understand, guide, and transform their organizations. *Change Agents* can help human resource professionals develop their expertise in interpreting forces for change, understanding the change agent role, developing change agents, and understanding and facilitating the change process. The book shows how the structure of the personnel department influences how the leader and line manager view their roles as human resource managers. It demonstrates how information from employees—gathered through attitude surveys and program evaluations—helps calibrate and reset the direction of the organization. In addition, this book describes how the personnel function assists in taking a forward look by forecasting external and internal trends and planning to meet the organization's future human resource requirements.

The competence of a change agent is dependent on skills, experience, and attitude. Change agents need the *resilience* to believe in themselves, to want to achieve, and to be willing to take risks in a changing environment. They need the *insight* into themselves and the organization to initiate change and make the change process successful. Moreover, they need a sense of *identity* to guide the organization through internal and environmental changes. This book describes these managerial characteristics and how they are developed.

My choice of examples and topics for this book stems from my experiences as an observer of change and as a participant in change processes—in some cases playing a major role in the design and introduction of change and in other cases playing the role of a manager anticipating and experiencing change. In this book, I have not covered all the ways human resource professionals can contribute to change but rather those that I know most about—that is, manager development, program evaluation, attitude surveys, organizational design, forecasting and planning, and quality of worklife or employee involvement programs. I have tried to communicate what I have learned from my own experiences in a way that will be valuable to human resource professionals in different organizations with different resources and problems. Overall, my goal is to show that being aware of change processes and ways to influence them will bind the human resource function to the mission of the organization and make human resources—both in terms of the function and the people—a driving force for successful change.

Audience

This book is for human resource professionals—personnel managers, researchers, and organization development specialists. It is also for leaders, managers, and students who want to understand how they might contribute to organizational change.

Overview of the Contents

Part One sets the scene and describes the characters in the change drama. The introductory chapter examines the roles of the human resource professional in the context of organizational change. In this chapter I summarize the human resource professional's responsibilities for understanding and responding to the forces for change; the importance of employee involvement to effective organizational adaptation; and the ways organization design, survey feedback, program evaluation, and forecasting and planning contribute to successful change. I discuss several reasons why human resource professionals need to be concerned about change: even in a stable environment, skills must be replenished as people leave the organization; business environments change; organizations must respond to competition, new markets, new customer expectations, new technologies; and more. The personnel function must help provide the people needed to accomplish the organization's changing business strategies. In addition, our way of doing business is changing. The global, high-technology environment demands strong workteams that bring together diverse functions to customize solutions to business problems. In Chapter One I discuss the multiple roles of human resource professionals for bringing about such changes today and in the future. Thus, human resource strategy becomes an extension of a corporation's business strategy, and human resource professionals are full partners with leaders and line managers in setting the organization's objectives and achieving success.

Chapters Two and Three outline the forces for change and the roles and characteristics of change agents. In Chapter Two I examine the major forces of the last ten years and then anticipate future trends. The outside environment is increasingly complex, with managers facing multiple constituencies, changing social values, governmental control, and stiff competition for top talent. Inside the organization, there are the need for more interdepartmental cooperation, the need for an increased market orientation, the need for a recognition of employees' quality of life inside and outside of work, and the need to respond to the changing environmental forces. In this chapter I describe how business direction—decline, mergers, acquisitions, growth, start-up, and redirection—influence corporate leaders' actions, employees' reactions, and human resource strategies. I conclude the chapter by anticipating the need for changing work structures to match internal and external forces.

Chapter Three focuses on the roles of corporate change agents—leaders, managers, and human resource professionals. The chapter begins with an examination of the influence of a leader on the company's direction. Using the examples of several CEOs, I show the leader's influence on the culture of the organization, the support given to employee development, and the rewards for participative management. I discuss the importance of a leader's resilience, insight, and sense of identity as ingredients in establishing a successful course for the organization. In this chapter I also outline leaders' and managers' roles as change generators, implementors, and adopters. Also addressed are the roles of human resource professionals as organization-effectiveness consultants and contributors to the accomplishment of business objectives. The personnel function is viewed both as supporting the leaders' and line managers' efforts to introduce change and as having a major influence on the firm's strategic direction.

Part Two describes how human resource professionals

change people and organizational cultures. In Chapter Four I consider how to prepare managers to handle change and how to develop competent change agents. This chapter shows how leaders, managers, and human resource professionals alike learn to envision and implement change and, in the process, educate others to new ways of managing. I offer guidelines for developing and reinforcing employees' resilience, insight, and sense of identity by providing job opportunities, performance feedback, information about the organization, and rewards and recognition. Change agents develop through job experiences that include ambiguous, unstable situations that require flexibility, perceptiveness, conviction, the ability to communicate clearly, a willingness to share information, and a willingness to involve others in problem solving and decision making. Overall, in this chapter I consider ways to accelerate manager development through critical job experiences and training. As a result of using these methods, managers can be better prepared to respond to environmental change.

In Chapter Five I examine cases of slow, progressive organizational change and rapid, dramatic organizational change. The former, called *incremental change,* maintains the values and mission of the organization while responding to changing marketplace demands and more efficient methods of operation. The latter, called *frame-breaking change,* radically alters corporate goals, organizational structures, and ways people work together. The examples I have chosen show the effects of technological change on employees and how employee involvement in technological design and implementation enhances its acceptance and value.

Chapter Six examines employee involvement programs as an important direction for organizational change. In this chapter I begin with how the role of managers is changing in many organizations from that of by-the-books bureaucrats to that of participative change agents. I then describe quality circle (QC) and quality of worklife (QWL) programs, which involve employees in improving the work environment and achieving business goals. QWL programs call for managerial behaviors and attitudes that support a participative environment. I discuss methods of facilitating the introduction of QWL programs and ways to avoid program decline and failure, applying the stages of change introduced in the previous chapter. Chapter Six also describes the evolution of QWL programs. I use examples to show the different degrees to which QWL can be incorporated into the work environment, including an example in which union officials and middle managers work together in common interest forums to accomplish business and union objectives. In this chapter I offer a method to evaluate the progress of a QWL effort and suggest ways to develop a QWL program, moving it from a structured process focusing on environmental issues to a dynamic, open process focusing on ways to improve productivity.

Part Three examines some other human resource interventions for change: organizational design of the personnel department, human resource forecasting and planning, and evaluation and survey feedback. In Chapter Seven I demonstrate the influence of a corporate personnel department's structure on how well human resource professionals work together to ensure responsiveness to the employees and departments they serve. The personnel department's design reflects the company's philosophy about who should be in control of human resource management: the personnel department or the line departments. Moreover, the example I have chosen shows how employees can be involved in the process of designing a department's structure and how a company's vision for the future should be evident in its plans for an evolving organization that matches environmental changes. For instance, the organization may require that human resource professionals take control of policies and programs. As the organization matures, the structure design can allow these professionals to become facilitators and consultants to managers in other departments who have the knowledge, skills, and awareness to meet organizational needs and can be held accountable for organizational outcomes. Thus, organization design becomes a vehicle for change, and involving employees in the design process is a way to bring about this change.

In Chapter Eight I return to a discussion of the forces for change I introduced in Chapter Two. Chapter Eight describes the human resource professional's role in forecasting and planning for the future. In this chapter I emphasize the value of linking human resource planning to the business plans of the corporation—that is, making the people in the company a major, strategic resource for accomplishing business goals. Environmental scanning and internal labor force analysis are outlined, and the roles of the line departments and corporate headquarters in applying this information are considered. I then describe the establishment of a human resource forecasting and planning function as a vehicle for change and give several different suggestions for starting up such an effort: collecting data on employee retirement eligibility over the next ten years, conducting an environmental scan of issues affecting the organization, using outside experts, visiting other companies to find out how they do human resource forecasting and planning, holding a conference for the company's business planners and personnel managers on environmental trends, and building scenarios for the future.

Chapter Nine covers ways to evaluate change. I begin with an overview of evaluation methods and designs, which can be used by human resource professionals to educate line managers about the importance of tracking program success. In this chapter I highlight the manager's role as experimenter and program evaluator. Leaders and managers faced with scarcity of resources and the need for cost control must establish criteria for the success of their change efforts. I review measurement techniques, evaluation procedures, research designs, and the applicability of results. The traditional scientific method of evaluation is compared to an action research approach. In this chapter I also cover ways to assess the cost-benefit ratio of a change effort.

In Chapter Nine I also give examples of program evaluations. The projects I describe were conducted by an organizational unit devoted to helping managers in line departments evaluate change programs. While such a unit does not exist in every personnel department, this kind of evaluation can also be conducted by human resource professionals, external consultants, and line managers who understand the evaluation methods detailed in this chapter. The projects I review in Chapter Nine show the impact of changes on employees: examples include evaluating a new job design, a training program for how to use a new telecommunications system, the change in organizational culture resulting from merging departments, and the process of socializing new managers. Finally, Chapter Nine describes survey feedback as an evaluative process for tracking the effects of change.

Chapter Ten highlights the conclusions of the book and offers advice for the future. Leaders, managers, and human resource professionals should understand change processes and effective intervention points. As change agents, they create opportunities and move the organization forward in response to environmental trends and customer needs. Human resource professionals should be role models, showing leaders and managers how to create and facilitate change and demonstrating the importance of human resource management to accomplishing business objectives.

The guidelines in Appendix A show the value to managers of feedback from employees, who have a valuable perspective on the way work is done. For instance, the results of employee attitude surveys help managers understand the extent to which managerial actions and strategies in response to environmental changes are understood by workers. Moreover, the survey process itself is a change intervention, which serves to increase worker involvement and to identify worker needs and expectations. In Appendix A I describe different uses for attitude survey information, for example, general diagnosis and problem focus; conditions for obtaining high-quality information; methods of data collection; the importance of feeding back the overall results to the employees who supplied the information; and methods to apply the results.

In Appendix B I summarize the literature on feedback as the foundation for evaluating change in general and for understanding the effectiveness of survey methods.

Acknowledgments

Many of the ideas and examples in this book stem from my experiences at American Telephone and Telegraph. I am grateful for the support and encouragement of the people I have worked for, most recently Curtis Artis, G. Robert Dobbs, and

John Fernandez. I fondly recall the memory of Bent Jensen, my former boss, who taught me to value differences in people, to create a participative work environment, to serve the people I lead, and to understand the needs of the clients I serve. I am indebted to the people who have worked for me, many of whom are acknowledged at relevant points in this book, for their contributions to the programs and research I discuss. Four members of my workgroup have been especially helpful: Anthony DeNicola has been a source of new ideas and a wealth of practical knowledge concerning organization effectiveness; Rosemary O'Connor and Linda Streit are highly competent professionals whose insights and successful client applications contributed to the success of our workgroup; and Annemarie Biondi has been invaluable in diligently organizing and proofreading the manuscript for this book as it progressed.

My wife, Marilyn, and children, David and Jared, deserve my love and gratitude for their patience and encouragement. I have spent most of my evenings and weekends engaged in professional activities, including writing, and they have understood my continuing need for professional involvement and contribution. Finally, this book is dedicated to my mother- and father-in-law for all their love and kindness.

Belle Mead   Manuel London
Montgomery Township, New Jersey
June 1988

THE AUTHOR

Manuel London is a district manager of planning and management systems for American Telephone and Telegraph's (AT&T's) Network and Operations Education and Training Organization. London has been involved in a variety of human resource functions at AT&T since 1977, including human resource forecasting and planning, organizational development, and personnel research. From 1974 to 1977 he taught in the business school of the University of Illinois in Urbana. He received his A.B. degree (1971) from Case Western Reserve University in philosophy and psychology and his M.A. (1972) and Ph.D. (1974) degrees from the Ohio State University in industrial and organizational psychology.

London's main research activities have been in manager development and career decisions. He has also conducted research on the relationship between work and nonwork behavior and has written on ethical issues in personnel decisions. He was a consulting editor for the *Academy of Management Journal* and is now a member of the editorial boards of *Personnel Psychology,* the *Journal of Applied Psychology, Administrative Science Quarterly,* and the *Journal of Management Development.* He has written more than thirty papers and thirty book reviews and is the author of *Managing Careers* (1982, with S. A. Stumpf), *Developing Managers* (1985), *Career Management and Survival in the Workplace* (1987, with E. M. Mone), and *Career Growth and Human Resource Strategies* (forthcoming, edited with E. M. Mone).

CHANGE AGENTS

1

Introduction: Human Resource Professionals and Organizational Change

 Change is inevitable in all organizations. Even in periods of stability, change occurs to replenish lost skills as people leave due to retirement, death, disability, and resignation. This ongoing change requires continuous recruitment, selection, socialization, and training strategies.

On a more dynamic level, environmental change requires that the organization formulate, revise, and reformulate strategies. Changing competition, marketplace demands, new products and services, labor market availability, and economic conditions are examples of factors that cause an organization to adjust or redirect its business approach. In addition, the business environment is likely to change in an effort to reduce costs and maintain competitiveness. Organizational structures are likely to be flatter and staffs are likely to be slimmer. Employees will have to have a more competitive attitude. New technology will require continuous learning.

These changes often entail new ways of working for employees in general and for human resource professionals in particular. For example, consider the advent of the information "node." This is essentially the intelligence behind information

1

transmission. A nodal system is a computer series that processes and directs information over different channels. The computers receive information, process it, specify channels for transmission, and then, at the receiving end, convert and/or combine the information to meet users' needs. There are many ways to transmit information, such as fiber optics, satellites, and cable. Opportunity for profit comes by adding value to the information—not just conveying it, but digesting it, and then determining how it should be transmitted for least cost and maximum efficiency. The computer processing may occur at the source of the information or at any point along the way to its final destination.

The battle is now on in the telecommunications industry between carriers of information that try to be dominant suppliers of the information node. Long-distance carriers, local telephone companies, computer manufacturers, large business users, and private exchange companies, to name some of the players, are vying for a role in supplying this profitable value-added resource to the customer. In one case, several organizations have established a joint venture to build a teleport that will analyze, merge, and process information and then transmit it by alternative routes.

The nodal system changes the nature of the work and the way organizations work together. Customers and suppliers become business partners as they attempt to supply networking solutions to information management and movement problems. The numerous possible configurations increase the number of players involved and the alternatives available to customers. Both managers and technicians must learn new ways of working together to keep up with technological advancements and to respond knowledgeably and quickly to customer demands. Human resource professionals may be called on to facilitate work-team development, provide training, and design appropriate reward and recognition systems to reinforce effective team behavior. They will be expected by top management to understand the new directions of the business and what they mean for human resource strategies.

Some of these changes are incremental in that they happen slowly. We are also seeing broad, frame-breaking organizational changes. This is explained well by Robert Reich in *The Next American Frontier:*

> Once again the economic context has changed, and our institutions are coming under pressure to evolve. A rigid management-centered organization has become inappropriate to an America now linked to an integrated world economy. That pattern of organization can be duplicated anywhere on the globe, including areas with lower-wage labor and cheaper access to raw materials and emerging markets. Since 1970, therefore, the economies of America and every other industrialized nation have undergone a profound structural change, as the high-volume industries that underpinned these economies in the previous half century—steel, textiles, automobiles, rubber, shipping, and chemicals —have become less competitive in world markets. The only way industrialized nations can increase their citizens' standards of living in the future is to concentrate on the high-valued niches within these industries and to seize and keep world leadership in new industries based on advanced and emerging technologies. This requires a different form of organization, one far more flexible and adaptable then the structure designed to support high-volume, standardized production [Reich, 1983, p. 231].

Organizations are moving toward increased customization of automation. Just-in-time manufacturing systems are one example. General Motors' Saturn plant, for instance, was intended to manufacture cars directly from customer specifications typed into a computer on the sales floor. Customers want short delivery cycles and enhanced quality. In a global marketplace with inexpensive labor abroad and with routinized, automated work moving abroad to take advantage of that inexpensive labor, workers in the United States must cooperate with each other and with management. Rather than be constrained by the precise measurement of work possible from new technology, workers must be empowered to use their own judgment in applying these technologies (Howard, 1986). Individual needs and organizational goals must be complementary. Employees will have to develop their skills continuously. Their job stability will come from contributing to the success of the organization. The organization will evolve through new alliances and/or acquisitions, and employees will be called on to work together to make these alliances successful.

These changes will require leaders, managers, and occupational workers to apply whatever resources are necessary to provide a product or service. Customers will expect all employees they deal with (from technical workers to top managers) to be knowledgeable about their businesses. These workers will have to integrate diverse functions (finance, manufacturing, operations, and marketing). Workteams will include customers and suppliers. Prime attention will be paid to process quality and cost effectiveness. Employees will have to learn to diagnose and anticipate customer needs and champion innovations. The keynote of the corporate environment will be employee involvement.

In addition, employees at all levels will need multicultural skills. The growing number of minorities in the United States (see Chapter Eight), indicates the need to understand cultural diversity in customers and the labor pool. Also, operating in a global environment requires understanding how to do business abroad. U.S. managers have a long way to go to cross cultural and language barriers. Human resource professionals will help to provide the systems for attracting, developing, and motivating employees in this diversified climate.

Problems and Pitfalls in Managing Change

Introducing organizational change is not usually a simple matter of generating ideas, designing plans and programs, implementing them, and watching their adoption throughout the organization. Change often encounters resistance. The goals and benefits may not be clear. The people affected may perceive risk, perhaps to their job security. People resist change just because it upsets the normal way of doing things, and so they feel a sense of discomfort and possibly anxiety. There are many danger signals of resistance to change: complaints; slow responses to requests; avoiding the topic; attempts to exert influence; increases in medical problems; absenteeism; tardiness; and lower productivity. The many potential barriers to change create the need for consultants to help leaders and managers through the process.

The Dark Side of Change for Human Resource Professionals

Human resource professionals should not be discouraged by the dark side of organizational change. Like other managers in a changing organization, human resource professionals face uncertainty about their job security and ambiguity about what they are expected to do. Change often imposes time pressures to institute new policies and programs. Organizational growth may require beefed-up recruiting and selection systems. A change in corporate direction may require communications and training programs to reach large numbers of employees. An organizational start-up may give the human resource professional the latitude to set policies and institute new programs, but these programs must be responsive to the immediate needs of the corporation. Mergers and acquisitions may require bringing together two personnel departments, and may result in jobs lost, and winners and losers in terms of which firm's policies and programs are adopted. Organizational downsizing may call on the human resource professional to design ways to identify people who should leave and then shepherd them through the outplacement process. In one case a human resource manager with seven years' experience in her firm was in charge of firing many competent people with far more tenure than she had. In another situation, the personnel manager lost his own job after he completed removing others from the payroll. Another source of strain faced by human resource professionals is an early career plateau. Human resource professionals must help themselves as well as other employees whose careers are plateaued because of organizational cutbacks. In addition, human resource professionals may be called on to evaluate programs and employee attitudes. As a result, they risk being messengers of bad news, which is all the worse when they encouraged and forced the evaluation in the first place.

Characteristics for Managing Change:
Resilience, Insight, and Identity

Leaders, managers, and human resource professionals will need competence to manage change. This competence is not simply a matter of new or different skills that are needed under changing circumstances. For example, organizing, problem solving, decision making, negotiating, and leading are, and will continue to be, critical managerial skills. However, in fluid, often ambiguous environments, these skills may be applied in new and different ways. (Chapters Three and Four discuss the importance of resilience, insight, and identity as key characteristics for managing change.) Resilient people have a sense of self-confidence; they want to achieve; and they demonstrate willingness to take risks. They are able to withstand the stress of change. People with insight understand their strengths and weaknesses and the social and political environment in which they function. Moreover, they are able to rise above the fray and see the whole organizational picture. Those with a strong sense of identity have a clear direction for themselves and the groups they manage. The organization builds and reinforces these characteristics by the opportunities and rewards it offers and the feedback and information it provides. Action learning through planned experiences and constant questioning is a way to prepare for success in dynamic organizational climates (see Chapter Four).

In addition to these personality characteristics, leaders, managers, and human resource professionals will need job experience, knowledge, and value systems that prepare them to function in a highly charged, changing environment. They will be champions of innovation. They will understand systems and functional integration. They will understand organization development and know how to generate self-managing workteams.

They will have had experience in different business contexts (start-ups, growing organizations, mergers, corporate redirections, and declining units). They will see the "big picture." Rather than have a narrow product or service focus, they will focus on creative, realistic solutions to business problems, and they will develop and articulate visions for the future.

Knowledge may be required in specific areas important to a business, such as knowledge of asset management techniques to do a better job at cost control. Knowledge of foreign languages and how to do business in different cultures may be necessary in growing multinational corporations. Knowledge of public and government affairs may be critical because of regulation and legislation in such areas as prices, foreign trade, employee relations, and environmental safety.

Values are also important in organizations trying to become more participative in nature. It is not enough to understand the meaning of employee involvement and self-managing workteams or to have knowledge of team-building exercises. Leaders, managers, and human resource professionals must value the input of others and be willing to contribute to team success as leaders or participants—possibly at the expense of making themselves look better.

Multiple Roles for Human Resource Professionals

Given the diversity and change in individual characteristics and business conditions, there is no one role for the human resource professional. The response of a personnel department to its clients in the organization will depend on the needs of the client departments (Chapter Seven). For instance, how much should a human resource manager control line managers' freedom to make decisions about employees? This depends on the importance of the issues, the willingness of the leadership to hold line managers accountable for managing people, and the knowledge and ability of line managers to do so (for example, hire minorities, train and give feedback to subordinates, and allocate merit increases in pay).

In general, human resource professionals should be able

to analyze the corporation's needs, anticipate and communicate these needs, and raise them for discussion in the corporation. In the process, human resource professionals generate consensus on solutions to the issues. They establish accountability and provide the necessary support to the managers who are accountable for carrying out the solutions. Sometimes the solutions necessitate central control and uniformity, and the personnel department will be accountable for the outcome or for monitoring the outcome. At other times, the solution must be close to the line department, and the line manager will retain accountability and the freedom to act. Consequently the responses will vary from department to department and within departments. Human resource professionals add value by helping managers share ideas and experiences and by consulting with line managers and tailoring programs to meet their needs.

The extent to which line managers will adopt the role of human resource manager and developer will depend on the extent to which this role is valued (rewarded) by the corporation. This depends on the value the company's leaders place in employees, treating them as resources for the future or instruments to accomplishing immediate business goals.

Educators and Developers. Consider the human resource professional's role in educating line managers to develop employees for current and future job requirements. Human resource professionals design and deliver training programs to help managers understand their role as developers of people. A developer role is an important part of each manager's job. Yet it is a role managers are likely to ignore, given heavy job demands. Also, many managers do not feel as comfortable developing people as they do with other aspects of management, such as providing direction and control. Giving subordinates performance feedback and working with them to improve their skills and offer them broader experiences takes time and may seem to be at the expense of accomplishing short-term departmental objectives. The organization can make the development role salient by rewarding managers for developing subordinates.

Courses may be necessary to help managers understand

the meaning of developing subordinates and of allowing them to acquire and practice related supervisory skills. One company developed a one-day seminar to remind managers of their responsibilities as developers. The seminar gave participants an opportunity to discuss the barriers in the company to developing subordinates and ways to overcome those barriers. Corporate resources for improving managerial skills associated with developing people were highlighted, such as training programs, the staffing system, and career planning forms and procedures.

The human resource professional needs to understand the educational value of key job experiences. After all, employee development is more likely to take place on the job than in the classroom (see Chapter Four). Each job assignment has the potential for teaching the employee new skills.

Some companies want managers to have a variety of job experiences so they can handle any situation. Other companies want managers to specialize in particular situations. The human resource staff must understand the needs of the business and individual career needs. Also, the staff must recognize the educational value of different job experiences, such as spearheading a new venture, managing a fast-growing unit, maintaining the profitability of a stable unit, coordinating the merger of two departments or the acquisition of a subsidiary, or overseeing the dissolution of a department.

The future will require human resource professionals to understand and support a continuous learning environment where employees have opportunities to acquire and apply new skills. Corporations may support career changes by sponsoring courses and degree programs for retraining to meet the changing needs of the business. Also, periodic refresher courses may be crucial to ensure that managers have the latest technical and managerial skills. Another role for the human resource professional is to educate corporate leaders and line managers on the importance of valuing people, and educating managers in the tools, programs, and policies that support employee development.

Innovators. Just as any organization is concerned with meeting customer needs, a personnel department must anticipate its clients' objectives and provide innovative policies and programs in relationship to these objectives. The human resource professional must stay abreast of developments in such fields as personnel psychology, career development, organizational behavior, organizational development, human resource planning, and strategic management. The human resource professional must also study competitors and other companies thought to have excellent management. In doing so, human resource professionals maintain their own expertise and are able to make timely, creative contributions to their organization.

Evaluators. Top management will increasingly expect human resource professionals to evaluate personnel policies and programs in order to demonstrate the latter's effectiveness. Human resource professionals will have to show that personnel programs and policies meet the strategic directions of the business. They will also have to establish criteria for the success of these programs—criteria that are ultimately associated with bottom-line financial performance. Satisfaction measures can assess participants' attitudes about a career planning workshop or other training programs. Employee attitude surveys can tap feelings about career opportunities, the company's support for women and minorities, beliefs about the company as a good place to work, and perceptions about specific change efforts. Utility analyses can estimate the incremental cost-benefit of new selection and new training programs. Research designs can compare groups attending various versions of a training program against control groups who are withheld from the program (see Chapter Nine).

   The human resource professional may have to demonstrate the relationship between such research measures and bottom-line results. This is particularly a problem with data on employee morale. Several studies indicate that employees are happier in companies that have better financial performance. Whether such results indicate that high morale encourages good financial results is difficult to say. However, the human resource professional can make a cogent argument that enhancing employee morale is an integral part of the way top-performing companies do business. The human resource professional may also be asked to compare the company to other corporations in the same industry to assess competitive advantage (for instance, on executive compensation and the ability to attract top talent).

Leaders. Earlier in this chapter and later in Chapter Seven, I raise what is essentially a dialectic between the human resource professional as the conscience of the corporation, the advocate of the employee, and the ensurer of equitable treatment versus the human resource professional as provider of resources to the line manager who has the ultimate responsibility for human resource management and the freedom to act to carry out this responsibility. This dialectic is resolved by a delicate balancing act of human resource professionals who vary their stance (control versus facilitation) depending on the issues. (For example, equal employment opportunity probably requires more central control than employee development, although admittedly these two areas are related.)

The human resource professional faces another dialectic: providing staff support that is responsive to client needs versus providing strategic initiatives and directions for the corporation's leaders and managers to follow. This leadership will treat human resource management as a major business function and treat people as a competitive advantage. In this sense, the human resource department is responsible for integrating human resource management activities in all parts of the business. It is responsible for identifying and educating managers on better ways of managing, such as designing self-managing workteams, promoting quality of worklife programs, and instituting an employee development ethic in the business. This requires proving the value of personnel programs to the corporation. It also demands an acute awareness of the business as a whole, which can only occur if human resource professionals work as part of a team with leaders and managers in other departments to establish and implement a strategic direction for the organization.

Change Agents. Organizational change agents are leaders and managers who see a need for change, conceptualize and design

the change, implement it, and/or adopt the change. (See Chapter
Three's examples of leaders and managers as change agents.) Although human resource professionals provide support for these
change agents in the form of consultation and facilitation (as
shown in Chapter Three), these professionals may lead the change
or be coleaders with influential leaders and line managers. For
instance, in preparing people to handle change through training
and job experiences (the subject of Chapter Four) and changing
the culture of the organization by making it more customer responsive (Chapter Five) or by increasing employee involvement
and commitment (Chapter Six), human resource professionals are
change generators, implementors, and adopters (Ottaway, 1983).

As change generators, human resource professionals express the needs of the organization, demonstrate the change (for
instance, by creating a client-responsive personnel department),
provide funding for the change in other departments (for example, by paying for a survey feedback process, as outlined in
Chapter Nine), and/or defend the change to others in the organization. As a change implementor, the human resource professional may articulate a leader's vision and possibly assume responsibility for designing and carrying out the change in a client's
organization with client representatives. As a change adopter,
the human resource professional may be the first to try a program (for example, a new training program or a method for
forecasting human resource needs).

Consultants. The human resource professional can facilitate
change by helping managers share ideas and by helping departments coordinate their objectives for people development. For
example, departments are likely to vary in what they feel is
necessary for development of their employees. Marketing departments may want to develop marketing experts. Finance departments may want to develop financial experts. Other departments may prefer generalist managers who have a broad base of
experience in the company and who can pick up technical information quickly as they move from job to job. The human
resource professional can work with each department to design
appropriate development programs. The human resource profes-

sional can bring departmental representatives together to discuss their common needs and how they can work on joint programs.

The consultant's role may be directive or nondirective. In a directive role, the human resource professional initiates an action, often in concert with a principal change agent who may be a leader or line manager. As a nondirective consultant, the human resource professional provides information or suggests change. Consultant roles include asking clients reflective questions to help them think through the details of a change, and serving as a process consultant to improve interpersonal relationships. Human resource professionals as consultants are also fact finders, possibly evaluating the success of change efforts, as described in Chapter Nine. The human resource professional may be called on to identify alternatives, perhaps based on knowledge of what other companies are doing (for example, to plan for future human resource needs; see Chapter Eight). Also, the human resource professional may be viewed as a problem-solver in formulating a course of action.

The roles of human resource professional as change agent and consultant will be evident in the examples throughout the book. Chapter Three includes a section on guidelines for when a change agent should use a consultant and guidelines for selecting a consultant—information that can help human resource professionals be better consultants and choose consultants for themselves.

Futurists. The human resource professional is a futurist who analyzes internal and external trends, develops forecasts for future human resource needs, and incorporates these forecasts into business objectives to formulate human resource plans (Chapters Two and Eight). Human resource professionals must communicate the results of these analyses to leaders and managers. Thinking about the future helps people to interpret events. For example, knowing that there is an increase in the number of workers with children helps a manager understand why a subordinate with a child-care problem is frequently late for work. If choices are available, a view to the future helps managers make these choices—for instance, whether to initiate

an on-premises child-care program and/or to invoke punish-
ments for tardiness. Considering the future helps people identify where they have no control and where there is a need to
develop coping mechanisms (J. F. Coates, Jr., personal communication, July 16, 1987). It also shows opportunities for building success. For example, knowing that many of the brightest
new scientists are Asians suggests that developing an organizational climate that will attract and motivate them will be important to the company's success in research and development.

Conclusion

There are exciting possibilities for people in the human
resource field. Rather than just providing services to meet client
demands, the human resource manager helps clients to understand their needs and educates clients about appropriate ways
to develop people. In this sense, human resource professionals
have multiple roles in organizational change. They are educators,
innovators, evaluators, leaders, change agents, consultants, and
futurists. The human resource professional must be a monitor
of behavior and actions, and must empower managers with the
freedom to act in managing and developing the corporation's
human resources. Therefore, in the future, human resource professionals will be an integral part of the business—not part of
overhead, but a critical resource to enhance financial performance and to bring about needed change.   '

My goal in the chapters to come is to demonstrate this
expanded role for the human resource professional within the
context of organizational change. Forces for change suggest the
need to change people and change organization cultures. Change
agent roles and characteristics supported by the human resource
function influence these change processes.

2

Environmental Forces and Changing Business Directions

Change is a given in today's organizations. The question is not whether there will be change, but how much there will be and how quickly it will come. This chapter sets the stage for understanding change by exploring the outside and inside forces that prompt change. I will consider the standpoints of employees affected by the change; of the leaders and managers who take actions; and of the human resource professionals who both establish directions for change and support it.

In 1977, two experts in organizational development, Richard Beckhard and Reuben Harris, predicted likely conditions in the late 1970s and early 1980s that would give rise to organizational change (Beckhard and Harris, 1977, pp. 106–109). Comparing their predicted outlook in 1977 to the situation of the late 1980s provides a perspective on the rate and complexities of change. They distinguished between trends external and internal to the organization.

External Trends

1. The environment will remain complex. Managers will have to respond to the competing demands of multiple, inde-

pendent constituencies (for example, government, public opinion, and stockholders).

2. The numbers, values, and demands of minorities, women, consumer advocates, environmentalists, and other interest groups will influence the available labor force, the cost of labor, the nature of work to produce the variety and quality of goods demanded, and the climate of the workplace. Beckhard and Harris discussed the need for U.S. organizations to balance the traditional concept of the private-enterprise organization as having a mission of producing wealth for its owners or wealth (employment) for society.

3. Government intervention and (probably) control will increase. Beckhard and Harris believed that the power distribution among owners, managers, and trade unions will undergo agonizing reappraisals and adjustments.

4. Despite predictable high unemployment, entering employees will have high expectations for the corporation. Young people with bachelor's and advanced degrees will choose a first job not as a permanent career home but as a place that will provide meaningful rewards—both financial and intrinsic—in the immediate future in return for their efforts. "When a twenty-four-year-old masters student lacking significant work experience can immediately go into the marketplace at a starting salary of $20,000, it is not hard to understand why these high expectations exist," Beckhard and Harris stated (Beckhard and Harris, 1977, p. 108). Today, of course, that figure would be considerably higher.

5. Middle managers' and midcareer managers' priorities will change from devoting themselves to career advancement to thinking about a well-balanced life, and perhaps looking forward to early retirement.

6. The tremendous push from the 1950s for new technology will level off. The human component of high creativity and motivation will be more important to competitive advantage than technological developments, even though there will still be a steady stream of new technologies.

7. People entering management from colleges and universities will have high expectations, but young people entering

lower-level jobs will have lower expectations. Their goal will be to earn money, not to work productively for product quality or company profit. Consequently, ways to improve the quality of work will be very much needed.

Beckhard and Harris were on the mark in most of their predictions, and other management commentators and researchers agree with them (for example, see Didsbury, 1983; Hammett, 1984; Howard and Bray, 1981). Indeed, Beckhard and Harris's ideas may only need adjustments for inflation to reflect the starting salaries for today's business school graduate. Several of their ideas are themes in this book. Beckhard and Harris are correct about the importance of people to maintaining a firm's competitive advantage. Advancing technology is a given for all viable competitors in an industry, but being able to apply the technology to meet customer needs is a major differentiating factor in the marketplace. Involving employees in improving product quality (and, in general, quality of worklife) has become critical in today's global business environment. This chapter will deepen these ideas by exploring the changing nature of work, the heterogeneity of the workforce, and globalization as external forces for change. But first, let us examine Beckhard and Harris's predictions about inside forces.

Internal Trends

1. Specialists will be required to bridge their technology with a market orientation. A professional will not be able to function only in a narrow discipline but will have to work cooperatively with other professionals on a variety of tasks.

2. The organization will recognize the interface between work and family, meeting employees' needs for a balanced life. This will be reflected in personnel practices, reward systems, vacation and retirement policies, and similar programs.

3. The organization and the people in it will have more need for "creative coping." Organizational structures, job designs, and workgroup interfaces will have to be flexible and adaptable to generate and release creative capacity.

4. There will be an imbalance between the skills possessed

by college graduates and the organizational requirements for their utilization. As noted in the first point, young people will find that the organization expects them to do more than apply their narrow discipline.

5. There will be a continuous need for change technologies—organization development, information systems, and operations research—to solve organizational problems. Beckhard and Harris envisioned that leading-edge organizations will have a "department of the future" sitting "next door" to the chief executive officer. The staff department will have planners and experts in change management, information systems, and applied behavioral science to help the organization cope with ever-changing conditions.

6. The organization will experiment with new work designs and organizational structures to provide more autonomy and influence for people at all organizational levels.

A decade after these predictions were published, we find that organizations have changed internally as Beckhard and Harris foresaw. Often, these changes occurred because organizations were forced into them by employee demands, financial crises, and increased foreign competition—rarely because of forward-thinking management. We still find many organizations dragging their feet in recognizing that employees' needs extend beyond their worklives. Innovative programs for child care, job relocation plans for spouses of transferred employees, and alternative work schedules such as job sharing and flextime are not yet the norm.

The need for specialists to work together in recognition of tight market windows has certainly happened. We have also seen the displacement of workers with obsolete skills and the need for midcareer training programs. Often, companies find it cheaper to offer these employees financial incentives for early retirement than to invest in retraining them.

We have seen increased attention to environmental trends and forecasts as we approach the twenty-first century. These trends will be discussed in this chapter as well as in Chapter Eight's focus on forecasting and planning.

Some change agents are specialists, and this book focuses

on the supporting role of human resource professionals as one type of specialist in designing and implementing change. However, the powerful change agents are corporate leaders and managers, and their role and preparation for this role are addressed in this book (see especially Chapters Three and Four).

Organizational Transformations

So far, this chapter has considered the multiple forces causing organizational change. Before exploring the forces faced by today's organizations, consider the transformations that organizations have experienced recently.

There are many examples of corporations changing internal systems and structures to match changes in the environment. Some of these changes are in direct response to environmental events. Sometimes such events do not change the corporation as much as they should. At other times, companies change in anticipation of environmental shifts. In other cases, the need for change is due to an internal failure, perhaps insufficient research and development or inadequate managerial ability. Here are a few examples.

• General Electric Company (GE) recently sold its small appliance division to Black & Decker. This sent the message to investors, customers, and employees that GE wanted to be number one or two in large-scale businesses (major appliances, lighting, and consumer electronics). GE's later purchase of RCA, another corporate giant, supports GE's leadership role in the electronics industry. Such frame-breaking changes have a profound effect on the corporate culture of these organizations.

• General Motors (GM) is undergoing tremendous change as it streamlines and restructures its divisions. Other important decisions at GM include establishing a joint venture with Toyota to build the newly designed Nova; working with another Japanese firm to develop robotic technology and to manufacture robots; establishing a new nameplate, Saturn, which uses the latest in computer technology and robotics to manufacture a car that competes with low-cost, high-quality foreign models; purchasing Electronic Data Systems (EDS) and trying to adopt its competitive, action-oriented, client-responsive management style; and purchasing Hughes Aircraft, essentially a high-tech R&D organization. Financial analysts who look for short-term shareholder return are quick to question the advisability of these major strategy shifts at GM. However, these are changes that take years if not decades to produce a return on investment. The changes go to the heart of how the company does business. For instance, the merger of GM and EDS has been likened to a Green Beret joining up with the Social Security Administration (Lehner, 1984). (We will return to the GM case in Chapter Three's analysis of leadership.)

• In the early 1970s, Arm & Hammer shifted its corporate direction from an industrial base to consumer marketing. A new company chairman recruited a new marketing vice-president to develop a string of consumer products that took advantage of the tradename. The first success was Arm & Hammer laundry detergent.

• New officers at Montgomery Securities Company converted the firm from a California securities research concern to a national player in block trading, corporate finance, and venture capital. Management style had a lot to do with the successful shift. Thomas Weisel, a senior partner, said he had no patience for people who rest once they reach a goal. "You've got to attack constantly. Sure we are aggressive. We like to think it's done with taste and tact and subtlety and finesse. But we are aggressive, and we are attacking, all the time" (Zonana, 1985, p. 1).

• The airline industry, a traditionally bureaucratic industry, has faced deregulation in the areas of price and routes. The resulting increase in competition gave way to numerous price wars and route changes. People Express became a growth company in this environment, and did it without the development of a bureaucratic structure. This employee-owned company was a flexible, entrepreneurial organization; every worker was a manager and no more than three organizational steps away from a managing officer or from Donald Burr, the chairman of the company. All workers performed both customer-related services and classic administrative chores, which led to greater creativity and innovation (Burr, 1985). Employees purchased 100 shares of stock when they joined the company, committing themselves to the organization's progressive management approach. The regulatory and economic environment was right for a competitive upstart, and the management philosophy of People Express at first allowed the efficiencies of operation to succeed in the fast-paced, rapidly changing industry. However, as People Express expanded by heavily borrowing capital to service more cities and by purchasing other airlines, and as the number of employees grew, the participative environment became less efficient. The company's inability to earn enough to carry the debt led to the brink of bankruptcy and eventual takeover.

• Internal problems can cause failure even when the external environment is optimal. A prime example is Trilogy Ltd. This organization was founded by Eugene Amdahl, the computer genius whose successful Amdahl Computer Corporation builds computers that are compatible with IBM computers but are less expensive. Trilogy proposed to build a supercomputer around giant silicon wafers. The financial forecast predicted that Trilogy's sales would reach $1 billion by 1986, two years after introducing the computer. Companies such as Honeywell and Digital Equipment Corporation (DEC) bankrolled Trilogy to the tune of $276 million, the largest start-up in the history of Silicon Valley and possibly the United States (Berg, 1984). In 1984, two years after the company was founded, Trilogy abandoned its supercomputer and concentrated on developing the chip. Technical problems abounded, but there were management problems as well. Carlton Amdahl, the founder's thirty-two-year-old son and Trilogy's vice-chairman and top scientist, left the company. The company had grown to 600 people in four years, with as many as fifty separate development teams that were impossible to coordinate. Carlton Amdahl concentrated on the computer's technical architecture rather than team coordination. In marked contrast, computer development in Data General, documented in Tracy Kidder's *The Soul of a New Machine,* showed how effective the management of a dedicated yet fairly small workteam can be successful (Kidder, 1981).

• Ford Motor Company has reformed itself internally,

changing from a notoriously rigid bureaucracy to a decentralized, high-employee-involvement organization straight out of *In Search of Excellence*—perhaps the most significant economic recovery in U.S. history (Easterbrook, 1986). In the early 1980s, Ford went for broke in its development of the Taurus/Mercury Sable line. This was Detroit's first attempt at a car with European handling characteristics aimed at the typical family buyer. At a time when Ford was sustaining record losses, it invested a record $3 billion into Taurus development. A union-management agreement resulted in an employee involvement program that put production workers into product design and marketing. Different groups of workers, designers, and managers were responsible for different stages during the five-year product development process. In another case, workers redesigned the Ford Escort EXP, which was due to go out of production. Management was persuaded to keep the redesigned car in production, thus avoiding layoffs and increasing market share because of the car's popularity with younger buyers.

Ford has made a number of management style changes. For instance, a single product manager was put in charge of each new project, rather than having managers in charge of small parts of a project. Quarterly departmental goals were replaced with general company-wide goals and guiding principles, which increased the managers' discretion of action while obtaining managers' assent to corporate objectives. Compensation for the company's top managers was altered to focus on five-year gains rather than on short-term results. Several thousand Ford managers were sent to a week-long "reeducation" program on the unstructured, participatory management approach.

These examples suggest different directions for organizational change and different management strategies. These changes are usually prompted by environmental trends. The changes represent the leaders', managers', and workers' responses to these trends. The next section considers more systematically several alternative business directions and their implications for managing change. Five business directions are examined: decline, mergers and acquisitions, growth, start-up, and redirection. The roles of managers (both leaders and mid-level managers) and human resource professionals are examined.

The Impact of Business Direction on Managing Change

Table 1 outlines the different business directions, typical employee reactions for each, the actions often taken by managers, and needed human resource strategies. (See Table 1 in the appendix at the end of this chapter.) The table and the discussion below show that changing business conditions entail a dynamic relationship between workers and managers and that human resource professionals play an important role in the organizational change process.

Declining Organizations. There are several types of organizational decline (Ferris, Schellenberg, and Zammuto, 1984). *Erosion* refers to continuous changes in the environment that result in decreased organizational performance. The reactions of employees are likely to be denial or avoidance of the problem or, if the problem is faced, the reaction might be hyperactivity as a sense of anxiety and the need for positive action emerge.

There will be less in the way of opportunities for career growth and development in an environment of erosion. In general, the environment is likely to be one of rigid cost control as people are required to do more with less. Management's strategy is likely to be to squeeze all it can in the way of profit margins. Perhaps an extreme example of an illegal, unethical business reaction to an eroding market is the baby food company that recently was accused of selling sugared water as pure apple juice.

Contraction occurs when there is a sudden, unexpected change in the environment. This change rapidly reduces the level of organizational performance. The 1985–1986 decline in the personal computer market is one example. Layoffs are one way companies seek a quick fix to the problem, and many employees are suddenly faced with a loss of their jobs, or at least their job security.

Dissolution, a third type of decline, is a continuous shift in acceptable levels of performance in the marketplace. This occurred in the automobile industry when high-quality, competitively priced foreign imports entered the U.S. marketplace. Under such conditions, employees must deal with increased standards, and those who cannot meet the standards may lose their jobs. The corporation tries to create a new market niche through innovation and improved production methods to meet the new quality standards. New talent is needed to develop and implement innovations.

Collapse is an immediate threat to organizational survival. The typewriter industry faced this threat with the advent of word processing machines. Movie theaters may be on the verge of such a collapse because the home video industry is competing for entertainment dollars; however, the complete story of this market is still evolving. Atari Corporation faced the collapse of the home video game market with the introduction of personal computers (Sutton, Eisenhardt, and Jucker, 1986). One corporate reaction to collapse is to seek a new leader. In Atari's case, the prior management was unable to design a viable computer product to compete in the fast-paced computer market. The corporation was essentially unable to abandon its stake in its video game products. After a period of severe cutbacks in force and production, the company was eventually sold, and the new management redirected the corporation by designing a low-cost personal computer that at this writing is gaining market share and making Atari profitable again.

Organizational decline is often blamed on poor leadership. Apparent lack of direction or frequent changes in direction are causes for loss of faith in management. Corporations on the verge of collapse are ripe for a merger. People Express's financial problems resulted from its rapid expansion and difficulty in managing its growth (Bennett, 1986). The management found that the only solution was to sell the company. Texas Air was able to borrow the capital to acquire People Express. However, Texas Air's financial position is dependent on its creditors' goodwill, and its success depends upon the business decisions made by the corporations' leadership.

Mergers and Acquisitions. Table 2 presents some facts about mergers and acquisitions and their implications for corporations and change agents. Corporate mergers occur more frequently today than ever before. (See Table 2 in the appendix at the end of this chapter.) Although mergers are a form of corporate growth and a means to increased financial power, an estimated one-third to one-half of all mergers fail. Employee-related problems are often the reasons for failure. Such problems include a lack of mutual understanding and a clash in corporate cultures. Mergers and acquisitions create an accelerated tempo of change and an environment of overwhelming uncertainty. Time is needed for the joint management team to work together for a new management team to gain power.

Acquisitions are often cleaner than mergers because there is certainty about who is taking over whom. However, GM's purchase of EDS shows that this is not always the case. The differences in corporate culture and leadership philosophy (specifically the differences between Ross Perot of EDS and Roger Smith of GM) resulted in several years of bickering before Perot was bought out by GM.

Mergers and acquisitions create a sense of loss as corporate identity changes and employees' sources of support and influence disappear. New organizational structures and new job designs create a further sense of change and loss.

Internal battles over turf, job assignments, and personnel are likely as a merger unfolds. Communication deteriorates as information is withheld and rumors fill the gap. Uncertainty leads to inaction, and productivity and morale decline. Employees find themselves paralyzed as managers delay decisions until the new top management team takes control. Self-interest becomes paramount, and team efforts suffer. Overall, mergers lower employees' commitment to the organization. Corporate goals become obscure, and there is the perception of a weakened sense of direction. The best performers are likely to leave the company.

Marks and Mirvis (1985) refer to such reactions as the *merger syndrome.* When the syndrome is unchecked, the outcome may be lower employee performance and poor financial and operational results. Organizations involved in mergers need to devise a thoughtful integration of the corporate entities to minimize the upheaval and provide due consideration for the effects of the change on employees. Strategies for accomplishing this include continuously providing employees with information about how the merger is likely to affect them. Effective communication reduces ambiguity, helps mesh corporate cultures, and increases openness and honesty. Another strategy is to facilitate upward communication. Attitude surveys give employees a way to voice their opinions. Survey results provide data for discussion. The results allow managers to monitor the integration process and send a message that employees' opinions are valued (see Chapter Nine). Joint transition teams staffed by personnel from both firms provide another successful approach to merger management. These teams counteract the "us-versus-them" feelings and broaden the planning of the merger by including more people in the decision process (Mirvis and Marks, 1986).

Concern for employees is a philosophy that pervades Delta Air Lines' personnel policies. When Delta acquired Western Air Lines in 1987, it formed teams of Delta nonmanagement workers (flight attendants, pilots, and ticket counter agents) to visit Western Air Lines employees. Twelve "spirit teams" were formed with five people each to visit their peers in the acquired airline. Delta also extended formal job offers to each of Western's 12,000 employees. The offer was made in writing and in person by the employee's supervisor, explaining the new salary structure (which was higher because of Delta's higher pay rates), the job the individual would have, and its location. Ninety-three percent of the Western employees accepted Delta's offer.

Organizational Growth. Periods of rapid growth are an exciting time in an organization. Employees have a heightened feeling of security. Those who were with the organization from the start are proud of their accomplishments and are likely to be rewarded with bonuses, opportunities for advancement, and a sense of challenge and accomplishment. Management should continue to do what worked so well and search for ways to expand the business, either by improving the successful product or service, by reducing its cost to meet increased competition, or by seeking new areas for investment (developing new products or purchasing existing corporations).

There have been many examples of rapid growth. Xerox, Polaroid, and Wang are a few companies that enjoyed long-term success because their growth was managed well and the demand for their products continued. However, in each of these cases, competition grew and new technology outpaced the corporations' growth, eventually requiring them to reduce operations. Xerox, faced by expanding competition in the copier business, tried to fill the gap by entering the automated work station business. However, limited demand required them to downsize substantially. A renewed sense of the importance of leadership and responsiveness to customers has envigorated the firm's profitability.

Other companies, such as People Express and Atari, managed their rapid growth poorly. I already described how Atari failed to recognize the changing marketplace for video games. People Express failed to recognize the need for new management strategies. The early job structures gave People Express personnel broad, interchangeable job duties. Workgroups managed themselves with little supervision. As the company grew, the tight-knit, common bond among employees weakened, and self-managing workgroups became less feasible. The need for standard practices and procedures between workgroups was not recognized. In addition, the company found it increasingly difficult to find prospective employees who would invest their time and money by purchasing stock to work for the company. Moreover, the company's financial position was strained to the limit as it acquired other airlines and expanded to serve new cities. The reward of profit sharing became less attractive as profits were plowed into the corporations' growth.

Start-Ups. New ventures usually start small, and with a sense of excitement and anticipation. Employees are challenged by their jobs and the chance for sharing in the firm's success. The venture may be formed by an existing corporation or by an entrepreneur who obtained capital to develop a new product or service. Managers of new ventures are keen on monitoring their progress, often because they must produce results within a certain time limit imposed by investors. The new venture must be very selective in hiring employees with the right skills, talent, and motivation.

A notable exception to the rule of minimizing overhead in a new venture was the initiation of AT&T's unregulated, separate subsidiary to manufacture and market telecommunications and computer equipment.

Here a very large corporate entity was created over several years. It was large because AT&T intended to be a major national force in the market, and it had the financial resources to create the enormous support staff needed for the extensive manufacturing, sales, and service operations. But new product development was slow, prices were high relative to the competition, and demand was soft, causing the company to downsize its force and operations considerably.

Organizational Redirection. Corporate leaders are paid to envision the future and make decisions about their organization's direction. Sometimes this entails major shifts in business plans. Employees struggle to understand the change and interpret how the change is likely to affect them. Management needs to spend time communicating its plans, as well as implementing and monitoring the changes. Second-guessing, back-stepping, and altering the course are likely. Careful evaluation of existing personnel is necessary to establish the match between the current skills of employees and future skill requirements. Obtaining the right people may mean laying off current employees and hiring others. Downsizing and relocations may occur if the corporate plans call for closing facilities. Atari, Xerox, AT&T, GM, and Ford, all discussed earlier, are examples of corporate redirections.

One of the most critical tasks of many successful firms, even fairly new firms, is keeping swiftly changing priorities clear to all employees. An example is Convex Computer Corporation in Dallas (Hayes, 1987). The firm introduced the first of its new breed of high-speed computers in 1985, after spending $32 million of venture capital during its three-year development phase. The firm became the industry leader in the scientific research computing market with its scaled-down version of the well-known supercomputer manufactured by Cray Research Inc. The minisupercomputer is likely to continue as one of the fastest-growing segments of the computer industry well into the 1990s, and Convex's chief executive, Robert J. Paluck, knows that other firms, such as DEC, which dominates the scientific computer market, are likely to counterattack. Paluck's goal for the firm during its early years was to establish high-quality manufacturing systems and a knowledgeable salesforce. Next the goals were to build a global sales unit and make money. Then the firm concentrated on increasing profits while bringing a more powerful computer into production. Convex had 425 employees in the spring of 1987. Only thirty employees had left the company since its start in September 1982. One reason for the stability in the workforce has been a generous stock bonus plan. Another reason may be the floundering Dallas economy and tight labor market.

Summary. The different types of organizational change described above demonstrate the need for different managerial behavior and human resource strategies to match business conditions. The leader's role is crucial in establishing a corporation's competitive advantage. I will return to the five business directions again in Chapter Four's discussion of the leader's support for employee development under the different business conditions.

The above typology of business directions suggests that change can be neatly categorized. However, what is not immediately evident is that the forces of change produce very complex processes that affect many different parts of the organization simultaneously. The outset of this chapter reviewed environmental trends that have changed organizations. The last section of this chapter explores current trends, reviewing their implications for changing business directions and their impact on multiple elements of the organization—the people, the work, the structure of the organization, interpersonal-intergroup relationships, and human resource strategies.

The Challenge of Postindustrial Society

Five, ten, or fifteen years from now, some organizations will face the same type of environment they do today. Other organizations will face very different environments that will change their structure and process of operation. Organizations that have structures and technologies suited to their environments will be more likely to survive than those that do not.

The postindustrial environment is characterized by increasing knowledge, complexity, and turbulence (Huber, 1984). Knowledge is increasing exponentially in many fields, and communications and computer technologies increase its availability. The organizational components necessary to deal with this growing knowledge are becoming more specialized and interdependent. Also, events occur more rapidly. Important discoveries and their applications happen faster and faster. Therefore, increasing knowledge eventually leads to increasing complexity and more turbulence.

For instance, in the telecommunications field, advances in technology make it possible to merge the transmission of voice and data information over digital networks. Moreover, telecommunications companies can now do more than transmit information. They add value by the computer processing of that information—analyzing it, aggregating or disaggregating it, and directing the transformed information to multiple uses. New and increased telecommunications technology enhances the complexity of dealing with information. The result is a new, competitive, very turbulent environment that consumers, government regulators, and the computer and telecommunications companies themselves are struggling to manage. Although this example is a simplified description of a complex situation, there are multiple forces at work that change how organizations are designed and how they operate. Knowledge, here in the form of new technology, is a primary and causal force.

The future presents us with the challenge to apply new technology in a way that expands opportunities rather than limits freedom and individual contribution. In his book *Brave New Workplace*, Robert Howard (1986) writes about how the United States' corporate utopias create inequalities and social conflict in our working lives:

> The allure of the brave new workplace is that it promises a wholesale transformation of working life precisely when we need it the most. When the legitimacy and effectiveness of traditional forms of corporate power and practice have been worn thin by the simultaneous impacts of rapid social, economic, and technological change, here is a brand new model of corporate life promising to reconcile equity with efficiency, meaningful work with high technology, worker satisfaction with corporate profit, and social renewal with economic prosperity.

> The corporate utopia for work denies the essential fact that work in America is a relationship of unequal power, that conflicts of interest are endemic to working life, and this new model of the corporation, much like the old, is founded on the systematic denial of influence and control to the large majority of working Americans [p. 10].

Howard believes that recent attempts by corporations to "humanize" technology and work are fundamentally flawed. Rather than the encouragement of self-development, he warns of a new dependence on corporate power, exploitation, and special dominance.

In this last section, I consider several trends that combine environmental events and internal business decisions. I discuss their potential implications and ideas of action with a view to avoid debilitating or constricting work and enhance the link between individual employee success and business success.

Changing Work Patterns. Organizations are experimenting with new work patterns—different work schedules, more temporary workers, self-managing workteams, flextime, job sharing, telecommuting, and four-day work weeks (Didsbury, 1983; Finkelstein and Newman, 1984; Hammett, 1984). Here are some examples:

> DEC uses self-managing workteams in its Enfield, Connecticut, plant. This approach to high-tech manufacturing has also been applied by other firms such as Volvo, GM, General Foods, and American Transtech.
>
> DEC has a no layoff policy for its regular employees. It uses temporary employees rather than hiring regular staff for some operations. Apple Computer does the same thing with professional and technical employees. At Delta, all employees start as temporary. They are eligible for permanent status after eighteen months. Currently, about 13 percent of Delta's workforce is temporary. They hope to bring that up to about 20 percent to give the firm flexibility in weathering difficult economic conditions by laying off those on temporary status and securing the employment of the permanent employee core.
>
> Travelers Corp. has an on-call worker pool of retired workers. American Transtech has a trained cadre of on-call, permanent part-time employees for peak demand periods.
>
> A Los Angeles–area medical office (The White Memorial Otolaryngology Foundation) "leases" its entire office staff including nurses and office managers. This frees doctors from administrative responsibility and allows them to have a lucrative pension plan for themselves.
>
> Many firms allow employees to modify work arrival and departure times. Such flextime programs

ease employees' child-care burdens. Smith Beckman Corporation cited improved productivity as a result.

Other scheduling alternatives include job sharing, homework/telecommuting, and voluntary reduced work hours. For instance, Pacific Bell began a telecommuting program in 1986 for ninety programmers, engineers, market planners, and others who work at remote sites or at their homes.

A unit in AT&T Bell Laboratories experimented with a four-day work week. Employees initiated and implemented it with management's approval and then returned to the old schedule when they did not like the new schedule.

What are the forces for change? There are many forces behind such changes, some of them externally driven and some of them internally driven. They include the following.

A highly competitive marketplace exists.
Emphasis is placed on high-quality, low-cost production to allow flexibility in the marketplace.
Customers demand responsiveness.
Different types of expertise are brought to bear on corporate projects. The mix of skills required varies from project to project.
Employers need greater staffing flexibility.
Employees need greater flexibility in work schedules.
New work technologies (for example, the personal computer and word processor) allow flexible work arrangements.
The growth of intermediary businesses, such as temporary help agencies and employee leasing firms, act as catalysts for change as well as the result of change.

What are the implications for management? Consider demographic trends in the labor force as precipitators of organizational change. One trend is the so-called baby bust—the rapid drop in the birth rate around 1964 that marked the end of the baby boom that followed World War II. This means that corporations are starting to compete fiercely to attract the best new entrants to the labor market. Although some corporations need fewer people, they often need different skills than already exist among employees, and so recruitment and selection are still important. The aging of the workforce is another trend as the baby boom cohort moves through the life cycle (the so-called pig in a python). Older workers suggest the need for training and retraining programs so that mid-career employees avoid the stagnation of career plateaus and continue to make a contribution to the organization. Another trend is the increasing number of women in the workforce. As a result, work/family issues, such as child care, are becoming increasingly important in some corporations. The challenge for responding to these forces and managing the changes effectively requires answering some strategic questions (Schuler and MacMillan, 1984; Yankelovich and Immerwahr, 1983). For instance, how do corporations prepare and recruit employees to work in changing conditions? What types of reward structures must be created? How can managers develop effective self-managing teams? Can managers change their style over time as the team develops or will different managers be needed at different stages? What types of people will be amenable to new work and schedule designs? Do skilled workers or professionals want temporary employment?

What do companies need to do? There is no one response to these trends. Corporations need to provide managers with differing key on-the-job learning experiences, for example managing newly formed workgroups, temporary workers, self-managing teams, downturn situations, growth situations, and so on. (These and other ways to develop change agent managerial skills are reviewed in Chapter Four.) Companies should experiment with new work schedules—first by identifying employees' interests in alternative schedules and then by experimenting with them. In addition, managers as change agents need to learn how to generate new job designs and workgroup structures, such as challenging individual assignments, matrix reporting relationships, and participative/employee involvement programs. (Such programs are the subject of Part Three of this book.) Managers and human resource professionals are the purveyors of corporate values through policies, programs, and actions. For instance, Merck & Co.'s belief in employment security had them announce a plant closing several years before the event. The union vowed to work closely with Merck to close the plant with dignity, and help employees find alternative employment with the company or another firm. This was possible because of management's long-term human resource planning and its respect for employees' need to know about decisions that would affect their lives.

Other Trends. Certainly there are other trends that must be treated as challenges to effective management. Mergers and acquisitions were discussed earlier in this chapter as a common business trend today. Table 2 reviews some facts about mergers and acquisitions and the general need for downsizing and cost control. The table covers relevant strategic questions, implications for management, and likely corporate actions. Other trends could be analyzed in the same way. The goal of trend analysis is for corporate leaders, managers, and human resource professionals to identify and implement ways to manage change for the mutual benefit of the individual and the organization. (See Chapter Eight for a discussion of the need to incorporate environmental trend analysis into human resource plans.)

Corporate Evolution: Preparing to Manage Change

The problem of corporate change can be viewed as evolution, similar to the origin of species. Corporations, like species, experience periods of equilibrium and transition. This has been termed "punctuated equilibrium"—a concept formulated by Harvard biologist S. J. Gould and explained to me by a corporate planner, Peter Schwartz, in a personal communication in July 1987. Over time, capabilities become embedded in the organization, but they are not tested or expressed. Punctuation refers to a major change in the environment. An anthropological example is a lake drying up during a drought, forcing adaptable species of prehistoric fish to live on the land. An organizational example is a sudden economic shift in exchange rates that floods the U.S. market with inexpensive foreign goods. The question is, how prepared are we for such changes?

Organizations that survive sudden changes have strategies that ensure they have sufficient financial and human resources. They have the resilience to withstand the shock of change and they are able to adapt. The leaders of the organization know its strengths and weaknesses, and they recognize the need for change. Also, the leaders are clear about the corporation's identity and the direction of change.

Maximizing Individual and Organizational Growth. In general, people need to be resilient in the face of work and life barriers. They need a sense of accomplishment and reason for self-confidence. They need insight into themselves and their environment, and they need a sense of identity or direction. Corporations need employees with these characteristics. Moreover, corporations support these characteristics through the challenges and rewards that are offered, through information that is provided (for example, performance feedback), and through opportunities for alternative career directions. These individual and corporate needs are independent of changing conditions. However, leaders, managers, and human resource professionals must know how to meet these needs under changing conditions. To do this they must understand the forces for change, the skills they need, and how these skills can be applied to the change process. These issues are the subject of the rest of this book.

Summary

This chapter found that forces for change recognized in the mid 1970s have materialized and deepened. External forces include complexity, changing values, government intervention, new technology, high expectations, waning corporate loyalty, and the importance of people to competitive advantage. Internal forces include the need for teamwork, recognizing employees' nonwork needs, more flexible job and workgroup structures, retraining, and consciously planning for and managing change.

Examples of organizational transformation and alternative business directions showed relationships between employee reactions, management actions, and human resource strategies. Managing these changes and taking advantage of new technologies and related work structures will require attention to multiple individual and organizational needs. This requires being able to analyze the forces for change and recognizing their implications for management.

So far I have set the scene for organizational change by discussing the forces for change (environmental trends and business directions). The next two chapters focus on the "characters" of our "drama": leaders, managers, and human resource professionals who initiate, implement, and support organizational change. Chapter Three examines organizational change agents' roles and characteristics. Then we will be ready for the heart of the "play"—an in-depth examination of ways to prepare people to handle change, introduce cultural change, and use the human resource function to support change.

Appendix

Table 1. Effects of Changing Business Conditions.

Business Conditions	Employee Reactions	Management Actions	Needed Human Resource Strategies
Decline			
• Erosion (continuously declining marketplace)	Denial Avoidance Hyperactivity Learning to do with less	Improve efficiency	Productivity improvement efforts Reliance on employees for ideas
• Contraction (sudden decline)	Fear Anxiety	Quick-fix Cost reduction	Layoffs
• Dissolution (slow alteration of performance standards)	Uncertainty Searching for direction	Innovation Seeking a market niche	Recruitment of people with needed skills Retraining

(continued on next page)

Table 1. Effects of Changing Business Conditions, Cont'd.

Business Conditions	Employee Reactions	Management Actions	Needed Human Resource Strategies
• Collapse (immediate threat to survival)	Threat Fear Panic	Change direction Close operations Merger New leadership	Layoffs

Mergers and Acquisitions

• Accelerated change	Uncertainty Perceived loss Personal risk Suspense Anxiety	Unclear direction Establishing control Redesigning the corporation Integration planning Redesigning jobs	Assessment of people and matching to new jobs Layoffs Hiring right people

Growth

• Rapid increase in demand	Excitement Security Pride in company Sense of accomplishment	Maintain operations Take advantage of market window Search for new investment opportunities Search for ways to expand the business	Hire people to meet growing human resource needs

Start-ups

	Anticipation High energy High sense of risk Challenge	Pressure to produce Time spent planning and designing Keep overhead low	Selective hiring Search for creative, talented, and skilled people

Redirection

	Anticipation Excitement Insecurity	Establish a plan Communicate changes	Evaluate current force to match new

Table 1. Effects of Changing Business Conditions, Cont'd.

Business Conditions	Employee Reactions	Management Actions	Needed Human Resource Strategies
		Implement plan Refine plan Close or sell parts of the business Start up new ventures	skill requirements Lay off those who do not match skill needs

Table 2. The Trend of Mergers and Acquisitions and the Need for Cost Reduction.

Some Facts

Corporate mergers are occurring more frequently than ever before:

- 2,543 mergers/acquisitions were recorded in 1984; 1985 set a new record.
- 23,000 mergers/acquisitions occurred in the decade preceding November 1985.
- Merger/acquisition activity is expected to continue at a significant rate for some time.
- Revenues of outplacement firms tripled from 1980 to 1985.

Many mass-employment jobs are being replaced by new technological developments.

Reducing costs in order to become more competitive will become more necessary with the growth of the global marketplace.

The trend toward more education, training, retraining, cross-training, and contracted employment will counteract the corporate downsizing phenomenon to some extent.

After downsizing, the use of temporary workers increases in order to avoid adding to "headcount."

Relevant Questions

How does a corporation determine when it needs downsizing?

How will downsizing affect the social climate in the workplace? How will it affect the workforce?

How does the corporation deal with the new problems and situations that employees will face?

How does the corporation maintain employee dedication, support, and morale in times of change and uncertainty?

(continued on next page)

**Table 2. The Trend of Mergers and Acquisitions
and the Need for Cost Reduction, Cont'd.**

What needs to be done in the area of human resource forecasting and planning to ensure proper resources for the corporation?

What types of career planning programs are necessary to handle shorter career spans?

What can be done to reduce the risk of downsizing?

How does a corporation prepare its managers to become facilitators or coaches rather than administrators?

Under what conditions are temporary personnel brought in? How will they be brought in? What will be offered to them?

How can a corporation use downsizing to create opportunities for creative management?

How can a corporation assess the real costs and benefits of a more flexible workforce?

Implications

Fewer layers of direct supervision needed when mass employment jobs are replaced by new technological developments.

Shorter career spans—more career shifts.

Need for human resource forecasting and planning to ensure proper resources in accord with the business plan of the corporation and to achieve competitive advantage.

Shift in boss-subordinate role in which the boss becomes more of a coach and facilitator and the subordinate plays a more interactive role.

Shift towards less rigid, team approach from hierarchal bureaucratic approach.

Employees may experience low morale, role uncertainty, high level of stress, and job uncertainty—at least temporarily.

Temporary assignments will become an important part of routine operations.

Individual lives will be affected by more complex decisions in career choice.

Use of temporary workforce will increase, and corporations will be forced to compare the expense of paying large numbers of temporary employees higher salaries than they would pay permanent employees doing the same work.

The most competitive firms will be those that are able to truly increase efficiencies (work "smarter") rather than just shift expenses from salaries to another budget line (contract workers).

Table 2. The Trend of Mergers and Acquisitions
and the Need for Cost Reduction, Cont'd.

What Companies Need to Do

Make force management a strategic issue.

Learn the issues of downsizing as they affect the company today.

Educate and prepare all employees on issues of downsizing and what its effects will be.

Incorporate team building efforts to support the workforce as well as the quality of work output.

Develop career planning programs to support both outgoing and remaining personnel.

Develop an extensive human resource forecasting and planning program.

Develop plans to deal with employee problems.

Determine need for temporary personnel and examine flexible workforce alternatives.

Use human resource indicators such as employee attitude surveys to track employee issues.

Support and reward managers who create efficiencies in their work units as a way of doing business.

3

Change Agent Roles for Leaders, Managers, and Human Resource Professionals

 This chapter and the next focus on the people who initiate and implement change—their roles, their characteristics, and their development. I begin with examples of chief executive officers responding to the forces of change and in some cases affecting these forces by creating conditions that support their organization's success. Characteristics that foster the success of these leaders as change agents are identified. Next, leaders' and managers' roles as change agents are outlined. Finally, I highlight the importance of human resource management to organizational change by describing the role of the human resource professional as a support for, and major contributor to, successful change.

Leaders as Change Agents

The role of the leader as change agent can be described best by examples of corporate officers who, as key change agents, initiated change and directed their corporations through the implementation process. Although the outcomes of the cases described below are not yet known because the changes are still in progress, the examples demonstrate the leaders' visions for the future of their businesses and the influence of changes in corporate direction on management actions and human resource strategies.

Jack Welch, Chairman, General Electric Company

When Jack Welch became GE's chairman in 1981, his goal was to move the company in a direction more attuned to the hotly competitive environment of the 1980s. He shut down unproductive plants and sold businesses that were marginally profitable. He reduced GE's total employee body by 18 percent. Welch's goal was to make every part of GE first or second in its market as measured by market share. GE is a highly decentralized company with a lean corporate staff, and holds its lines of business accountable for human resource management and business planning. The company recently acquired two major corporations—Employee Reassurance Company and RCA. GE has improved its manufacturing business by automating plants and enhancing product quality. In one case, a worker-paced assembly line was implemented. This allows workers to assemble machines at their individual stations long enough to do the job properly (Lueck, 1985).

Roger Smith, Chairman, General Motors

Roger Smith is the chief executive of the world's largest corporation. (GM employs over 750,000 people and sells $84 billion worth of products a year.) Since assuming the chairmanship in 1981, Smith has presided over a top-to-bottom reorganization, shaking up the company's bureaucracy and demanding that its staff become more entrepreneurial (Reich, 1985; Burck, 1983). Early in his tenure as chairman, Smith laid off 27,000 white-collar workers and 172,000 blue-collar workers and cut $3 billion from the corporate budget. GM's five car businesses and its Canadian car operations were reorganized into two groups, each of which would have total responsibility for the cars it produced. The assembly division and the body division were disbanded, and their functions were taken over by the two new groups—the Oldsmobile-Buick-Cadillac division and the Chevrolet-Pontiac-GM of Canada division. The overriding goal of these corporate changes was to increase the decision-making power of the staff at every level of the company and to loosen the chain of command, giving subordinates more direct access to their bosses.

By 1987, Smith's efforts were faltering. GM's acquisition of EDS was intended to improve GM's vast data processing requirements. However, the result was a widely publicized culture clash between bureaucratic, committee-managed GM and its newly acquired, more entrepreneurial EDS, with its outspoken founder, Ross Perot. The result was a $700 million payment to dissolve Perot's affiliation with GM.

There have been other setbacks. After the first year's operation of "The Factory of the Future" in Detroit, the facility was running at half speed because many sophisticated machines were breaking down. In addition, business slumps forced layoffs at Hughes Aircraft, another recent GM acquisition. Also, GM recently decided to scale back Saturn Corporation, the project to produce profitable small cars in the United States (Hampton and Norman, 1987).

GM is known for its long view, and it is pushing forward despite these setbacks, which have led to quarterly losses in the hundreds of millions of dollars. Smith's vision for the future has entailed meshing technological advancement with understanding the requirements of its human resources. Economic conditions forced union concessions, which in turn allowed more automation and experimental work design programs. Smith's approach has been to be flexible, to make adjustments in his course, to slow down or change directions slightly, but with a continued vision of the ultimate goal: a competitive, profitable enterprise making maximum use of its technological and human resources.

Donald Petersen, CEO, Ford Motor Company

The other U.S. automakers have experienced frame-breaking change. I will spare the reader a description of Chrysler's legendary comeback led by Lee Iacocca. Ford Motor's Team Taurus and related management style and work structure changes have become another corporate miracle, as I have described in Chapter Two. The effort was led by Donald Petersen, who became Ford's CEO in 1985 after a thirty-seven-year career with the company. Petersen has been described as "soft-spoken, mild, really paternal: the kind of father figure who would insist that you do your homework, then bring you a cup of cocoa as you worked" (Easterbrook, 1986). An engineer by training, Petersen is the first Ford CEO since the company's founder to have in-depth product knowledge rather than training in finance or birthright as his primary credential. Petersen's exposure to Ford's European division on a rotational assignment prompted an appreciation of European functional design, resisted by U.S. automakers. Petersen wanted a car that would be European in every detail: tight handling, no mushy ride; exterior aerodynamic styling and interior ergonomic styling. The risk involved making Taurus and Sable Ford's primary offering in the intermediate class, where most auto sales occur.

With the enlightened assistance of Peter Pestillo (the firm's labor relations manager who was hired in the early 1980s) and the cooperation of United Auto Workers official Donald Elphin, Petersen instituted employee involvement and quality control programs. Petersen also initiated a more open, less bureaucratic management style for company managers. Unlike the flamboyant Iacocca, Petersen has been a quiet inside leader. He meets with employee involvement committees, and attends executive development sessions to discuss company decisions. However, Ford's transition has not been without pain. Ford employment declined 28 percent from 1978 to 1985, a reduction of nearly 143,000 people, equally distributed between management and labor. The reduced labor costs immediately increased profits, showing the prior featherbedding on the factory floor and in the management suite.

Although it took five years to produce Ford's new line of cars, the changes in the corporation, still ongoing, are frame breaking. (See Chapter Five's discussion of frame-breaking change.) Petersen bet the company, incurring losses to develop the new products. Ford would have broken even had the invest-ment in development not been made. Unlike GM's massive re-organizations, joint ventures, and new automation, Ford's effort was initially concentrated on a single corporate goal that in-volved employees at all levels of the company. If Taurus and Sable had flopped, the consequences would have been disas-trous for Ford. The success of these cars reinforced the new product design and work procedures and allowed extending them into other parts of the company.

Silicon Valley Leaders

Silicon Valley has had its share of failures. Adam Os-borne left the company he founded, Osborne Computer Cor-poration, in a dispute with the new management brought in by the board of directors to run the company. Nolan Bushnell, founder of Atari, left the company as it grew more complex. Both organizations subsequently collapsed. These entrepreneurial leaders were unable to envision the change needed to manage growth and adapt to changing technology and a demanding competitive environment.

Steven Jobs, Apple Computer. Steven Jobs is probably the most notable entrepreneur who was unable to adjust as his company grew larger and the business changed. He had difficulty seeing anyone but himself at the helm. His attention to pet products made it difficult for him to understand the needs of the whole business. Steven Wozniak, Apple's cofounder, left the company before Jobs for similar reasons. Wozniak had sharp disagreements with Apple's management over the company's direction and was frustrated with the regimentation of a growing bureaucracy (Bellew, 1985). In both cases, their visions failed to match the business's needs and they were ineffectual in molding the corpo-ration to those visions.

Now under the leadership of John Sculley, Apple is mov-ing from Jobs's one-man product design operation to a more tightly controlled, market-driven product design process (Schlen-der, 1987). Ten years after the company was founded, Sculley's goal is now to produce a steady stream of new products, as do other high-tech companies. Apple's goal is to maintain its innovativeness while meeting the needs of the marketplace. The industry is more competitive and the technology more widespread than when Apple introduced its first model.

New product development under Jobs was a secret mission. Engineers often clashed with marketers and production managers as the product was brought to fruition. Also, product developers worked in isolation of each other and often did not share ideas that could have been helpful.

Sculley is trying to replace Jobs's single-minded, often impulsive passion to create a few revolutionary products with a more structured, collegial approach. Sculley consolidated Apple's product line into a single group. One aspect of the new approach is reduced fear of negative consequences if a project fails to become a product. "The ability to fail is very important to a high-tech company. In fact, you can measure a company's creativity by its failures better than anything else," according to Alan Alcorn, an Apple Fellow (distinguished researcher) responsible for new product ideas (Schlender, 1987, p. 10).

Apple had the resources to adapt to a changing environment, but its founding CEO did not have the capability to change. A new leader was necessary to redirect the company and ensure that it was not only successful in the short run but also developed the capabilities to withstand and take advantage of change in the future. So far, Sculley appears to have the resilience, insight, and identity to accomplish this.

Scott McNeally, Chairman of Sun Microsystems. In another Silicon Valley example, the climate of the organization shaped by the firm's chief executive is turning out to be a determining factor in the battle with a major competitor. Scott McNeally is chairman of Sun Microsystems, a manufacturer of work stations —powerful personal computers used for such tasks as product design and investment planning. Sun has a 23 percent share of this booming market, which grew 65 percent to $1.5 billion in 1986 (Bulkeley, 1987). Sun was founded in 1982 by two engineers and two MBAs, all twenty-seven years old at the time. The corporate style at Sun is open-collar, open-door, and protocol free. Every Friday is dress-down day. Most workers wear jeans and sport shirts. McNeally favors open discussion among his managers and heated disputes in committees. McNeally has maintained the hot-house atmosphere of a start-up company. This corporate personality is reflected in Sun's products and market strategies. Recently, Sun cut its prices on its cheapest work station by 37 percent, making it competitive with some personal computers. It is now half the price of its competitor's cheapest machine.

A Competing Firm with a Different Corporate Culture. Sun's major competitor is Apollo, a Massachusetts firm that founded the work station industry in 1980. Its chairman is Thomas Vanderslice, fifty-three years old, who rose through the ranks at GE and was once president of GTE. Apollo's corporate culture is staid and professional. The atmosphere there is highly corporate with closed doors, scheduled meetings, and a sedate executive suite. Vanderslice believes that being professional does not mean losing the entrepreneurial spirit. The question in the market is whether Apollo can keep up with the flashier Sun and whether Sun could recover if the market took a downturn. Apollo faced a slump in the market in 1984 when its main customers in the semiconductor industry stopped buying capital equipment.

Robert Goizueta, Chairman, Coca-Cola

Goizueta (pronounced Goy-SWEH-tuh) wants to make sure he does not spend time trying to keep things the same (Anderson, 1984). Goizueta, who believes in "intelligent risk taking," has a strategy for the 1980s. Since assuming the chairmanship in 1981, changes in the company have included purchasing Columbia Pictures and introducing Diet Coke in competition with the company's own Tab. The unfavorable customer reaction to New Coke led to returning the old formula to the market in the form of Classic Coke. Goizueta believes that the only way to change the business is to change the people. For instance, he put a marketing expert in charge of Coke's Japanese subsidiary because the company, then run by an engineer, put too much emphasis on production. The new assertive attitude of Coke's managers contributes to its success, and success encourages the assertive attitude.

James Olson, Chairman, AT&T

Olson assumed the chairmanship in June 1986. He took over from Charles L. Brown, who had led the company through divestiture. Olson's mission was to establish a clear direction for the company, which found the postdivestiture marketplace to be far more limited than it had forecast. The company consisted of many diverse elements that were not working together, partly because the government required separation of regulated and unregulated sides of the business. After divestiture, these separation requirements were relaxed, allowing AT&T to operate more as a single company. Several months after assuming the chairmanship, Olson took his vice-presidential staff on a weeklong Cape Cod retreat to iron out a strategy for the company. A three-pronged approach emerged.

The first element of the strategy was to bolster the core businesses of AT&T, especially the long-distance network. The second element was data networking, which meant taking advantage of the company's expertise in designing communications networks for customers' data needs. The third element of the strategy was to develop a more global business and become a major force in the international marketplace. These goals were really directions for the business. The strategies for accomplishing them would unfold over time.

Another element of the vision was to merge departments wherever possible to reduce redundancies and eliminate unnecessary overhead expenses. However, rather than arbitrarily slashing departmental budgets and headcount, Olson recognized that each department would be different in its requirements for streamlining. Each department head was asked to redesign his or her own organization to match the needs of managing that particular part of the business.

Gus Blanchard, an AT&T Executive and Role Model. Some executives at AT&T have turned adversity into success. Gus Blanchard is one example. After the divestiture, he was put in charge of fixing a major problem: the difficulty the long-distance network portion of the company was having filling business customers' orders for private line service. One reason for the problem was the breakdown in systems required to implement an order. Coordination was needed between the divested local operating telephone companies and AT&T's long-distance network. Prior to the Bell System break-up, informal communication between units worked well to ensure on-line installation. This informal communication process broke down after divestiture. Blanchard, an AT&T vice-president, coordinated a nationwide task force to analyze the problems, design new systems, and monitor progress. Blanchard's style was to communicate regularly with his people, often using electronic mail to broadcast updates on progress.

In a later assignment, Blanchard headed AT&T's General Business Systems division, which manufactures and sells communications systems and services to small businesses. This part of the firm had been seeing rapidly diminishing profits and was heading into red ink (Kreiling, 1987). When Blanchard took over as head of the unit, he initiated a series of videotaped meetings with employees. His goal was to convince everyone that the problems were real and to ensure that everyone heard the same story. He started a rumor hot line for employees to call executives. Blanchard himself took over 300 rumor-killing calls. In an open letter to employees he squashed the rumor that AT&T was selling the General Business Systems unit. Blanchard used this open communication style to explain his new business plan and involve employees in the process. Employees in separate branches began to see that other branches had the same problems. The videotapes and newsletters were a way to share solutions and jointly track progress. Employees felt that top management cared about them and their customers. The result of Blanchard's leadership was above-target financial performance only one year after he took over.

Obviously, other examples of leadership, business strategy, and human resources philosophy could be cited. The above cases show the importance of the leader's vision for the future. However, having a vision does not mean the company will follow it. On the one hand, a company in need of a major shakeup may drift under a managerial chief executive—an executive who focuses primarily on process, argues Abraham Zaleznik of the Harvard Business School (Wysocki, 1984). On the other hand, a company in need of a slight change may steer off course with a maverick leader. If the leader is out of touch with the demands of the business, he or she endangers the company as well as him- or herself. Moreover, a leader who has the confidence of the company's employees and stockholders may be in for setbacks as the direction for change needs to be altered to respond to environmental shifts.

Characteristics Needed to Lead Organizational Change

The leader's personality, insight, and clarity of direction can have a major influence on the success of a corporation. One important element of a leader's personality is *resilience* (London, 1985a). This is a combination of self-confidence, desire to achieve, and willingness to take risks. Resilience is needed in a changing environment because the leader usually does not have immediate feedback on the success of his or her strategy. The leader must be able to persist in the face of constant questioning from stockholders, managers, nonmanagement employees, customers, and suppliers.

Jack Welch at GE and Roger Smith at GM took the long-term view of what their corporations needed to do. This is often at the expense of short-term profit. Stockholders criticized Welch for making slow acquisition decisions. Smith faced criticism from Ross Perot, who for a short time was a member of the GM board and the largest GM stockholder as well as the head of GM's newly acquired EDS subsidiary. Perot argued in public that GM's bureaucracy continued to overwhelm any attempts to take action in response to customers' needs. Coca-

Cola's Robert Goizueta believed in risk taking and expressed no love for keeping things the same. Ford's Donald Petersen quietly created a renewed mission and management style for the firm, incurring stiff costs for a tremendous benefit.

Jobs and Wozniak at Apple Computer believed in themselves and their vision for the future of their company, and thus demonstrated resilience—persistence in their desire to achieve what they knew best. But they each lacked insight into the extreme conditions faced by their company. *Insight* is a second characteristic needed by leaders in a changing environment. The leader must have a clear concept of the goals of the business and be able to see the whole organizational picture. Also the leader must have insight into him- or herself as well as staff members. Adam Osborne (of Osborne Computer) and Nolan Bushnell (Atari) lacked the insight needed to understand the changing marketplace.

Resilience and insight are, in my view, the foundation for a meaningful corporate identity or direction. That is, the leader of the business must have a sense of the company's identity. *Identity* refers to the goals the leader has for the corporation. The term *identity* is appropriate because it implies that corporate direction must be internalized by the leaders of the corporation. Stated another way, the corporation and its goals must become part of the leader's identity. This is one reason why successful entrepreneurs such as Jobs had trouble changing direction. Their view of corporate identity was entwined with their individual identity, and changing the corporation implied changing their self-concept.

Entrepreneurs such as Jobs and Wozniak were not able to adjust to the needs of a growing business. In a sense all environments are emerging. They are constantly changing, some more rapidly than others. Leaders need resilience, insight, and identity to establish a corporate direction that matches the needs of the business at the time. Leaders must have confidence in themselves, a desire to achieve, and a willingness to take the necessary risks. They also must be able to accurately perceive their strengths and weaknesses. Moreover, they need an understanding of the internal and external politics of managing people and generating commitment to corporate goals. They need a sense of identity—a clear vision for the future. Resilience and insight are the basis for a meaningful identity. However, despite strong resilience and insight, once identity has been established, it is often difficult to change. This is because leaders with resilience believe in what they are doing and are able to resist forces against that direction. A rude awakening, such as when Iacocca was fired by Ford, may be required for the leader to make a meaningful change in personal and corporate direction.

A new environment requires that leaders and managers be flexible and adaptable. Resilience and insight imply that the leader understands the environment and has the motivation to take the needed risks.

Also, resilience and insight imply that identity is appropriate to the nature of the environment. Otherwise, the corporate direction would be out of synch with the demands of the situation. This is what happens when leaders do not adjust their behavior to a changing environment. Their insight is blocked by their identity. Thus, although insight contributes to identity, identity may become a barrier to continued insight over time.

Leaders who have strong resilience may be able to avoid this problem. Resilience implies a sufficiently strong self-concept that allows a person to admit mistakes and accept failure without becoming debilitated. In this sense, resilience is the foundation that allows continued insight and periodic adjustment in identity. We have seen that this combination is hard to come by. One could possibly argue that success makes a leader inflexible. The leader naturally wants to continue behavior that was rewarded in the past. The self-concept prevents the leader from making the changes that would avoid failure in a changing environment. This theorizing needs to be further developed and tested. For now, my intention is to emphasize that emerging environments require top managers with resilience, insight, and identity to take risks, understand the environment, and establish and implement a vision for the future. The difficulty is that people have trouble changing their style of management and their goals.

Lower- and Mid-Level Managers as Change Agents

The first part of this chapter focused on the leader as a change agent. Effective organization-wide change must be managed from the top (Beckhard, 1969). However, other managers throughout the organizational hierarchy will be involved in introducing change (Beckhard and Harris, 1987). This section describes the roles they play at various points in the change effort.

Managers' roles are changing from controlling, organizing, planning, and decision making to facilitating relationships. Managers need to create an environment for goal accomplishment. They design jobs, make assignments, suggest linkages between people and groups, enhance the work environment within their units, and help their units work smoothly with other groups internal and external to the organization (Kotter, 1985). Responding to environmental change requires managers to be flexible and able to cope with uncertainty.

Level Differences. Managers' level in the organization makes a difference in their willingness to handle uncertainty. Lower-level managers are likely to have more well-defined jobs, and they generally spend less time interacting with others than do higher-level managers. Perhaps because of this, lower-level managers are reluctant to seek out others when they are dealing with matters about which they are uncertain (Hannaway, 1985). Because lower-level managers are not consulted to the same degree as upper managers, lower-level managers must take the initiative when they need information or want assurance. Upper-level managers are constantly being called on to meet with other managers, and they have less need to share or seek information that resolves uncertainty. For them, uncertainty is resolved in the course of daily activity.

A danger is that because lower-level managers are more reticent under conditions of uncertainty, higher-level managers may not be aware of a problem until it becomes a fire to fight (perhaps a reason why "putting out fires" is a big part of managerial work). If lower-level managers are suppressing problems, higher-level managers must take action to solicit the views of lower-level managers and encourage greater communication between levels. This is also a reason why lower-level managers, possibly more than those at higher levels, need to be educated in how to analyze the environment, determine needed changes, and bring them about.

Rational Managerial Behavior in a Changing World. Organizations such as GM undergo frame-breaking change because they fail to anticipate changes in the environment, such as international competition, the cost of raw materials, and societal values that change customer demands (Burck, 1983). GM has begun to adjust and is on a trajectory for further change. However, the corporation will have to be resilient in the face of financial expectations on Wall Street. High-profit years may create complacency; low-profit years may create temptations to change the course for short-term gain at the expense of long-term success. This is not to say that GM should stick to its new direction no matter what. Rather, a new type of rationality is demanded, one that is based on insight into the reasons for organizational strategies, how well they are working, and how these strategies mesh with the environment. This new rationality also requires flexibility in direction, the same flexibility that brought about the change in the first place.

This need for understanding corporate direction and flexibility in response to a changing environment is not confined to the amorphous "organization as a whole" or to the top leadership of a corporation. Managers at all levels bring about the change. They have to understand how their behavior contributes to their unit's goals and ultimately to the organization's objectives. Managers face the need to reduce costs, to do more with fewer people, and to give employees more autonomy in making decisions affecting them. Corporate change cannot occur without managers understanding and being willing to change their behavior. However, old habits are tough to break. One GM executive commented in the fall of 1982 (as GM's new management strategy of more employee participation was unfolding) that only about half of the company's 45,000 managers had really grasped the need to change old ways of operating. "Over-confidence dies hard, particularly in an organization as conservative as GM. And of course, it dies all the harder when sales and profits are moving up" (cited in Mitroff, 1985, p. 196).

Managers used to a bureaucratic environment are reluctant to give up control. They cling to structure and a by-the-books mentality. Sudden shifts in corporate strategy or a unit's direction are difficult for them to envision, let alone initiate. Rational behavior is synonymous with cautious study and calculated efforts.

Today, rationality is taking on new meaning.

> Thinking rationally in today's world basically means being aware of the key assumptions that one is making about the critical stakeholders that impact on one's business. It also means engaging in a continually ongoing process of challenging one's assumptions. It does not mean following some rigid financial method of analysis for the critical assumptions upon which every organization's policies depend are broader in scope than solely financial ones. It means being aware as much as possible of all the assumptions one is making. It thus means engaging in a process of critical reasoning, not following blindly some magic formula for success [Mitroff, 1985, pp. 198–199].

Desirable Managerial Characteristics. Certainly there are many desirable managerial and leadership characteristics. I like to focus on three clusters of characteristics: resilience, insight, and identity as important for leadership and management in this new environment (London, 1983, 1985a).

Managers must be resilient, meaning they must both want to achieve and be willing to take risks to achieve their goals. They must decide when it is important to act independently and when it is important to cooperate with others. They need insight into how they are doing, and they get that insight by asking for feedback from supervisors, peers, and subordinates. It helps to have clear goals, but it also helps to be flexible in altering or refining these goals as the situation changes. Moreover, managers need to have identity—a sense of direction for themselves and the organization.

Resilience, insight, and identity help in analyzing and resolving uncertain situations. These characteristics enable managers to experiment with different alternatives—not to vacillate, but to try an alternative with conviction, and if that does not work, to try something else. (See London, 1985a, for a description of how the organization reinforces and supports managers' resilience, insight, and identity.)

The concepts of resilience, insight, and identity parallel the desirable change agent skills identified by Huse (1975). He described the importance of a stable, secure self-image and flexibility, characteristics that are consistent with my concept of resilience. He emphasized self-assessment and the ability to see things objectively as other important characteristics. These fit with my notion of insight. Lastly, he highlighted imagination and consistency as other valuable qualities, which are in line with my view of identity. Huse also discussed the importance of honesty and trust, which perhaps cut across resilience, insight, and identity in that change agents need a clear and accurate picture of their values and goals.

Types of Change Agents. Managers have a role in identifying the need for change, establishing the direction for constructive change, and then making change happen. Change agents behave differently at different stages of change. At the early stage, the vision for the change is clearer. At later stages, the focus of change may become more ambiguous as it is altered in the face of resistance and begins to take on different forms. Ottaway (1983) suggested the following taxonomy of change agents that applies to leaders, to managers, and as described in Chapter One, to human resource professionals.

Change Generators

1. *Key change agents.* Those who convert an issue into a felt need. This is usually the role of a charismatic leader. An example is Lee Iacocca, whose methods, style, and values dominated the change process at Chrysler. Iacocca eventually became a symbol of U.S. pride and rebirth.
2. *Demonstrators.* These change agents demonstrate support for the change conceptualized by the key change agent. They are first in the line of confrontation to face those who prefer the status quo. The demonstrator's role is to provide visible, vocal support for the change.
3. *Patrons.* These individuals support the change process, financially or psychologically. For instance, a patron of change may provide the key change agent with a budget, a prestigious title, a promotion, or other symbols of support.
4. *Defenders.* This role entails defending the change at the grass roots—the lower levels of the organization. The manager-defender is caught up by the charisma of the key change agent, by becoming an adherent, and by spreading the word among the troops. Defenders may see how they can benefit from the change, or they may be pushed into defending the change by resisters.

Change Implementors

5. *External change implementors.* These individuals are invited from outside the organization to implement change. They may be consultants for organizational development efforts hired to articulate and implement the key change agent's vision. External change agents have the advantage of a fresh perspective and no vested interest in keeping things the way they are.
6. *External/internal change implementors.* These individuals develop internal implementors. Staff managers from headquarters, who are alien to the field organizations, may have the task of carrying the word from on high to the masses. They are external in the sense that they appear to

come from outside. Yet they are long-standing members of the organization with the traditional supports.

7. *Internal change implementors.* These are managers who assume the responsibility to implement the change in their own organizations. Convinced of the need for change, they model other change agents to move their units in the desired direction, often translating or redefining the change to meet their own needs.

Change Adopters

8. *Early adopters.* These managers practice the new change. The first adopters show the highest commitment and become the prototypes for the change. Going beyond implementation, they maintain the change, making it the norm in their organization.

9. *Maintainers.* These managers are primarily concerned with meeting current business needs, doing their jobs to keep the organization going. However, they are willing to adopt the change in the process, because they see how it contributes to their own work. Their objective is to sustain the organization, and they realize that the change is one of the things that you have to do now and then to assure the organization's survival. An example is how managers readily take on new or added responsibilities in the wake of a reorganization of functions and reporting relationships.

10. *Users.* Managers become users when they make a habit of the change. Initially, they have the least commitment to the change, and they are probably the last adopters. Yet they are likely to benefit the most from the change. Without them, the change would never be successful.

All managers may play these roles at different times. For example, generators become implementors who later (or simultaneously) become adopters. Alternately, managers may assume only one or two roles in a change process. The key point here is that managers must not only be aware of the need for change; they must create it, accept it, and play a role in bringing it about. They may get help from outsiders who are experts in organizational development or management strategy. But the manager is not just reacting or following another's lead. The manager must become a mover and a shaker. Even if the change is originated somewhere else, the manager creates the setting for making the change happen.

Top executives and managers may be the agents of change. They are the visionaries, the designers, and the implementors. Occupational employees may also be agents of change when they are given the opportunity to participate in decisions to improve quality of worklife and productivity. Organizational consultants and human resource professionals are another source of change. They work with the initiators of change to conceptualize, communicate, introduce, and operationalize the change.

The Role of Organization Effectiveness Consulting

Most organizational changes of any magnitude are not simple processes. Because the changes require the cooperation of many people along the way, they are likely to encounter numerous barriers, if for no other reason than people tend to resist altering what is familiar and comfortable. Therefore, change agents need help. This is often when the human resource professional comes in—either as an internal consultant or as an external consultant hired to work on the problem.

Consultation is a general label for many variations of helping relationships. A general definition of consultation assumes that the consultation relationship is a voluntary relationship between a professional helper (consultant) and the client, formed to give help to the client in identifying and meeting a challenge. The relationship is perceived as temporary by both parties, and the relationship is a collaborative one where the client and consultant concur in all major decisions throughout the effort. Also, the consultant is an outsider, that is, not a part of any hierarchical power system in which the client is located.

The consultant's role includes providing information, identifying and helping to solve problems, building consensus, facilitating learning (so clients can solve their own problems in the future), and ultimately improving organizational effectiveness.

As described in Chapter One, the human resource professional as consultant may be directive, by initiating action, or nondirective, by providing advice or information. Consultants help the client "see or hear" the situation more clearly by asking reflective questions. They are also group process consultants and fact finders; they offer alternatives and collaborate in solving problems.

Many large companies have internal organization effectiveness consultants. They may work in the human resource department or they may be employed by other departments in the organization. Such a consultant should be a person who is knowledgeable about the organization, its business, and its operations. This usually requires having some line experience. (For instance, a large stock brokerage firm requires its internal consultants to become stockbrokers and spend some time in various jobs dealing with customers and facing the daily problems of the business.)

The internal consultant may be a specialist in organizational behavior and development (for example, a person with a graduate degree from a business school or a psychology department with a specialty in organizational psychology). Or the internal consultant may be a line manager who is sent to short courses in organizational behavior and process consultation to prepare for the consulting role. One organization uses the consultant job as a training ground for fast-track managers. Becoming a consultant is viewed as a valuable experience that can help managers as they move up in the business.

The internal consultant is often most effective at lower levels in the organization. Higher-level managers often prefer to deal with external consultants—professionals who bring an objective, broad view of the organization and experience with other companies.

Consultants with human resource expertise played important roles in several of the change efforts discussed earlier in this chapter. Ford's increased employee involvement began with top manager teams that were facilitated by external process consultants; the top managers later trained internal managers to facilitate team interactions across levels. I have noted the importance of Ford's labor relations officer in working with the union. At

GE, Jack Welch's vision for the future is communicated through a series of training programs at their corporate training facility in Croton-on-Hudson, New York. Recently, Noel Tichy, a management professor at the University of Michigan, was given a two-year assignment as the head of GE's training institute. He had a major role in designing a curriculum and advising Welch about ways to communicate and enhance managers' commitment to GE's strategy.

Identifying the Need for a Change Consultant

As agents for change, leaders and managers originate, implement, and adopt change efforts. Organizational assessment and the advice of an external consultant may help in establishing directions for planned change.

There are times when leaders and managers have difficulty understanding leadership, structure, goals, climate, and interpersonal relationships. They may find it difficult to identify behavior patterns that affect the performance of their organization. These elements of management strongly govern individual and team capability, which in turn control performance. Because efforts to achieve customer satisfaction and profitability are priorities, a systematic approach for identifying areas of growth is essential to the success of a company. Organizational development consultants, one type of human resource professional, provide the resources and perspectives to enable organizations at all levels to achieve the excellent performance necessary to attain these goals.

All leaders and managers need to examine the possibilities of what they currently are versus what they can be. Once the possibilities are clear, they can start to think about what barriers, if any, are keeping their organization "stuck" where it is. Human resource professionals may be called on by leaders and managers to help them determine if a consultant is necessary and then to identify who should be commissioned. The following guide may help managers consider areas for needed change, and whether a consultant may be helpful for clarifying issues, solving problems, and generally improving organizational effectiveness.

Human resource professionals should encourage leaders and managers to think about how satisfied they are with themselves and their groups on the following items.

Morale
Productivity
Service/product quality
Work flow
Overall structure
Professionalism
Cost consciousness
Flexibility
Environment
Goal-setting skills
Management style
Supervisory-subordinate ratio
Supervision
Decision-making skills
Understanding corporate goals
Inter/intra-group communications
Commitment to corporate goals
Motivation to achieve
Ability to be creative and innovative
Ability to make timely decisions

Human resource professionals might ask their clients the following questions.

Are you on the leading edge of corporate visionaries who are well on their way to success?
Do you have a sense that you have a good organization that can be even better?
Do you have an organizational goal in mind?
Do small problems, such as communications difficulties, hinder your goal accomplishment?
Do you need a stronger goal, and do some barriers need to be moved out of the way?
Do you feel the organization needs redirection?

These questions should prompt leaders and managers to think about the complexion of their organization. Do they want to change? Are they *ready* to change? Is the workgroup ready to change? People are generally uncomfortable with change, and they must be able to overcome the urge to retreat at the first sign of uncertainty.

Leaders and managers who are ready to change should ask themselves whether they are prepared to devote their time and energy and their group's resources to the process. If they are, they are probably ready for an organizational development consultant. If they are undecided, they could talk to a consultant. An organizational development consultant's experience can help them to understand their feelings of uncertainty and perhaps enable them to decide if they are ready to change.

Once leaders or managers have decided to contact a consultant, they will need to have some information available for the first meeting. They should give some thought to what they see as their organization's potential and what is keeping it from getting there. The following checklist can aid in this examination.

1. What is the opportunity/challenge?
2. Whose opportunity/challenge is it?
3. What signs cause doubt about its achievement?
4. What is the cost of not achieving it?
5. How would the organization benefit if the opportunity/ challenge were realized?
6. Can the problem be solved internally?
7. How can the consultant's skills be used to benefit the group?

Guidance for Choosing a Consultant

The following guide should help in selecting organizational development consultants or consultants for specific purposes such as employee attitude surveys and program evaluation (methods covered in Chapter Nine). This should help human resource professionals both advise their clients in choosing a consultant and, as consultants themselves, to contract with clients.

Once a problem arises and the need for additional resources has been recognized, the search for a consultant begins.
Some consultants come with ready-made solutions, and the
choice of consultant depends on the solution deemed desirable.
For instance, a consultant who specializes in conducting training needs analyses would be desirable if the problem already
revolves around the need to examine training requirements.
Some consultants help formulate the problem, but they may or
may not be good at implementing a solution. Consequently, the
situation may call for different consultants at different stages of
the change process. The following are issues and questions to
consider in selecting a consultant.

  I.   Area of Specialization
       A.   Is the problem clear? If so, the need for a particu-
           lar type of consultant is probably evident. If not,
           someone with good knowledge of the organization
           or department may be desirable. Alternately, it
           may be necessary to invest in a consultant to bring
           him or her up to speed with the organization—the
           work, the climate, and so on.
       B.   Ethical consultants will inform you if the problem
           or issue is beyond their expertise, and they may
           recommend others who are better equipped to
           deal with the issues.
 II.   Sources of Consultants
       A.   Directories published by professional organizations
           (such as the American Society of Training and
           Development) are sources of names. A professional
           association may do some screening (for example,
           a consultant may have to be a member of the orga-
           nization and have certain degrees or have met cer-
           tain certification requirements to be listed).
       B.   Referrals are an excellent source of consultants.
           They provide a way to assess consultants' credibil-
           ity with top management and their effectiveness in
           producing a high-quality product on time.
       C.   Prior experience with a consultant is a good way

to select a consultant for a new project. However, if the project is substantially different from an earlier one, there is no assurance that the consultant will do a good job on the next project. Some leaders and managers develop relationships of trust and confidence with one or more consultants, and they tend to rely on them to meet almost any need. This is simple but does not always bring the best talent to bear on the project.

III. Evaluating Consultant Projects

    A. Inviting project proposals is a good way to compare consultants. This is possible when the project is fairly well structured and each proposal will be for similar work. The request for proposal should detail the sections that should be included in the proposals, such as the methods, time lines, analyses, and costs.

    B. Examining prior work outputs and talking to the consultant's clients are other ways to evaluate client efforts. Consultants like to list the company names of their clients, and they should be willing to supply names of key contacts in those companies. These contacts in turn may name others who have had experience with the consultant. One technique is to send out a "consultant appraisal and review form" asking about the nature of the assignment and an evaluation of the consultant's performance or the performance of the consulting firm's employees. This request should be made only with the prior approval of the consultant.

    C. Cost is another basis for comparison, but here the scope of the projects proposed by the consultants needs to be compared. Often, price is a reflection of the consultant's experience and reputation. Paying for reputation makes sense when the consultant has history of solid work performance.

    D. One potential indicator of consultants' worth is their willingness to evaluate their projects—in fact, to build evaluation into the project design. The astute manager should be willing to pay for evaluation, and the competent consultant should suggest objective, independent evaluation efforts. Evaluation is not just an indicator of the value of the final product, but also should provide information to refine and improve the project as it unfolds. This is termed *action research,* as described in Chapter Nine. The more costly the project and the deeper its impact on the corporation, the more important evaluation is to the project's success.

IV. Contracting

A. A formal contract for services is a critical but often ignored step. The contract specifies the services that will be performed, due dates, and costs. It is best to have an estimate of the total costs rather than a per-day rate that will continue until the project is completed. In addition, it is important to have projections of both professional fees and expenses (travel, printing, and the like).

B. A nondisclosure agreement may be important to a competitive enterprise because the specifics of the project may be technical or in some other way be a competitive advantage to the firm. A contract should also specify other legal relationships, such as liabilities in case of physical injury, product damage, and so forth.

C. At the very least, there should be a written letter of agreement specifying the work that will be done and the costs. This letter should be signed by both parties. Less formal and detailed than a contract, a letter of agreement outlines the work and price and provides written documentation.

D. Contracts should be established for internal consultants as well. Corporations with internal organizational development consultants are likely to charge back for those services at a competitive rate. A contract for such services is as important for the internal consultant as it is for the client because the consultant's reputation within the company rests on satisfying internal clients.

For more information on contracting with consultants see McGonagle (1981).

The Human Resource Professional as Change Initiator and Facilitator

Human resource professionals may serve as internal consultants when they are skilled in organization development, but other human resource specialists may be valuable consultants in other ways. For instance, analyses of employee demographic characteristics (for example, retirement eligibility during the next five years), studies of skills and knowledge in critical and emerging job areas, and reports on environmental trends (for example, labor force availability) are valuable data to business planners. In this sense, the company's human resources are viewed as strategic for accomplishing business goals, and human resource professionals educate the firm's executives on the importance of human resource forecasting and planning to developing business strategy. (See Chapter Two's discussion of environmental trends and Chapter Eight's overview of the human resource forecasting and planning function.)

Human resource professionals may also help set business strategy by introducing new organizational technologies and management strategies. Examples of these are employee involvement programs, participative management, job redesign methods, workgroup structure design, and team building. Because these methods can improve productivity, they are obviously linked to the success of the organization (Guzzo, Jette, and Katzell, 1985). Human resource professionals can lead the organization by training managers, analyzing and redesigning job and workgroup structures, diagnosing weaknesses in department operations, and recommending and implementing new methods and procedures.

Unfortunately, human resource professionals often face

the frustration of not being welcomed by line managers with open arms. The personnel function may be viewed solely as a support for routine transactions, processes, and policies, such as payroll changes for job transfers, job evaluation, affirmative action monitoring, supervisory training, health benefits, medical services, attendance practices, labor relations negotiations, and the like. Personnel department staff are not readily viewed as the source of new business practices and plans, especially when the daily transactions are a source of complaint.

Clearly, human resource professionals must do both jobs well. They need to enhance the quality of routine personnel services and they need to facilitate the transformation of the organization to prepare for the future. They also need to educate managers as change agents.

Business leaders who recognize that the firm's people are a key to competitive advantage are likely to look to the personnel department to identify human resource strategies to make the business successful. (See Chapter Seven's discussion of how the design of the human resource department can influence the role that line managers play in treating human resources as valuable assets.)

Summary

This chapter reviewed the roles that leaders, managers, and human resource professionals enact as organizational change agents. Examples of progressive corporate leaders demonstrated that direction from the top of the organization is critical in designing and implementing change. Nevertheless, managers at all organizational levels, and occupational workers as well, may transform the organization as change generators, implementors, and adopters. Resilience, insight, and identity are key personal characteristics to respond to and to create meaningful change. Human resource professionals' knowledge and skills can be a strategic resource for accomplishing business goals. As change agents they both direct and facilitate organizational change.

Chapter Four begins a section on changing people and organizational culture. It describes how the characteristics of resilience, insight, and identity can be supported and developed by human resource programs and policies. The chapter shows how exposure to different business conditions is important to managing change and recognizing the requirements of different business environments. The chapter presents methods and guidance for learning to handle uncertain situations and to establish organizational direction. As such it suggests strategies for human resource professionals to consider in designing training and development programs to encourage and prepare managers to be change agents. Chapters Five and Six then describe how organizational cultures are changed and how human resource professionals can support, and at times initiate, these efforts.

4

Preparing People to Handle Change

 This chapter describes what leaders, managers, and human resource professionals can do to prepare themselves and others to be change agents. Human resource professionals are often responsible for designing such development programs. The examples and suggestions provide directions for human resource professionals to help prepare people to deal with change.

Typical Development Processes

The belief shared by most companies is that significant development occurs on the job and that the ability to develop people should be a key element in the performance evaluation of any manager (Digman, 1978; London and Stumpf, 1982). In many companies, a newly hired manager attends a company orientation program and training sessions in his or her functional area. After a period of successful performance, the individual's potential as a manager is evaluated. Those identified early in their careers as having the potential to advance are placed on a high-potential list. People on this list are moved into a series of line and staff assignments, often moving between departments

71

to acquire a broad picture of the company. They may also attend executive development programs at major universities to better understand the environment in which the corporation operates. Only about 3 to 5 percent of new managers are placed in such high-potential programs. Others have opportunities for training and lateral transfers with the possibility of promotion, but generally at a slower pace than those identified as high-potential managers. Corporate development programs also rely on supervisors to provide on-the-job coaching and performance feedback as well as job assignments that are valuable for development.

To supplement on-the-job development, large companies have in-house training departments that offer courses in management skills such as decision making, time management, appraisal processes, oral and written communication, and the like. In addition, companies usually view self-development activities, such as attending evening courses toward an MBA degree, as an indication of the individual's commitment to professional development. At higher levels of the organization, succession planning is vital to ensure continuity of the corporation. Top managers may meet periodically to identify potential successors and determine further grooming needed for likely candidates.

Linking Employee Development to Business Needs

In today's environment of corporate change, many things create the need for new management development strategies: uncertainty, new technology, and tough competition between organizations and between the people within them. Managers must understand the process of bringing about organizational change in line with the changing environment. This requires being able to create a vision of the future and gaining the commitment and involvement of employees in the design and implementation of the change. Managers need to understand what is necessary to enhance competitive advantage—for example, reducing costs, differentiating the company's products and services from those of competitors, and being responsive to customers' needs. In addition, the manager must be responsive to the needs of clients in the company. This requires awareness of the interdependencies between individuals and between groups (Kotter, 1985). Managing in today's environment requires understanding the diversity of employees in terms of their skills, career goals, stages in life, and family responsibilities.

Introducing new technology may require redesigning reporting relationships and changing the skills employees need to do the job (see Chapter Five). In addition to learning about the technology and acquiring the needed technical skills, employees must adapt to changes in structure and possibly take direction from people who have less experience and fewer skills. Change agent managers need to understand how employees affected by such changes can be involved in the process of implementing those changes. The research I report in Chapters Five and Six shows that employee involvement can enhance commitment to new technology. However, the manager must be willing to allow employees to adapt the technology to fit their needs.

Quality of worklife programs require a participative style of management aimed at cooperation and integration of different points of view. Establishing self-managing workgroups (called "third-generation quality of worklife" in Chapter Six) requires attention to developing positive workgroup relationships and providing the group with information and resources rather than structure and control. Self-managing groups will ultimately be held accountable for their performance outcomes, but the process of accomplishing those outcomes will be up to the group. The manager needs to understand group development and the need to lessen the amount of structure and control as the group progresses. Moreover, the manager needs to change his or her focus, concentrating less over time on the immediate workgroup and more on intergroup issues. Self-managing teams are fragile. It takes time for group members to develop the necessary trust in each other and in management, especially when there is a history of close supervision and adversarial union-management relationships. The implication for employee development is that employees must learn how to work together as a group to solve problems.

Continuous Learning

Companies are beginning to understand the value of paying people more as they acquire new skills, even if those skills are not used immediately. As long as the skills are relevant to the business, employees with more skills give the organization flexibility for varying assignments depending on need. This must be balanced with the fact that some assignments require fewer skills, and these jobs can be done by less-educated, lower-paid employees. Consequently, the organization may find itself decreasing the qualifications required for some jobs while increasing the requirements for other jobs and encouraging employees on these jobs to acquire more skills.

Experimenting Organizations

Self-designing and self-evaluating organizations continually appraise and revise their behaviors and invent new directions to maintain their long-term viability (Bedeian, 1986). Continued experimentation becomes institutionalized. Managers ask themselves how they will know when they are successful, or put another way, when a new program is successful. Managers learn from feedback from their environment as new knowledge, tools, behaviors, and values are tested. Also, managers want rigorous, objective methods for measuring the effects of their actions (as discussed in Chapter Nine).

Valuing Employees

Chapter Two described how leaders' human resource strategies depend on business conditions. Managers' support for employee development will also vary with business conditions and on the extent to which top managers value employees' contributions to the organization—treating employees as resources for the future or as a way to meet immediate business needs.

Consider the difference between the extremes of a declining organization and a growing organization. A declining organization that supports employee development encourages employees to try new business ventures and to learn what is necessary to make them successful. The company prepares employees to leave when layoffs are necessary. Outplacement services and career counseling are offered. Retraining programs prepare employees for job vacancies in the company or in other companies. When support for employee development is low in a declining organization, employees are laid off with little or no warning. Only those employees whose skills and performance levels match business needs are retained.

Support for employee development is easier when the company is prospering. In a growing organization that supports employee development, education is a top priority. Supervisors encourage subordinates to take advantage of training resources within and outside the organization. Tuition assistance programs and career counseling support a continuous learning environment. Rotational assignments are created to develop employees' skills and their understanding of the business. The company may require each employee to have a certain number of hours of technical, sales, and/or managerial training, perhaps twenty to forty hours per year.

Where there is little support for employee development, training may be required only when it meets immediate business needs—for example, training in the technical aspects of a new product. Some top managers give their attention to developing only high-potential managers by moving them into different departments as they advance through the organization and by sending them to external training programs. But for most employees, opportunities to transfer to different jobs are infrequent and are not aimed at promoting new learning.

IBM. Support for employee development usually stems directly from top management, not the human resource department. For instance, IBM's support for employee education began in the mid 1950s when its chairman, Thomas Watson, Jr., recognized that the business was outrunning its supply of top managers. Today, IBM spends more than $600 million annually in employee development and training. The company's top managers believe that the educational system drives the business.

First-line supervisors receive eighty hours of classroom training during the first year on the new job. Within thirty days of a promotion, each manager must attend a one-week class at IBM's Management Development Center in Armonk, New York. The training covers the company's history, beliefs, policies, and practices in addition to basic managerial skills including motivation, appraisal, and communication. Each employee must attend at least ten hours of company-sponsored training per year.

GE. In the early 1980s, GE began to attack the problem of developing "information-age talent." It formed a partnership with Purdue's Krannert Graduate School of Management to provide courses for management information systems managers to train them on MBA subjects. The program lasts over three summers with six two-week sessions on campus. In general, training at GE is systematically related to the company's business goals. Each year, an annual review of development needs is conducted. Managers are held accountable to ensure that adequate training is provided to meet business goals.

Hewlett-Packard. Hewlett-Packard uses training not only to increase employees' knowledge and skills but also to perpetuate the organization's philosophy and shared values. In this sense, training and development are strategic. They help top management put business plans into action and share the vision of the organization's future. Training avoids costs that come from wasted time and poor customer relationships. Hewlett-Packard realizes that employees need a thorough understanding of the firm's businesses, the procedures used to produce its products and services, customer needs, and the strategies that are followed to grow their businesses.

AT&T. After the Bell System divestiture, AT&T's long-distance service departments realized that the increasingly competitive environment demanded new ways of managing. The fast pace of change and the need for rapid responses required that managers have as much decision-making discretion as possible. Moreover, the need to cut costs and cut people meant fewer middle managers, and the remaining managers would have broader spans of control. Consequently, managers could not bring every problem and decision to their bosses. As managers' responsibilities increased, so did the responsibility of their subordinates. The personnel department could not tell people how to manage in this new environment. However, it could outline the general outputs required of every manager with the understanding that the manager had to decide how to achieve the outputs for which he or she would be responsible.

The desired managerial outputs and underlying philosophy were published in a set of documents called the "Managing for Excellence Library." The booklets covered the company's business plans in general terms; important managerial outputs needed to accomplish the human resources component of the business plans; competencies required to produce those outputs; and recommended goal setting, appraisal, feedback, and career management processes and resources. The concepts were developed with input from line managers. The outputs that managers were asked to concentrate on were establishing performance goals; developing positive interpersonal relationships within workgroups; fostering networks and positive relationships between groups; designing challenging jobs; and achieving performance goals. The competencies needed to achieve these goals included decision making, leadership, and communication skills, among others. A training curriculum was established to offer courses on these competencies. A performance appraisal form asked managers to indicate development plans for subordinates in addition to evaluating their performance.

Another AT&T effort was aimed at assessing managers' contributions to their jobs and preparing them for future technological changes. It recognized that the meaning of employee development was changing from preparing for promotion to increasing employees' capabilities on their current jobs. It was a way to help avoid the career plateaus that many managers experienced because of declining promotional opportunities (Bardwick, 1986; Hall, 1985). The effort was to establish mastery paths for attaining job competencies (London and Mone,

1987). As applied to seven job families in one department, a mastery path for each job outlined skills and output expectations over time as the individual learned the job. Salary increases and promotions recognized the attainment of mastery. Developing the mastery paths required drawing on the expert knowledge of job incumbents. Personnel department managers and personnel psychologists helped in several ways. For instance, job analysis, job evaluation, compensation, selection, and appraisal systems were needed to develop the mastery paths.

The mastery path concept was one department's answer to enhancing professionalism. Another department established a "people plan" to highlight the importance of managing people. This provided career development and training programs to redevelop supervisory skills. A personnel manager was assigned the function of career development specialist. In addition, and perhaps most importantly, the vice-president of the department emphasized that managers would be evaluated and rewarded partially on how well they managed their people.

Honeywell. The importance of developing people was also emphasized at Honeywell. They established a $3,000 award for people development and announced thirty-seven recipients. The prize helped show how people development contributes to the bottom line. A single manager can foster the development of many others during his or her career, and make Honeywell a successful and exciting place to work.

Receptiveness to Learning

Major transitions are times for learning. People are particularly receptive to learning during times of transition perhaps because routines are altered and new behaviors are expected. This occurs when a person starts his or her first job, changes careers, or retires. Other changes (such as a new job or a new assignment) are also opportunities for learning, especially when the environment is different and behavioral expectations are altered.

Several years ago, I participated in the development of an orientation program for people recently promoted or hired into the first level of management. The goal of the program was to help new managers understand what was expected of them as supervisors and what they could expect from their own supervisors. Part of the two-and-a-half day program was a half-day module on understanding one's career motivation and how bosses affect the career motivation of their subordinates. We produced videotapes of new managers and bosses describing their experiences along dimensions that I had found in previous research to be important to career motivation.

The dimensions were resilience (a combination of self-confidence, a desire to achieve, and a willingness to take risks), insight (an understanding of one's strengths and weaknesses and an understanding of the political and social environment in the corporation), and identity (the direction of one's career goals—whether the person wants to advance, have a balanced worklife, and so on). (See Chapter Three's discussion of these concepts as desirable leadership characteristics; also see London, 1985a.) The orientation program described how these characteristics are reinforced by the bosses' behavior. For instance, positive reinforcement for achievement enhances resilience. Feedback on performance and information about the organization and career opportunities both foster insight. Challenging assignments and opportunities for advancement encourage identity with the corporation. The bosses' videotape showed that bosses are not perfect in enhancing elements of subordinates' career motivation. Also, self-assessment tools and discussion of the tape helped participants to set action plans to achieve higher levels of resilience, insight, and identity. For example, goals might be asking for performance feedback from the boss or providing subordinates with frequent feedback.

The manager orientation program emphasized that developing subordinates and enhancing their career motivation are each manager's responsibility. In addition, the program helped the participants think about their own development needs and how to affect the situation to accomplish their goals. Development is not necessarily geared to preparing for the next job or the next promotion. Rather, it centers around becoming more involved in one's work, understanding how the individual fits into the organization, and realizing the value of one's accomplishments to the corporation.

Developing "Complicated Understanding"

Leaders and managers need to see organizations from several perspectives to understand that problems may have different causes, and they need to determine the causes of these problems (Weick, 1979). Effective managers generate several interpretations of organizational events. When the variety in the situation is equivalent to the variety in the manager's understanding, the manager is able to accurately register the complex nature of the events he or she faces and to choose actions appropriate to the situation (Bartunek, Gordon, and Weathersby, 1983). This requires the ability to differentiate the dimensions of a situation and to integrate these dimensions. For example, cognitively complex managers (those who are able to differentiate and to integrate the dimensions of a situation) are able to judge employees' performance on the basis of several dimensions—for example, decision making, quality of output, speed of work, and interpersonal skills. These judges are also able to integrate the dimensions based on their interrelationships. For instance, attention to workgroup climate may initially reduce speed of output and increase quality of the group's work, while over time, speed and quality may both increase as workgroup climate continues to improve.

Development occurs when an individual is confronted with a slightly more complex and demanding level of work than he or she would ordinarily feel comfortable doing (Weathersby, 1980). Training to enhance complicated understanding should use multiple teaching techniques, such as case exercises that focus on real business problems accompanied by readings, speakers, and discussion. The assumption behind such training is that exposure to situations calling for greater complexity will help encourage understanding and integration of different perspectives.

The goal is to challenge the individual's current thought structure and behaviors. This is facilitated by being around people who take multiple perspectives and realize the value of others' different skills and viewpoints. The training requires complex learning environments. Such environments include opportunities for goal setting and self-initiated action. A supportive interpersonal climate allows risk taking and self-disclosure. There should be time for personal and group reflection as well as for opportunities to comment on others' evaluation of one's performance.

Strategic Thinking

A concept closely related to complicated understanding is strategic thinking. This is learning how to make sense of the complex environment and establish a future vision. Many low- and middle-level managers are concerned with daily activities because they are measured on various indices of their group's daily output. However, they are usually charged with understanding the strategic direction of the business. Therefore, they have to have both a short-term and a long-term view of their role.

One way to accomplish this is for top managers to communicate the business strategy and define it or ask mid-level managers to flesh out the strategy in their own terms. Group sessions may be held to discuss business plans and how they drive actions of managers in the field.

Executives also have to think strategically while responding to daily problems and unexpected issues that may not fit into the corporate strategy. This has been termed *strategic opportunism:* "the ability to remain focused on long-term objectives while staying flexible enough to solve day-to-day problems and recognize new opportunities" (Isenberg, 1987, p. 92).

Effective top managers search for and process information in ways that bridge the gap between short- and long-term directions. They establish plans but also remain receptive to new information and opportunities that may not have been accounted for in the plans. A strategic plan to them is more of a vision than a list of well-defined, measurable, and time-bound goals. The manager's vision is qualitative and general, for instance, becoming the "best" marketing firm or the highest-quality producer in a competitive industry. The vision shapes daily activities, but opportunities and new ideas shape the vision. Unforeseen events and changing circumstances are reasons for reformulation of plans and actions.

Thinking strategically and opportunistically "requires a

tolerance for ambiguity, intellectual intensity, mental hustle, and a vigilant eye for new ideas" (Isenberg, 1987, p. 97). It also requires a flexible organizational planning process. Rather than physically binding together detailed plans in a single volume that is difficult to change, the plans should be in a format (such as files or a loose-leaf binder) that is easily adjusted and communicated. Thus, both the executive's characteristics and the organization's planning system (which is likely to be a product of the executive's preferences) allow flexibility and encourage taking advantage of new information.

Action Learning

Perhaps the best way to learn how to manage complex problems is to have exposure to these problems. There are at least three ways to get such experience: working on such a problem on the job, analyzing business cases in a classroom setting, and simulations. These are essentially ways to accelerate learning to prepare leaders and managers to handle today's rapid pace of change.

On-the-Job Learning. Working in a complex, changing environment creates many opportunities for learning. For instance, a task force to redesign the structure of a department is an opportunity for the participants to think about corporate needs and their role in the corporation (see Chapter Seven for an example). It is a way to build linkages between individuals and groups within the department. It is a chance to create a positive working environment and challenging jobs. Also, it is an opportunity to outline the department's objectives and envision how the department should change over time to meet changing demands.

Working in an evolving environment requires managing ambiguity, uncertainty, and the people who face these conditions. It is a chance to act rather than to wait for direction, or a chance to interpret and implement a leader's vision for the organization.

Research on successful and unsuccessful executives has suggested the types of experiences that contribute to success

(Lombardo, forthcoming). Rather than focusing on the development of skills, the research indicates the value of different types of experience that prepare the manager for top executive positions. One set of experiences centers around a logical sequence of job assignments, including managing a newly formed group, then managing a new group responsible for developing a new product, to directing larger units with new product or new market responsibilities, and so on. Tough jobs and hard times also are beneficial, because they increase the manager's reliability in adversity or because they teach the value of persistence and openness to new ideas. Learning from classroom experiences and simulation can supplement learning from these action-oriented, on-the-job experiences. Interpersonal relationships are an additional source of learning positive role models; mentors help the manager learn behaviors that are rewarded in the organization. Negative role models demonstrate behaviors that are not rewarded. The manager's insight needs to be keen enough to distinguish between positive and negative role models.

Solving Real Business Cases. Reginald Revans, a British professor, conceptualized action learning as a way to develop a pool of seasoned managers. As applied in Great Britain's General Electric Company (no relation to GE in the United States), managers were selected for temporary assignment to a task force to solve problems in their own or other divisions (Foy, 1977). The efforts combined problem solving and management development to the benefit of the organization and the individual. One project examined the effects of the United Kingdom Post Office's technical standards on exports from one division in the General Electric Company. Export sales might be increased tremendously if the team could effect changes in the Post Office's technical specifications to better match foreign markets. The team learned to understand the social, political, and regulatory issues involved in an interface with an agency external to the company.

In a sense, this is do-it-yourself management education (Mumford, 1987). The task forces were encouraged to meet regularly to evaluate programs, analyze their own strengths and weaknesses as individuals and as a group, and plan future actions. In the British General Electric case, each task force was under the direction of a trained leader who facilitated the periodic group self-analysis.

This idea of working on real business issues as a developmental experience has been incorporated into management development courses. One such program, run by the University of Michigan, brings together teams from five or six companies with five managers on each team. The course focuses on tying human resource strategies to business objectives. Each session begins with a week of presentations, exercises, and group discussions at a conference center. The participants then return to their respective companies to work on a real human resource problem (for example, the design of a new sales incentive compensation program). A consultant from the university works with the team for several days to help members evaluate how well they are working together and to help them work toward accomplishing their goal. Because the team members may be from different parts of the organization, the joint project is a way to help them learn about the entire corporation. After four or five weeks, the teams reconvene for a second week of project analysis, experience sharing, and further presentations.

Simulations. Optimal adult training probably involves some elements of diagnosis of individual strengths and weaknesses and actions needed for personal growth and development. Also, a training technique should draw on life experiences and integrate theoretical concepts with hands-on practice. Simulations can be used in training programs to provide this combination in a short time, according to Stephen Stumpf, professor of business administration at New York University. Stumpf (forthcoming) distinguishes between large-scale behavioral simulations and computer-based organizational simulations. Both types are realistic, provide participants an opportunity to see an organization from a senior management perspective, and seek to involve participants emotionally and intellectually.

A large-scale behavioral simulation is Looking Glass, Inc. (McCall and Lombardo, 1978). Designed by the Center for Creative Leadership in Greensboro, North Carolina, Looking Glass includes roles for twenty top-level managerial positions across four hierarchical levels, three divisions, and three functional areas. A trained staff observes the participants during the six-hour interactive simulation and provides group and individual feedback on more than a dozen managerial skills. Another simulation, based on the Looking Glass format, was designed by Stumpf for use by financial service managers. Large-scale behavioral simulations, such as Looking Glass, are usually part of three- to five-day training programs. They are also used in advanced business courses that focus on the application of management theory to actual business situations.

Computer-based organizational simulations focus on formulating strategy through analyzing marketing, financial, and corporate information, and then put the decisions into a computer model of the business. Questions addressed might include "How much raw material should we buy?" "What price should we charge?" and "Should we invest this year or next in plant and equipment?" Individuals or groups may compete with each other, and decision effectiveness is generally measured against the model's design rather than through interpersonal interactions with participants, as in behavioral simulations (Stumpf, forthcoming). Behavioral simulations can become outmoded as managerial skill dimensions change in their importance to effective job performance. Consequently, the simulation may require updating to match the situation relevant to the participants.

"Top Gun" School. The learning experiences discussed above may be combined in an accelerated learning experience for leaders and managers who demonstrate highest potential to be effective change agents. Named after the Air Force fighter pilot training program during the Vietnam War (and later the movie *Top Gun* depicting the experience), the approach is to improve organizational performance by special training for the crème de la crème, and to expect them to demonstrate the new behavior and educate others. So, for example, several top corporate officers may be sent to visit other companies, where they observe and participate in international assignments. They might meet

with a series of top consultants to learn global business strategies, new product design and manufacturing procedures and ways to promote cross-functional integration within the corporation. They learn from the best, and they are then charged with applying the new learning within their organizations.

Relapse Prevention

The intention of the various learning experiences described above is to bring about long-term behavior change. However, after the training, the learning must generalize to on-the-job behavior and continue over time, especially when the learning is meant to bring about long-term organizational change. The new behaviors are likely to continue when they are rewarded. In addition, behavior is likely to be enhanced by anticipating and monitoring past and present failures (Marlatt and Gordon, 1980). Also, managers need to be equipped with appropriate coping skills for dealing with future difficult situations. There are several self-control techniques for relapse prevention (after Marx, 1982).

• Awareness of the relapse process can help avoid relapse. This entails describing previous slips or failures in detail and considering how such slips can be prevented in the future. This heightens awareness of the environmental and emotional circumstances surrounding the failure to use the learned behavior.
• Identification of high-risk situations prevents relapse by sensitizing the manager to work environments that are most likely to result in a temporary or permanent lapse in experimenting with new learning. High-risk situations include time pressure, angry subordinates, and lack of support from bosses.
• Developing coping responses goes beyond anticipating a relapse to actually coping with it on the job. Skill deficits need to be assessed and additional training obtained in such areas as time management, assertiveness, and strategic planning.
• Enhancing one's sense of self-efficacy is important because occasional relapses are likely to be frustrating and lead to rationalizations for why the new behavior will not work. Mastery of complex skills is a trial-and-error process requiring moni-

toring and coping skills. Role playing and self-reinforcement are valuable for even minor improvements to emphasize skill acquisition.

• Setting goals is a way to keep focused on the learned behavior. Assigning goals to students and having them set their own goals are effective ways to promote transfer of learning to the job situation (Wexley and Baldwin, 1986).

• Realizing the possible effects of behavior change is also important. The long- and short-term advantages of the new behavior must be considered. Introducing organizational change and solving complex problems often have short-term difficulties, and keeping an eye on the long-term benefits is valuable to continuing the effort.

• Paying close attention to one's own emotions and decisions, even minor decisions, is necessary to calibrate future actions. When managers deviate from their plans, they are likely to blame themselves. They need to understand their emotional reactions to failure and develop competing interpretations—for example, concentrating on ways to avoid slips in the future. Monitoring the process, with particular attention to decisions made along the way, can be useful. For instance, in trying to become more participative, a manager may be overzealous and insist that each subordinate say something at every group meeting or that each subordinate be assigned a task for which he or she alone will be held accountable. Managers need to be aware of the impact of actions that may appear inconsistent to subordinates and damage the manager's credibility.

• Life-style interventions may be necessary. Managers creating change are likely to pay more attention to work than to their own or others' personal needs. In the process, they may impose unreasonable requirements on their management team, for example, the expectation that people will work from 7:30 A.M. to 7:00 P.M. and be available to any team member on demand. Life-style interventions such as development workshops and counseling services for burnout and career planning may help managers see how they can tie personal objectives to the learned behaviors.

• Programming a failure without the usual stress that

accompanies it can help the manager analyze the slip and develop effective strategies for dealing with failure in the future. A failure, such as resuming an autocratic leadership style after learning to be more participative, can be role-played in a training situation and then carried out in the work setting. The resulting behaviors can later be explained to group members and then analyzed in the group.

Group members should be involved in the above relapse prevention processes. The group members can reinforce each other's behaviors, provide a sounding board for new ideas, and offer the feedback to improve the accuracy of self-analysis.

The Change Agent as Educator

As the initiator of organizational change, the leader, manager, or human resource professional establishes the vision for the future and involves others in the process of creating that vision. Then, again with others' involvement, he or she develops action plans and carries out those plans. In the process, the manager is *modeling* a style of management that may be new to many in the organization. Perhaps with the encouragement and guidance of an organizational effectiveness consultant, the manager or "top gun" creates a work climate that is conducive to learning. The manager both demonstrates the new behavior and rewards those behaviors in others.

Peter Block, in his book *The Empowered Manager,* describes how managers can move from a bureaucratic mentality to self-empowerment and positive politics (Block, 1987).

> The key to positive politics, then, is to look at each encounter as an opportunity to support autonomy and to create an organization of our own choosing. It requires viewing ourselves as the primary instrument for changing the culture. Cultures get changed in a thousand small ways, not by dramatic announcements emanating from the boardroom. If we wait until top management gives leadership to the change we want to see, we miss the point. For us to have any hope that our own preferred future

will come to pass, we must provide the leadership
[pp. 97–98].

Block argues that managers should create an "entrepreneurial cycle." This starts with establishing an implicit contract
with the organization that encourages employees to be their
own authority, to engage in self-expression, and to make commitments.

The next step in the entrepreneurial cycle is "enlightened
self-interest." This includes engaging in activities that are needed
and that are meaningful to us. The goal is to contribute and be
of service to the organization, not only to our own self-aggran-
dizement. Maintaining integrity, having a positive impact on
people's lives, and learning as much as possible about one's job
and profession are other hallmarks of enlightened self-interest.

The third step in the entrepreneurial cycle is to engage in
"authentic tactics." This includes saying no when we mean no,
sharing as much information as possible, being frank in communicating, and not repositioning our opinions or programs just
to be popular.

The outcome of the cycle is a growing autonomy and
teamwork—an environment in which the people are involved in
meaningful work, are informed about events and consequences
that affect them, and are committed to organizational goals.
These outcomes parallel the three domains of career motivation: resilience, insight, and identity.

Developing Employees' Career Motivation

Chapter Three argued that corporate leaders and managers need resilience, insight, and identity to establish and implement business direction. Earlier in this chapter, I described how
a new manager orientation program helped managers understand their role and their bosses' role in reinforcing these characteristics. Resilience, insight, and identity are the cornerstones
of career motivation and are valuable characteristics for change
agents (London, 1985a). Each of these concepts has multiple
components. People who are high in career resilience believe in
themselves, need achievement for its own sake (not for external

reward), are willing to take risks, and know when to act independently and when to act cooperatively. People who are high in career insight establish career goals and have an accurate perception of their own strengths and weaknesses and of the political and social environment in the corporation. Career identity refers to the direction of one's career goals. Employees with high career identity are involved in their jobs, the organization, and/or their profession. One form of career identity is wanting to advance in the corporation, and wanting the recognition, leadership, and money that usually accompanies advancement.

Resilience is the foundation for career insight in that people who are high in resilience are receptive to information about themselves and the organization, and they incorporate that information in formulating a career identity that is meaningful for them.

The organization prepares people to handle change by reinforcing and supporting their career resilience, insight, and identity. Change agent managers need to understand how the work environment reinforces career resilience and provides information to support career insight and identity. This reinforcement and support may come from the supervisor, the job itself, or the policies of the corporation. Organizational leaders who are themselves high in resilience, insight, and identity are likely to create an environment that reinforces and supports their employees' resilience, insight, and identity. These leaders are likely to realize the importance of employees' contribution to accomplishing business goals, and hence they place a high value on developing and rewarding their employees.

Types of support for resilience, insight, and identity may take different forms and may occur in different combinations. Taken together, they represent the value the organization places in its people. Employees' career resilience is reinforced by characteristics that encourage self-confidence (positive reinforcement for a job well done) and that generate opportunities for achievement (for example, an assignment to direct a special project). Resilience is also reinforced by creating an environment for risk taking and recognizing the potential value of risks when they are not successful and providing especially strong rewards when they are. Independence and cooperation are encouraged by rewarding both types of behavior as appropriate. Career insight stems from supporting career development, encouraging goal seting, and giving information about the organization and about the subordinate's performance. Work involvement is encouraged through opportunities for job challenge (which should also contribute to career resilience) and opportunities for professional growth. Opportunities for leadership, advancement, and other extrinsic rewards (for example, monetary bonuses) also contribute to career identity.

Human resource professionals support career motivation through a variety of policies and programs. Compensation and recognition systems provide resources and methods for leaders and managers to build career resilience. Staffing systems and job and organizational designs help leaders and managers create opportunities for achievement. Performance appraisal procedures and career paths provide ways for supervisors to enhance subordinates' self-insight and identity through feedback, career counseling, and goal setting. Training and development programs both provide direction for the individual's career identity and help managers learn how to support their subordinates' career motivation.

These environmental characteristics constitute the foundation and direction for the corporation's human resource strategies. Encouragement of individual contribution, personal growth, career development, and work involvement suggest policies, programs, and actions for managing the corporation's human resources. The actual strategies used will depend both on the value the corporation places on people and on the business needs of the corporation. Business conditions and the company's philosophy of valuing employees (reinforcing and supporting their career resilience, insight, and identity) influence the human resource strategies adopted by the corporation.

Tying Together Business Conditions, Human Resource Strategies, and Support for Career Motivation

Figure 1 describes the relationships between business conditions, human resource strategies, and employee outcomes. As stated in Chapter One, human resource strategies depend on the

Figure 1. The Influence of Support for Career Motivation
on Human Resource Strategies.

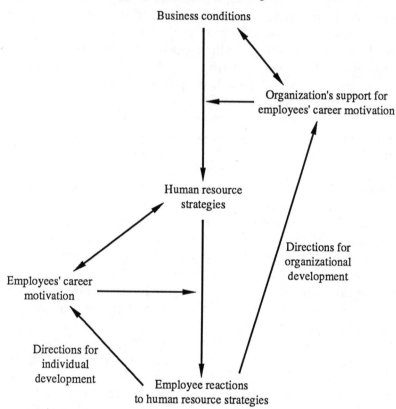

needs of the organization (whether the firm is just starting, growing, declining, merging with another firm, or establishing a new direction). Human resource strategies in turn affect employees' career motivation and employees' behaviors (for example, performance, turnover, and absenteeism) as well as their attitudes (for example, job satisfaction and commitment to the organization). Career motivation also affects the relationship between human resource strategies and employee outcomes in that a high level of career motivation helps human resource strategies work. Over time, a consistent corporate philosophy of support for employees' career motivation through human resource strategies will increase that motivation. However, support for career motivation comes from different sources in the organization, all of which may not be consistent. For instance, an employees' immediate supervisor may discourage risk taking, provide few opportunities and rewards for achievement, and offer little information about organizational conditions despite a leadership philosophy to the contrary. In general, the organization should strive for consistency in its human resource policies and programs and the role of the manager.

Employees' career resilience, insight, and identity also stem from sources other than the corporation. Career resilience is likely to be fairly well established by the time an individual starts working, and it will change only after consistent reinforcement. Career insight and identity are probably more easily changed because they result largely from information and opportunities available in the work environment.

Employees' career motivation may also influence the human resource strategies top management is willing to adopt as well as vice versa. This is noted in Figure 1 by the two-way arrow between employees' career motivation and the company's human resource strategies. For instance, new leaders coming into an environment that supported employees' resilience, insight, and identity may be likely to continue such support because employees are motivated to succeed.

There is also a relationship between business conditions and the leader's support for employee career motivation—being supportive of employees in a positive business environment (for example, organizational growth) is easier than it is in a negative business environment (for example, organizational decline). Also, the reaction of leaders under different business conditions will depend on the leaders' background. However, the actions taken will vary with business conditions (London, forthcoming). For instance, under conditions of organizational decline, leaders may communicate openly, discuss career possibilities, and involve employees in a restructuring and/or downsizing. This would indicate high support for employees. On the other hand, leaders facing organizational decline may provide little information on organizational plans, make no effort to retrain or place laid-off employees, and deride people who leave as "deadwood." This would indicate low support for employees.

Under conditions of growth, leaders may reward employees for their contribution to the organization, since new enterprises generate increased growth opportunities for the employees and for the organization. Or leaders may treat employees solely as instruments to meeting current business needs and not provide them with extra rewards or growth opportunities.

Start-up business conditions may prompt the supportive leader to involve employees in planning, encourage innovation, and form self-managing workteams. Low-support leaders starting a business unit may hire or fire people as needed with little or no investment in employees' development. Moreover, the leaders are likely to make all major decisions with little or no involvement of employees.

Under conditions of merger and acquisition, leaders who support employees' career motivation are likely to communicate information about the changes and appoint joint planning committees. Leaders who do not support employees' career motivation are likely to reveal little information, make decisions unilaterally, and not involve employees in the reorganization process.

Organizational redirection coupled with high leader support for employees' career motivation may lead to programs for employee retraining, employee involvement in planning, open communication of corporate goals, and trust in employees to implement the new strategy. However, redirection coupled with low leader support may lead to hastily made decisions from the top, rigid management control, and layoffs rather than offers to retrain employees.

Change Agent Roles

Change agents prepare employees to handle change by providing support for learning and development. This may mean making new job assignments, creating experiential exercises (for example, case discussions and simulations), and/or designing and conducting training experiences (for example, a "top gun" school). Human resource professionals may lead the organization by introducing new concepts, such as "the empowered manager" and "career motivation," and by formulating programs to support the organizational change.

Change agents learn this role by sending themselves to school and by seeking experiences such as the ones described in this chapter. Human resource professionals must learn how to be consultants by educating themselves in the roles of reflector, process specialist, fact finder, alternative identifier, and collaborator. They do this by practice and by formal education, for instance attending short-courses sponsored by the National Training Laboratories or by universities. Of course, the human resource professional who is also an organizational development specialist should come to the organization with the education and background in team building, negotiation skills, conflict resolution techniques, and problem-solving methods.

One organization hired a consulting firm to work with experienced internal organizational development consultants in a three-week consultant-development workshop. Conducted by members of the consulting firm and by the internal consultants, the workshop was for novice internal consultants—recently appointed managers from other functions who were moved into the job as a developmental experience. The workshop focused on such topics as adult learning processes, management style self-assessment instruments, group dynamics, facilitation skills, self-evaluation, and self-empowerment.

The ways change agents prepare employees to manage change should depend on the needs of the organization. The form development takes is an intervention in itself that must be in line with business direction, just as different leader behaviors are needed to support employees' motivation under different business conditions. Organization start-up, growth, and redirection are likely to require ways for managers to learn how to think and act strategically and involve their subordinates in the enterprise. Organizational decline and mergers are likely to require teaching managers to communicate openly, to work as a team to establish and renew creative energies.

Summary

This chapter described development strategies to meet a corporation's need for new styles of management (for example, participative decision making, support for continuous learning, and self-managing teams). Managers must learn how to experiment and evaluate the success of their actions. Successful firms devote considerable attention to employee development because they see it as integral to accomplishing their financial and market objectives. Corporations need to understand when managers are most receptive to learning, and then provide training during these critical periods. Organizations create opportunities for learning by assigning managers to complex, unstructured tasks. This type of action learning is a way to develop "complicated understanding" and strategic thinking about how to generate and achieve business goals while keeping the organization running on a daily basis. Change agents educate by example and by involving their teams and peers in creating a new environment to match the changing needs of the corporation. The manager needs resilience, insight, and identity. Leaders' support for these elements of career motivation influences the human resource strategies that are implemented under different business conditions and the reactions of employees to these strategies. Thus, the change agent must realize the relationships between business needs, concern about developing people, human resource strategies, and employee outcomes. As such, human resource management is a critical lever for accomplishing corporate objectives and preparing people for change. This will become clearer as we move into the next two chapters on organizational change processes.

5

Managing Incremental and Frame-Breaking Changes

Earlier chapters set the scene for organizational change by describing environmental trends, directions for change, the roles of change agents, and how change agents learn their roles. This chapter looks more closely at types of organizational change and how change is introduced.

Some organizational changes are incremental. They entail incorporating new technologies with existing missions and strategies. The risks are fairly low, and the speed is generally slow. Chapter Two described organizational erosion and dissolution as incremental processes. Organizational growth and redirection may also be incremental, but not necessarily. Other organizational changes are frame breaking. Economic, political, and technological developments may be so dramatic that they require an immediate response from management if the organization is to survive. The risks are high, and events happen quickly. This usually means a change in the organization's goals and operations. Organizational start-ups and mergers are likely to be frame-breaking experiences.

Building on the ideas of incremental and frame-breaking change, as originally outlined by Tushman, Newman, and

Romanelli (1985) and Kanter (1983), this chapter describes examples of these two types of change. I will show how the forces of change affect the people in the organization and organizational processes. The examples focus on the ways leaders, managers, and human resource professionals, often working together, change the attitudes and behavior of organization members.

Incremental Change

The fit between an organization's strategy, structure, people, and processes always needs some adjustment. This entails refining policies and methods (for example, a revised benefits plan, or a new advertising campaign); creating special units to handle specific needs (for example, a task force to solve a major production problem or a new quality control unit); or developing people to meet current needs (for example, improved personnel selection and training). New products, new manufacturing procedures, or changes in competition and the economy are reasons for such continued changes. But organizational changes that are made in response to these occurrences must be consistent with the existing, successful organizational structure and strategy.

The advent of new information processing technologies requires the slow realignment of organizational systems as they take advantage of new technological capabilities. The adoption of these technologies (for example, intra- and interoffice networks of personal computers) is often slow because they are initially costly and unfamiliar. However, the increasing accessibility and efficiency of new technologies and the need to keep up with a fast-paced environment will accelerate the adoption of technologies such as electronic mail, voice mail, radiophones, personal computers, advanced software to aid design and decision making, and yet-to-be-developed technological generations (Huber, 1984).

Teleconferencing, videoconferencing and computer networks will facilitate group discussion and decisions. For instance, the U.S. Department of Labor recently sponsored a computer network of about forty-five chief executive officers of major U.S. corporations across the country. Terminals were placed in the CEOs' homes for about six months. The CEOs were free to log on and off as they wished, to read the thoughts of their colleagues, and to express their own views on major business, technological, productivity, and human resource issues. Such computer networks inside organizations will facilitate making more complex decisions that require participation with a variety of experts.

Formalized project management methods, using computer networks and other integrated technical links, may be designed to handle complex designs, communicate progress, and obtain authorization. For instance, a national organization might establish a business planning council of top executives across the country to regularly review and update corporate plans, establish financial commitments to stockholders, and evaluate capital budgets and expenditures. Information technology may be adapted to communicate data, express opinions, and to vote on or establish consensus on issues driving the business.

The joint organizational and technological configurations used in these management processes are likely to change as new technologies are developed, different managers take over with their own decision-making styles, and business conditions place new burdens on the corporation. Electronic mail and video-conferencing may work well in the planning stages or for routine meetings, but periodic face-to-face conferences may be needed to hash out disagreements and develop and implement internal local strategies. In some cases, electronic communication systems may work well for collecting and synthesizing varied opinions. One such procedure, the Delphi technique, calls for collecting written opinions from group members, feeding back synthesized data, and collecting further opinions. This continues several times as issues are clarified and a clear direction is established (Martin, 1981).

An Example of Incremental Change: Rejuvenating the Boy Scouts. A mainstay in the life of U.S. youth, the Boy Scouts of America (founded in 1910) is dedicated to such traditional values as honesty, integrity, discipline, excellence, fairness, diligence, respect, and self-confidence. The continued success of this national youth organization depends on attracting membership, contributions, and volunteers. The Boy Scouts is coordinated by a professional, paid staff that is funded primarily through the United Way and other local contributions. Recently, the national headquarters started its Shaping Tomorrow program. The goal was to investigate ways to "propel the organization into the next century" (Boy Scouts of America, 1984). The mission of the organization was not in question; in fact, nothing was radically wrong as perceived by the national staff. The problem centered around delivering services to the ultimate consumer—the youth members. Many separate small changes were needed to make the organization more effective in local communities.

Starting with this broad objective, a national steering committee was formed. A survey was conducted, and the organization received more than 4,000 responses from people involved in a wide range of scouting-related activities. Fifty-five project teams were recommended to the executive board to work on such activities as improved funding, better recruitment and utilization of professional staff and volunteers, higher-quality programs, and a clearer idea of how the organization's programs can still meet traditional values.

The executive board recognized the need to tailor the organization's goals to individual situations. Joint ventures were strengthened with educational, veterans', civic, and social organizations to better serve the needs of minority, handicapped, and disadvantaged youth. Needed actions were interpreted in marketing terms, such as the "delivery" of services. A national vice-president of marketing was appointed to "apply the organization's considerable knowledge of customers (the youth and parents) to provide services they are willing to buy" (Boy Scouts of America, 1984). The feeling was that though the cherished values transcend the mechanics of delivering services to youth, the values are meaningless if they fail to reach the intended audience.

As a major effort at self-reflection, evaluation, and action, the components of the Shaping Tomorrow program represent incremental change. New programs are being meshed with the old. The standard formats continue. The goal is to strengthen the traditions of the organization and to make them more widely applicable—not to change the image. The marketing department's job is to focus existing functions (for example, public relations and program development). Meanwhile teams are working on revitalizing many aspects of the organization. This renewal is long term and continuous, not a one-time change. As a consequence, the results will take years to materialize. Also, the Shaping Tomorrow program is a reaffirmation of the organization's traditional direction, not a rejection of it. The old guard as well as the new can feel comfortable with the need for change. Moreover, involving both volunteers and professionals at all levels of the organization and soliciting the input of thousands of others create a sense of a dedicated team working together to accomplish a common goal.

Although incremental change is slow and not immediately evident, it still requires forward thinking and risk taking. In some ways it is more difficult than more immediate, extensive change because it happens slowly and is subject to the scrutiny of numerous vested interests.

Change Agents in the Boy Scouts. The Shaping Tomorrow program was not just the vision of a single individual at the top of the organization, although certainly support for change started at the top. Because the Boy Scouts is an organization steeped in traditional values, the stance of the leadership was that nothing was seriously wrong. No major change in direction was foreseen. Rather, this was an effort at becoming more modern and more responsive to the current needs of youth. The youth were viewed as clients—they were seen from a marketing perspective. The organization is still paternalistic. The leaders are still guides and role models, certain in their convictions and more concerned about how they continue to "spread the word" than they are in changing the message.

The key change agents were the professional staff who direct the organization from its headquarters in a Dallas suburb. Working with volunteers at high levels of the Boy Scout hierarchy, many of whom were top executives of major corporations, they formed committees to evaluate the shape of tomorrow. In other words, they were to identify areas needing work—for example, new programs, better methods of fund-raising, and better training of the professional staff and community volunteers. Thus, the generators of the change were both internal and external to the organization, and they were generally influential people in their communities. The strategy was to ask the opinions of literally thousands of volunteers, and then to form task forces on the various issues.

Other change agent implementors and adopters were the local professional staff. Each community has a professional staff attached to a regional Boy Scout office. This professional staff is responsible for recruiting and coordinating a hierarchy of volunteers, from high-level elected officials in the local Boy Scout organization to the scoutmasters. The professional staff establishes new units, trains volunteers, runs regional programs, and raises funds.

Thus, the change implementors and adopters were diverse groups (professionals, volunteers, and youth) with diverse needs —all linked by a common mission. Many of the problems faced by the professional staff were typical of any employee body (for example, concerns about rates of pay, career development, transfer policies, recognition for doing a good job, and feedback from supervisors). They must work with community volunteers and leaders as well as the headquarters staff to bring about change.

As the Shaping Tomorrow program continues, it must be open to new ideas and must convince others to experiment. New areas for change will be identified and implementation committees will be established at the local and national levels. Unlike other more radical change, no single person will be the champion of the change. Change will not be perceptible immediately. Also, it will require persistent effort, as multiple facets of the organization are explored, scrutinized, and ultimately refined. There will be considerable discussion, debate, and argument as well as compromise. Just as there will be multiple directions for change, there will be multiple pockets of resistance —some small and some large.

Incremental change is never fully complete, but rather is continuous, and is aimed at maintaining a sense of growth and stimulation. The process of change is likely to vary over time. The Shaping Tomorrow program will eventually die down and new efforts will take its place. Also, change will take place at different levels—at headquarters, at the local professional staff level, and at the troop level. Each level will perceive the need for different changes, at least if the organization continues to be populated by concerned, active, and dedicated people.

Changing the Employee Relations Strategy at Merck. Another example of incremental change is an ongoing effort at Merck & Co., a leading drug firm, to enhance the importance of people management in the firm. In 1985, the chairman of the firm, Roy Vagelos, recognized that remaining competitive and becoming the preeminent health-care company in the world would require not only the highly qualified technical people already in the company but also people who were motivated to extend themselves for the benefit of the organization. The company's emphasis had been on technical competence, not on an ability to manage people.

Vagelos appointed an employee relations review committee to examine the company's current policies and programs. Six line vice-presidents, two personnel executives, and the corporate controller sat on the committee. They reviewed written personnel policies, compared these policies to the literature on effective policies, talked to leading consultants, interviewed 300 employees, and identified models of excellence inside Merck as well as at other companies, including AT&T Bell Laboratories, TRW, and IBM.

The task force concluded its work in six months and issued a report with fifty recommendations. This effort and the summary of recommendations were communicated throughout the firm in newsletters and a special videotape. Employees could see that top line managers, many of whom advanced to higher levels because of their technical ability, were involved in the process and committed to changing the organization.

During the next year, the company began to act on many of the recommendations. It strengthened the employment process by clarifying criteria for filling jobs, and improved the interview process by requiring agreement from several interviewers and not just the hiring supervisor. The company improved employee communications and involvement by instituting team problem-solving groups, quality circles, and focus groups. The performance appraisal system was changed to force a greater distinction among people and provide higher financial awards to the exceptional performers. Training and development were expanded to improve supervisory skills and explain the new personnel policies. An opinion survey was instituted as well.

Although these are many policy changes during a relatively short time, the firm has not yet made people management a priority throughout the company. The performance appraisal process does not yet measure managers on how well they develop their people. Employees are not yet comfortable with the forced distribution appraisal categories because they put 70 percent of the people in a "high Merck standard" category, only 15 percent in a "performed with distinction" category, and 5 percent in an "exceptional" category. The old system allowed bosses to rate everyone highly and in fact most people received ratings that made them feel special. The new system recognizes outstanding performance, but it leaves many people feeling average despite the company's attempts to explain that Merck believes that all its people are a cut above those in other firms.

The change at Merck will be gradual. New programs supporting better people management will be tried, improved, and in some cases replaced. The increased emphasis on people management will become a reality as it pervades many corporate decisions and actions over time. The company has a history of consistency in its policies, for instance, continuing to invest in research even in hard economic times. The stage has been set by the CEO and top officers, employees have been involved in policy evaluation, and the firm is experimenting with new programs. This is an incremental process as the company moves toward its goal of being the top firm in its industry. (It was already recognized in *Fortune* as among the best 100 U.S. employers.)

Frame-Breaking Change

A problem occurs when an organization's strategy is no longer appropriate and when changes that are inconsistent with existing strategies are needed for survival and growth (Tushman, Newman, and Romanelli, 1985). Such drastic changes include major events in regulation, economics, technology, and society. These changes happen slowly, or they may be rapid. For example in the early 1980s (before divestiture), the Bell System responded to the new competitive environment by creating unregulated subsidiaries that would be allowed to market products free of government restriction. This was an incremental change because the company still believed in the slogan "The System Is the Solution." Of course, this belief changed with the divestiture of the Bell Operating Companies from AT&T. This was a frame-breaking change if there ever was one, and it was a dramatic, almost immediate break with the century-long history of the Bell System. There were less than two years to plan and implement the actual divestiture.

Roadblocks to Frame-Breaking Change. Although a company's leaders may understand the need for change (for example, because of a slow market with intense competition), the change may require dismantling the infrastructure that supports a business environment that no longer exists. This is likely to be difficult for some of the following reasons (after Ames, 1986).

• *Inadequate attention to the importance of being fully cost competitive.* For instance, costs build up during the years when readily accepted price increases covered staff additions. (In the case of the Bell System, regulation allowed full cost recovery, a condition that no longer exists. The postdivestiture AT&T now finds itself with a swollen force of middle managers.)

• *A bureaucratic approach to managing the business in a way that resists change and frustrates the entrepreneurial spirit.* For instance, large corporate organizations are bloated with redundant middle managers doing many of the things line managers could be doing, such as staffing and other personnel functions. This is confounded by excessive layering between top management and the line. Although they are likely to be reluctant to do so, managers must break down their businesses around a number of discrete profit centers that avoid the middle-management drag on decisions and establish clear-cut responsibility and accountability.

• *An overdependence on products, policies, and procedures that do not offer anything new.* Standard operating procedures instituted to meet certain needs quickly become habit. When the old needs change and new needs are ambiguous, managers may still rely on the old operating procedures. Managers must learn to interpret new environmental demands and create appropriate structures.

• *A lack of drive, urgency, and competence in employees who have become conditioned to earning a living simply by taking orders.* One explanation for this is that a new, often uncertain environment is stressful, and the one way to deal with stress is to continue doing what worked in the past. Another explanation is that employees simply fail to perceive a need for change. The threat of lay-offs and the hiring of new employees with the needed competence may be necessary to shock employees into awareness that new behaviors are required.

Requirements for Frame-Breaking Change. Frame-breaking changes are best implemented all at once to take advantage of the synergy and exhilaration surrounding the challenge to change. Also, pockets of resistance should not be given a chance to develop, and dwelling on the uncertainties and risks of a change should be avoided. There are at least five elements of frame-breaking change (after Tushman, Newman, and Romanelli, 1985).

• *Reformed mission and core values.* This refers to a new definition of company mission. In AT&T, this meant a new course bent on competition, aggressiveness, and responsiveness as well as a new set of values centering on customer satisfaction rather than the old value of the highest-quality service to all regardless of the cost to the company.

• *Altered power and status.* New strategies shift power within a company as well as change the position of the company as a whole in the economic and corporate community. Financial analysts first thought that AT&T would be unstoppable when freed from regulatory shackles. It turned out that the regulated operating companies did far better financially in the two years following divestiture than did the remaining AT&T. AT&T had to cope with continuing regulation, high overhead, substantial and erratic charges from the local operating companies for tying the long-distance network into the local networks (charges that were higher than those paid by long-distance competitors), and difficulty in responding to market shifts and customer demands.

• *Reorganization.* New strategies require changes in structure, systems, and procedures with added activities in some areas and fewer in others. AT&T formed many joint ventures with firms in the United States and abroad. It established new subsidiaries to handle its data needs and to provide large business customers with credit. It redesigned its corporate headquarters, at first limiting the size of the headquarters, and when that resulted in redundancies within the various entities of the company, it centralized more functions to avoid duplication of effort. Also, regulatory relief allowed the regulated long-distance service part of the company (AT&T Communications) to merge with the premises products entity (AT&T Information Systems). This led to more unified efforts to market communications products and service customers.

• *Revised interaction patterns.* New procedures are established to facilitate internal communications and decision making. Managers establish new networks of relationships. In the case of AT&T, one major internal revision was establishing a more user-sensitive financial system with internal cross-charges so that departments could be held accountable for the costs they incurred, including building rents and other support services that were previously charged at the corporate level. Additional changes dealt with encouraging new ways of managing. For example, emphasis was placed on managers' fostering supportive work climates and developing alliances between units within the company. Goal setting and performance appraisal procedures were established to make these values part of the managers' responsibilities. (A vehicle for communicating this was the Managing for Excellence Library described in Chapter Four.)

• *New Executives.* Often new executives are needed because the old guard finds it difficult to make the shift to the new corporate strategy. Here again AT&T is a particularly interesting case. About ten years before divestiture, a marketing vice-president was hired from IBM to make AT&T more market driven. The clash between his personality and business philosophy and the prevailing organizational culture was a shock to the system. Although this marketing executive, Arch McGill, had a major influence on the marketing department, the company was not yet ready for the vast changes he wanted. The manufacturing side of the business seemed to win the power play for predominance in setting organizational priorities. Even though AT&T was entering the new, increasingly competitive realm of marketing directly to business and residence customers, it was difficult to lose the research, development, and manufacturing orientation (the "we know what's best for you" mentality). Not long after McGill left the company for greener pastures, divestiture was announced. The way had been paved for the necessary change and orientation to market-driven R&D —product development responsive to client needs and attuned to market windows. Manufacturing also had to become more aware of the need for quick delivery of products to take advantage of the competitive edge. Any new developments would likely be matched by competitors or by other new technological advances in a short time. Despite efforts to downsize the company, needed gaps in required expertise were filled by hiring people at all levels of management, contrary to the previously ingrained philosophy of promotion from within the company. In line with that, a new chief financial officer, Robert Kavner, was hired from outside the company to bring more rigorous attention to cost control and cost management.

How a Company Knows When a Change Is Necessary. The need for frame-breaking change generally stems from catastrophic events or pending catastrophe. For the Bell System, divestiture seemed to be the least of several evils in a rising trend of change that was impossible to stop, despite many costly advertising campaigns and lobbying efforts. Considering some other examples, the changes at GM arose from financial crisis, but rebounding profits seemed to make GM slow to implement its reorganization. Ford started on heavy investment that meant incurring severe losses. They had reached the point of no return, and had few options other than to persist in their new strategy.

Marketplace and economic conditions may demand frame-breaking changes, as when it is impossible to increase profitability by increasing prices because of strenuous competition and the only alternative is to reduce costs. Or perhaps the introduction of a technology in the industry makes it necessary to redirect the company's business strategy. This happened when the advent of personal computers undermined the video-game business and cut heavily into the profits of Atari; the company did not foresee customers moving away from video games as much as they did.

In still other cases, the corporation may be doing well, but its leaders have a vision for redirecting its efforts. This may be the most risky route, and it requires considerable strength of leadership. This "intrapreneurial" spirit is beginning to pervade organizations at all corporate levels because of the need to be innovative to remain competitive. People in the company begin to respond to what they believe needs to be done even if it goes beyond their responsibilities. This may result in major organizational transformations, such as the introduction of new products or services and the corresponding establishment of new organizational units. This same spirit generally guides the development of new businesses, but it is more difficult to accomplish when it faces existing, incongruous organizational structures. Championing change is the stuff corporate heroes are made of, as when RCA's David Sarnoff envisioned the commercial value of radio and later television and understood the importance of manufacturing and marketing electronic equipment rather than just transmitting electronic signals. The result of course was the growth of RCA and its subsidiaries, now absorbed by another giant corporation, GE.

American Transtech: A Frame-Breaking Change. American Transtech grew out of the old AT&T's stock and bond department and the need to provide shareholder services for the new regional operating telephone companies as well as for AT&T after the Bell System divestiture. The old AT&T stock and bond department had handled 3.2 million shareholder accounts, but the volume would rise to a staggering 18 million accounts after divestiture. The new entity had to handle all the transactions involved in conversion of accounts according to each stockholder's wishes (for example, splitting shares in different combinations among the telephone companies). The old department was too small to handle the volume, so some change was necessary.

Rather than simply increase the size of the organization, top management realized that it was necessary to take maximum advantage of economies of scale. Otherwise, large banks and other competitors would grab the business away from AT&T (Henderson, 1984). Also, transactions would have to be handled quickly and accurately. American Transtech's goal, and name, stemmed the need to process *trans*actions using high *tech*nology. The result was significant frame breaking in how to organize and operate the business unit. This was accomplished in several unique ways by the unit's operating officer, Lawrence Lemasters. Here are some of the major changes.

• American Transtech became a new, wholly owned subsidiary of AT&T. Its formation began about the time AT&T agreed to the divestiture in August 1982. American Transtech had to be in operation in time to conduct the necessary stock transactions for divestiture on 1 January 1984.

• The stock and bond department in Piscataway, New Jersey, would be closed. The new operation would be established in Jacksonville, Florida, where labor costs were lower and temporary employees were plentiful. The business volume would fluctuate, so the company thought it would be reasonable to hire and train many part-time people who could work when needed. Teams of managers who currently worked in the New Jersey stock and bond department were formed to choose the personnel who would relocate, design the building and layout, prepare the required training programs for the new staff, and plan for the necessary transitions.

- Because only about 200 employees would be relocated and many more were needed, training would be necessary to prepare the 800 new employees. These employees would have to handle large volumes of complicated questions and transactions. The current procedures were complex and contained in volumes of material. Additional procedures would be added to handle the changes resulting from divestiture. The new employees would be operating the latest computer equipment, so it seemed logical to develop computerized delivery training packages, instead of using human instructors and printed materials.
- Lemasters rearranged the tradition-bound chain of command. In place of six layers of management with each employee in a neat organizational box reporting to a single person, the new structure organized employees into teams or "families" of 15 or 20 people doing similar work. The layers of supervision were reduced to three: 97 team managers, 23 directors, and 5 officers. Each team would make its own decisions about how their work space would be divided and how often the team should meet. The team would resolve problems and make suggestions to help reach its sales and profit goals.
- Teams and team managers were rewarded for innovations that increased productivity. Initially the enthusiasm was so great that productivity was 100–120 percent higher than in the prior location. This productivity gain decreased over time but still remained high (350,000 transactions a day—60–80 percent higher than before the move).
- Each team was a profit center, and the team manager was accountable for the team's productivity and profitability.
- The entrepreneurial spirit was encouraged. One enterprising manager sold the services of his operations to other companies for telemarketing. He reasoned that during off hours, when the force was not fully utilized and telephone lines were available, the operators could make calls for other firms to advertise or sell services.

Thus, American Transtech realized that the competitive edge was high-quality, low-cost service. Using high technology and a participative style of management, the organization was able to streamline its operations to meet the challenge of the new business environment. In part, early success was due to the start-up. The fresh location and carefully selected employees fit into the new organizational structure and style. However, many of the old employees made the transition happen, and they were excited by the change and welcomed their involvement.

Change Agents at American Transtech. As the chief architect of American Transtech's philosophy of management, Lemasters was the key change agent and principal role model (demonstrator) of the change. Given the freedom and financial support of the parent company, Lemasters was creating an organization that departed radically from the traditional, by-the-books bureaucracy of the old stock and bond department. He showed that even in an area of the business governed by tight time schedules and volumes of rules and regulations on securities exchange, there was tremendous freedom to involve workers in establishing their own procedures and ultimately increase productivity. The speed with which the new organization had to be up and running (less than two years) probably helped Lemasters implement the change. There was little time for resistance. The organization literally had to be built from the ground up. People had to be relocated to a different state, a building had to be designed and built, numerous new employees had to be recruited and trained, and complex computer systems (both hardware and software) had to be installed and debugged.

Lemasters had the help of several external and internal consultants. However, rather than rely on these experts to design and implement the change, Lemasters depended largely on existing employees. Some of these employees would not move to the new location because of family obligations or other personal reasons—not because they would not fit the new organization. (The people who would not relocate would have to find new jobs in the company and some would be laid off.) Lemasters recognized that the current employees had the most knowledge of what work was required in handling the company's stock and bond transactions and responding to stockholders' questions, and this knowledge had to be the foundation of the new organization. Perhaps because of the demands of the change, the employees were able to leave behind their old patterns and structures of management and work with each other to create new, flexible, and participative organizational structures.

Some of these designers and implementors of the change became the early change adoptors as they moved to Jacksonville and began to operate the new organization. One lower-level manager who worked in the stock and bond department for many years was rapidly promoted three levels to director. His open, people-oriented style of management was just what the new environment needed. New employees were quickly socialized to the demands of the organization so that the ultimate "users" of the change did not experience a major transition between one way of doing business and another. There was no tolerance of laggards or resisters. The spirit of responsiveness to the needs of the business and the clients was highly positive, and productivity initially skyrocketed.

American Transtech had difficulties several years after Lemasters was transferred to a new position in AT&T and later retired. American Transtech continued to do an excellent job handling stock and bond transactions—the work it had been designed to do. However, it did not do as well at marketing new services, such as telemarketing.

Technological Change

Technological innovation is a major force for change in many organizations. Today's companies face an increasingly competitive environment that requires using technological and human resources to the best advantage. Innovations in technology and management must be implemented quickly and cost-effectively (Tornatzky and others, 1983). Yet many organizations often face barriers to change. For instance, technological and/or managerial change may affect the nature of the work (making it more or less routine), alter supervisors' control, and create employee resistance. Implementing innovations in organizations requires understanding how technical and human resources work together. Consider the following two cases (adapted from London and MacDuffie, 1987):

• The internal telecommunications group of a large nationwide organization designs and implements a system for desk-to-desk electronic mail, word processing, filing, and announcements. Only three years after its introduction in the company, this electronic message system is available to 15,000 users. Any manager with a terminal connected to a telephone can apply for an ID and password to access the system. New users receive an instruction book and attend a two-hour training course. Some top managers use the system to communicate to their entire staff at once. Other managers use it to communicate quickly with co-workers about meetings, status reports, and even personal messages. The system has considerable potential for expansion of users and technical enhancements. It also has the potential for changing management style and organizational design by opening lines of communication between management levels, and, because of the ease of communication, increasing supervisors' spans of control.

• Sophisticated computer technology allows the central monitoring of electronic, telecommunications switching equipment in remote locations. This has the potential for reducing force levels and decreasing the expertise needed at local sites. However, the local technicians resist the central monitoring centers. They fear forced relocations, job loss, the inability to keep up their skills, and decreased control over their work while still being held accountable for the local operation. When a central monitoring center is implemented by management fiat, the process fails. Technicians resist working in the center and taking orders from it. When the technicians are involved in a center's implementation (that is, deciding who staffs it and when it has control over the local site), the concept succeeds.

These two cases are examples of innovations, yet each affects the technical and social aspects of work. The electronic message system is a software-based innovation affecting the process of work—that is, how people communicate. An incremental change, its principal goal is to improve efficiency. The central monitoring center involves technological and organizational change. It is a frame-breaking change, and its primary goal is cost reduction by changing the organization and the content of the work, reducing overall skill requirements, and decreasing the number of employees. It also affects reporting relationships and employees' feelings of status.

Of the two examples, probably the most pervasive change for the people involved was the implementation of the central monitoring centers. Telecommunications switching technology (the equipment that directs calls over lines to reach their appropriate destinations) has undergone a transformation from electromechanical switches to electronic (digital) switches. Electromechanical switches were maintained by technicians who actually made changes on the switches using various tools, such as soldering guns. Technicians were responsible for monitoring, testing, analyzing, and servicing the equipment. The advent of the electronic switch changed the nature of this monitoring and service process. The technicians could now work in an office environment to monitor the electronic switches (now large computers) and make changes in their software systems. The notion of a central monitoring center was a further development made possible by electronic switching technology. Now electronic switches can be monitored from a remote location. Some adjustments in the switch can be made from the remote site, whereas other adjustments require on-site work. Fewer technicians are needed at each site, saving substantial numbers of people.

The central monitoring center gives the technicians at that center exposure to more problems, allows them to keep their skills at a high level, and gives them a much better understanding of how the switches operate. However, the technicians at the local site require much less expertise. Before central monitoring, they needed six months of training. Now most on-site technicians get only about six weeks of training. The local technician's work consists mainly of following the orders of the monitoring center. The local site work is often nothing more than inserting packets in the computer. Like the "Maytag repairman," the switch technician becomes bored and rusty in using his or her skills. However, one or two experienced technicians are still seen as essential at each switch site in case major problems arise.

Several years ago, three pilot central monitoring projects were established. First-line supervisors at the local sites were concerned they would lose control over the technicians who would now take direction from the central monitoring center. Technicians worried that the switches would be increasingly vulnerable to problems. If something could not be fixed at the monitoring center and not enough properly trained technicians were available at the local site, the company ran the danger of having a major switch down for an extended time.

In addition, local technicians had pride in their electronic switches. They installed them, worked out the bugs, and felt they knew them best. The monitoring center concept implied that this history was not important. Central monitoring devalued the jobs of local technicians and enhanced the jobs of those in the monitoring center. The new system changed reporting relationships, and created a new hierarchy of expertise and authority (central monitoring center personnel over local personnel). Local technicians feared they would lose their skills, and monitoring center technicians feared they would lose hands-on experience.

Overall, the monitoring center concept had clear goals. But the costs to the technicians were clear. They perceived high risks to their jobs, and their resistance meant slow adoption of the idea.

In one case, technicians refused to transfer to a monitoring center, so the company hired and trained outside people who had no experience working on a switch. Yet, the outsiders had to give direction to the more highly experienced, highly skilled technicians in the field. In another case, a monitoring center was staffed by people from an urban area and the switches were in a rural area miles away. This introduced a cultural conflict that further increased resentment of both groups. In yet another case, local technicians refused to respond to monitoring center directives.

Next, consider the electronic message system. The electronic message technology has a clear purpose, visible applications, and few demands and costs. Also, it is comparatively easy to implement. It involves few risks to participants. They can obtain an ID, learn how to use the system, and then it is up to them to apply it to their jobs. Some managers use it frequently, others find it of little value. Usage often depends on the extent to which other managers in a department rely on the system. For instance, if top management uses the system to communicate with lower-level managers, then it is important to be part of the system and obtain and send messages through it. Although the system allows higher-level managers to communicate directly with large numbers of people in their departments, the nature of this communication is impersonal. However, this is likely to be better than no communication at all or infrequent communication via memo. Managers can use the system to communicate to individuals or to groups of people at once. The system can have an important impact on the amount of communication and ease of dealing with information, but it is not an intrusive change. For the most part, each individual has the discretion to decide when and how to use it. Instead of having technology imposed on them, people choose to be part of the system.

The more a change affects people, the more they should be involved in all aspects of the change, from design to implementation. The central monitoring centers provide a good example of what happens when users are not part of the design process. The centers tended to be more successful when technicians were involved in implementing them. In one case, center technicians were eventually given responsibility for a local switch. This enabled them to maintain their hands-on skills. In another case, technicians rotated between the center and local sites. This maintained skill and experience levels. It also increased the commitment of all technicians to the central monitoring center concept. They understood what the technicians in the center were doing, and center technicians understood the local situation. This enhanced cooperation.

In another central monitoring case, conflict between the center and local technicians resulted in the general manager deciding to shut down the center for one year to explore alternatives. The process resumed when the general manager asked the field offices to volunteer to be covered by the center. Local technicians could choose the shifts the center would cover. Often, they chose to ask the center to let them cover the switch during the night shift while they were making repairs that could set off alarms. During the day, central monitoring allowed on-site technicians to leave their terminals and do other work. Another site used a similar process by allowing the local technicians to decide when they would be responsible for monitoring the switch, when the center would have sole responsibility for monitoring, and when they would both monitor.

Central monitoring centers were designed by scientists and engineers. The decision to implement the monitoring center concept was made by management. The user-technicians involved had nothing to do with it until the first center was implemented. At first, the monitoring center concept was viewed by the company as fixed (that is, inflexible). The goal was to implement it exactly as it had been designed. However, some general managers who faced resistance to the concept realized that it could be adapted to meet the needs of the situation.

The electronic message system was designed by telecommunications experts. Users became involved after the system had been designed, and now users are asked to contribute by determining what enhancements should be added to the system. For instance, it is possible to use the system to access various data bases. The legal department worked with the system experts to tie legal data bases to the system for easier access by the corporate attorneys. Another adaptation was putting the company telephone directory on the system so that changes in location and telephone numbers could be made rapidly and would be immediately accessible to everyone on the system. Another idea was to put the company's managers' personnel guide on-line. The guide, usually updated several times a year, is a document of several hundred pages detailing personnel policies, such as vacation time, information about various benefits, safety regulations, procedures for transfers, and the like. The policies change frequently, but the updates and the changes are not immediately available to the field because of the expense of printing and distributing the document. Putting the personnel guide on the computer system would give employees immediate access and facilitate announcing personnel policy changes.

Those affected by a change must be committed to the goal of the change (the intended outcome) and the process of bringing about the change, as we saw in the case of the central monitoring centers. The degree of commitment to the change is likely to depend upon how apt the change is in the prevailing culture. In the monitoring center case, the change was incongruous. Monitoring centers were perceived as a break with the service ethic—that is, providing the highest-quality service at almost any expense. It was also a break with the tradition of high job security; or at least that is what the technicians feared.

In contrast, the electronic message system was highly congruous with the prevailing corporate culture. It did not require changing structures or reporting relationships. Most of the employees had technical backgrounds, and so using the computer terminals and learning the software were not problems. The technology could be imposed easily and adapted to local needs.

The central monitoring center case shows the importance of not taking the design of technological improvement as given or fixed, merely to be imposed on the organization. The importance of the social impact of technological introduction could also be applied in other cases where technological change affects the numbers of people needed, their qualifications, and their relationships with each other.

The electronic message center case shows the flexibility of the technology in adapting to the needs of the users. Electronic messages were used in different ways by different managers. Some made it their principal mode of communication, whereas others used it sporadically or not at all. While enhancements to the system were being added to meet the needs of specific departments, more attention was given to expanding the network and increasing the number of users.

Change Agent Roles

Incremental change requires patience and step-by-step planning. Leaders and managers must be demonstrators and defenders, and be willing to analyze the situation and adapt as needed. They may ensure that the spirit or purpose of the changes is maintained or they may alter the direction of the change to suit the needs of the organization. Leaders, managers, and/or human resource professionals may set the stage by articulating the goal(s). They must then elicit the support of their colleagues as change implementors and adopters over time. Thus the human resource professional may be both generator and supporter of incremental change.

Frame-breaking change requires bold articulation and clear demonstration of the vision. Leaders must be key change agents and demonstrators for frame-breaking change. Consultants can facilitate frame-breaking change, but most employees must "buy in" quickly and become defenders and adopters of the change. Human resource professionals support frame-breaking change by providing personnel selection, performance review, and reward systems to reinforce the change and ensure the right talent is available to implement the change. Human resource professionals are less likely to be key change agents than they are to be defenders, demonstrators, and implementors of frame-breaking change.

Technology makes some organizational changes possible, as was the case in the examples cited in this chapter. However, leaders decide to implement the change by investing money and people. This chapter showed the importance of users as change adopters and adapters in ultimately making the change successful. In general, leaders and managers may demonstrate the change and defend it. Human resource professionals may provide training, team building, the structure and process for employee involvement programs, and evaluations. These professionals must understand the technology and how it adds value to the organization.

Recommended Actions

Incremental change is less dramatic than frame-breaking change. Leaders of incremental change should take ample time to plan strategy and involve managers and support staff in the development of plans and actions. Small demonstrations should showcase the value of the change to others who may be skeptical. Human resource professionals who have their own agenda for organizational change may spearhead the effort if they can get key leaders as patrons and defenders and if they can create early success stories.

To accomplish frame-breaking change, leaders need to be direct, vocal, and convincing. They need to elicit the support of key managers and staff, and may find external consultants helpful to carry the message and build team support. Human resource professionals can add to their power base by showing leaders how their programs depend on attracting, motivating, developing, and retaining the right people.

The following are some general guidelines for human resource professionals, leaders, and managers involved in introducing change.

   • *Evaluate the characteristics of change.* Consider the complexity and cost (psychological as well as financial) of the change, the extent to which the purpose and intended outcome are clear and agreed to by everyone. Change that is complex, costly, and uncertain of purpose and outcome is likely to meet more resistance, be more time consuming, and in general have fewer positive outcomes. Developing realistic expectations of what to expect from the change and trying to evaluate the characteristics of the change at the outset may suggest actions that will facilitate the change process.

   • *Consider who and what is affected by the change.* Try to determine how the change affects the work that is done, reporting relationships, and other interpersonal relationships. In general, the more organizational systems affected by the change, the more difficult it will be to implement. The more the user is affected by the change, the more the user should be involved in its design and implementation. Change will be more difficult when it is externally driven yet dependent on user commitment and action.

Users should be involved early in the change process, and user modifications of the change should be considered carefully. One strategy is to hold users responsible for implementing the change, but this should include allowing users to modify the change as they see fit.

Consider the match between the change and the organizational culture. Expect difficulty when the change conflicts with the culture and climate (for example, if it requires a participative management style though the organization is highly bureaucratic).

- *Envision how the change will be implemented.* Try to reduce uncertainty or keep it to a minimum. Try to build on experience. This is particularly important if the change is to be implemented separately in different locations. Communication is the key here. People want to know what the change is supposed to accomplish and what their roles will be.

Consider the level of support for the change and what is needed to gain support. Also, consider the organizational climate. Change will be more difficult when the environment is fraught with conflict. Unless the climate can be altered, the change may be doomed to failure and make things worse. This suggests that supportive social interventions may be needed to facilitate electronic innovations, or that several different, mutually supportive social interventions may be needed simultaneously (for example, supervisor training to support an employee involvement program).

- *Select interventions that recognize the multiple facets involved in the change.* A single intervention may not be enough. For instance, trying to change people through training may have no effect if the social system or the reward structure prevent implementing the behaviors trained. As suggested above, several mutually supportive innovations may be needed simultaneously. Be aware of the costs and benefits of interventions. For instance, involving users in the change process to enhance user commitment increases the likelihood that the change will be modified, possibly for the better in terms of the change's impact on the organization as well as employees' commitment to the change. Finally, an intervention that is too late or misfocused may do more harm than good.

Summary

Incremental change merges the new with the old. It requires a willingness to be open to new ideas and to continuously refine and possibly extend the goals of the organization. Frame-breaking change is dramatic and often sudden. Though resistance is likely, the organization's survival depends on re-creating the organization's mission, structure, staff, and modes of operation. Involving users in the design of the change and recognizing the interplay between the technology and the social aspects of the change are crucial to the success of the innovation. The earlier users are involved and the earlier the social impact of the change is considered, the more successful the change is likely to be. The cases showed the value of learning from experience and applying the results in later applications of the innovation. The next chapter examines the evolution of employee involvement programs and ways to evaluate and enhance the success of these programs.

6

Increasing Employee Involvement in the Change Process

 Leaders, managers, and human resource professionals as change agents must understand environmental forces and changing business directions and introduce new ways of managing that recognize these changes. This chapter examines the move toward more participative styles of management with a focus on the introduction and evolution of employee involvement programs.

The term *postindustrial society* refers to the current and future technological and knowledge boom, the increased competition in a vacillating economic environment, and changes in people's career attitudes and expectations. Key descriptive words are heterogeneity, turbulence, uncertainty, transition, and linkages. People vary in their values and life-styles, and their values and life-styles change over time depending on career opportunities and life stage. Force and cost reductions, mergers of corporate cultures, and reductions in government regulation in some major industries (for example, airlines and telecommunications) have created turbulence and uncertainty. However, these environmental factors have generated opportunities for organizational transitions.

Companies faced with changing environments are "re-inventing" their style of management (Naisbitt, 1984; Elkins, 1985; Finkelstein and Newman, 1984; Hirschorn, 1984; Martin, 1981).

> In the re-invented corporation, top-down, hierarchical, authoritarian management styles have given way to a networking style of management, where everyone is a resource for everyone else. The baby-boomers grew up on the networking style in the anti-war movement and the women's rights movement, and they're now carrying that style into the business community. In the re-invented corporation, we are shifting from "manager as order giver" to "manager as facilitator." In the '80s, we are moving from the manager who is supposed to have all the answers and tells everyone what to do to the manager whose role is to create a nourishing environment for personal growth. We have to increasingly think about the manager as teacher, as mentor, as resource, as developer of human potential [Naisbitt, 1984, pp. 19–20].

Modeling a Participative Style

The American Transtech example in Chapter Five described Lawrence Lemasters's efforts to develop a flat organizational hierarchy with semiautonomous workgroups. From the organization's start, the goal was to enhance responsiveness to the client while keeping costs down. The goal was also to design challenging jobs that demonstrated trust in individual employees and in workgroups to make decisions and take actions. This required a participative management style—one that recognized employees' contributions to the organization and gave employees discretion to act. Lemasters was a role model for communicating and enacting the new organizational design and management style. He also rewarded managers who were able to manage effectively in this new environment.

One such manager, Jim Williams (name disguised) had been in a second-level management position for many years in the old AT&T stock and bond department in New Jersey. He quickly caught on to the meaning of participative management and demonstrated this style as the early workgroups met to design the new organization and plan for the move to Jacksonville, Florida. Jim was invited to be part of the new organization, and he relocated to Florida. Lemasters eventually promoted him to the director level—a three-step jump. When Lemasters was transferred to be the executive vice-president of the administrative section of Bell Laboratories, Jim once again moved with Lemasters. They both tried to use the participative management approaches in this new environment. However, unlike American Transtech, which was literally designed from the ground up to be a sophisticated, participative organization, Lemasters's participative style needed to be superimposed on the existing bureaucracy of the administrative side of Bell Labs (as opposed to the research side, which has a more fluid, less bureaucratic work environment). This was analogous to keeping a 747 in the air while converting key aeronautical systems to the newest technology (Maccoby, personal communication, May 1986).

One of Jim's early experiments was to allow a group of nonmanagement employees the freedom to experiment with scheduling their work time. The group of employees had asked Jim if they could change from a five-day work week to a four-day week and work ten hours a day. The employees manned a computer center that had to be operational around the clock. When Jim consulted his fellow directors, he was told that changing the work schedule was impossible because of union rules, normal administrative procedures, and equity with other groups that would not have the same flexible work schedule. Also, the employees asking for the change in work schedule admitted that not everyone in the unit was sure about a four-day work week.

Jim's response was to review the pros and cons of the request with the employees and tell them they could pursue the idea themselves. They would need to gain the commitment of everyone affected, obtain union consent, and work through the red tape involved with time reports and payroll changes. The group took on the task, overcame the obstacles, and implemented the new work schedule, to the surprise of Jim's peers.

Three months after the trial, the group members decided that the four-day work week was not what they expected, and they asked to return to the old schedule.

Jim's peers laughed at this failure, but Jim did not see it as a failure at all. The experiment demonstrated his openness to new ideas, his trust in his employees, and his unwillingness to let the existing system prevent innovation. He was a model to supervisors in his group as well as to other managers in the organization who observed the process. Of course, he also demonstrated the frustrations of going against company norms and peer pressure, thus clarifying the potential negative as well as positive consequences of a participative style of management.

The Human Resource Professional's Role in Employee Involvement Programs

The idea for an employee involvement program sometimes comes from the human resource department—perhaps because the underlying principles of psychology and group dynamics elicit stronger employee commitment, and perhaps because human resource professionals are called on to provide the needed support for group development. Nevertheless, an employee involvement program will not succeed without the demonstrated support of key top managers or the active and continued involvement of managers as users.

Leaders and human resource professionals should partner as key change agents in the introduction of an employee involvement program. They should evaluate whether the organization needs or can tolerate employee involvement as a frame-breaking or incremental change. If the prevailing management style is counter to participative management (that is, hierarchical and bureaucratic), incremental change is more appropriate with efforts focused on making early adopters successful and then rewarding and communicating the success. Human resource professionals may design supporting systems such as training for problem solving, negotiating skills, new performance measurement, and reward systems (for example, all team members sharing a bonus based on team performance). Selection and assessment processes may identify participative managers early in their careers, and development programs can ensure that these managers are rewarded for their team development and participative management successes.

Self-Managing Teams. New participative situations demand different management behaviors. For instance, managers do different things when leading a self-managing workteam than when directing a more typical workgroup. What does the leader do if the team is supposed to manage itself? To answer this question, organizational researchers Charles Manz and Henry Sims (1987) observed and measured the behavior of team "coordinators" (the position analogous to foreman in a traditional plant) and the behavior of elected team leaders of self-managing groups. The coordinator has the responsibility of getting the group to manage itself by encouraging self-reinforcement, self-criticism, self–goal setting, self-observation and -evaluation, and rehearsal. The team leader, elected from within the group, facilitates the group's organizing itself, trains inexperienced employees, coordinates job assignments, and makes sure that needed materials are available.

Productivity Improvement Efforts. Productivity and product quality have been pervasive problems during the 1970s and early 1980s, with the United States falling to the sixth position among seven leading industrial nations (Ferris and Wagner, 1985). Although technological advances in robotics and computerized manufacturing are increasing productivity and quality levels, there is general agreement that U.S. workers can produce substantially more.

One reason for the low productivity levels is the distrust between union and management. This stems from the early days of the industrial revolution when workers were treated as robots are today and employees feared for their job security as new technology was implemented. For decades, U.S. management has been concerned with standardizing and routinizing the human factor in the workplace as much as possible. As a result, workers spent more time looking out for their own interests than they did worrying about the viability of their employers.

Today, the distrust between management and workers is breaking down as corporations realize that workers have valuable knowledge, and that their contribution is crucial to ensuring responsiveness to customer needs for high-quality products and competitive prices. Also, unions are beginning to realize that the jobs of their members depend on the members' commitment and involvement in the corporation. As a result, workers are joining forces with management in cooperative efforts in place of the traditional adversarial relationship. Employees are learning about the economic conditions of their companies and of their industries. They are adding to their skills so they can be of more value to the organization. In addition, they are working directly with customers to understand how their products are being used, and they are conceding wage increases and in some cases actively becoming partners in the corporation to ensure continued employment. Management is empowering workers to do a better job. Work is becoming so specialized that decisions about products have to be made closer to the work itself (Roth, 1986). Consider the following examples.

• Westinghouse Electric Corporation sent machine operators to Japan to see firsthand how the competition produces turbine engines. The company also sent thirty hourly workers who produced subway generating equipment to New York to evaluate the quality of their product in operation in the city's transit system. Workers saw the difference between "putting wires into a black box and riding the product through the South Bronx" (Roth, 1986, p. 1).

• Bethlehem Steel Company started a program for workers to visit major customers. Steel workers were jolted after seeing defects in their sheet steel show up in the customer's products.

• Technicians installing telecommunications services (for example, private data lines) in telephone company switching offices were encouraged to visit customer sites with service problems rather than work through service representatives and learn about the problems indirectly.

Quality Circles. Following the lead of the Japanese, many companies have established quality circles (QCs). These are small groups of employees, usually ranging in size from three to fifteen members, that meet periodically (for instance, one hour each week) to identify and resolve job-related problems. In 1980, there were 3,000 QCs in more than 500 U.S. organizations (Ramsing and Blair, 1982).

QCs are more than just a technique. They are a way of life in many corporations—a way to integrate people, information, knowledge, and skills to effectively accomplish a common purpose (Landen, 1982). The technical knowledge and problem-solving skills people acquire by participating in QCs transfer to all phases of the corporate enterprise.

Quality of Worklife Programs. QCs are often one tool used in organization-wide quality of worklife (QWL) programs. These programs include structural changes such as management-worker steering committees, semiautonomous workteams, employee ownership and profit sharing, joint goal setting, and other forms of industrial democracy.

QWL programs can be highly structured and based on joint union and management agreements. For instance, the Communications Workers of America and the Bell System companies agreed in 1980 to establish a QWL program. The structure of the program specified that local workforce committees (LWCs) would be established to work on problems of their own choosing. An LWC might include representatives (volunteers or elected workers) from different workgroups or it might be a natural workgroup (that is, the people who generally work together as a team). A local union official would be present at all group meetings. Also, facilitators, either union or management employees trained in group development skills, would work with each LWC. Common issues undertaken by the LWCs tended to be environmental concerns, such as decorating break areas, because such issues were common to all group members. Productivity issues were often ignored because they were not interpreted as part of QWL and because they were viewed as management's responsibility. Natural workteams were more likely to address productivity concerns because they could share the nature of the work and understand common problems. However, time pressures to get the work done and scheduling difficulties to allow for continued meetings, plus the pervasive adversarial nature of the union-management relationship and the traditional bureaucratic-autocratic management style in the company, made it difficult to maintain QWL. (Later in this chapter, I will describe how QWL evolved into a more flexible, productivity-oriented effort responsive to client needs and geared to taking advantage of new technology.)

Comparing QCs and QWL/Employee Participation. QCs are a type of QWL group (Landen, 1982). A major difference between the two is that QCs focus on productivity issues whereas QWL groups may focus more on improving the work environment than enhancing group productivity. Consequently, QCs' productivity is tracked, and increases in productivity resulting from QC-generated changes are measured. QCs may be compared with each other, and the groups doing the best may be rewarded financially. Annual banquets are often held to recognize the top groups. Also, each group may benefit financially by sharing a portion of the savings generated by the group's increase in productivity or cost reduction.

QCs are usually natural teams; QWL groups may consist of representatives from different units. The QC membership is fixed; the QWL members usually rotate, perhaps serving on the QWL committee for a year. QCs are led by the supervisor, but the QWL groups may be led by a member elected by the group. Supervisors may or may not observe and participate in the meetings. Training for QC members emphasizes problem solving. Training for QWL groups is often broader, including team building, decision making, and problem solving. QWL training is also likely to be continuous or be offered whenever it is needed; however, some QWL groups receive no training. Companies with QWL often employ group facilitators. These may be professionals in organizational development or they may be employees trained in group facilitation techniques. In both QCs and QWL groups, authority is generally limited to making recommendations. QCs operate on their own; QWL groups are usually tied to a network of higher-level union and management teams.

The QC procedure is static, with its role limited to identifying problems and areas for productivity improvement. QWL groups are dynamic. What they do is limited only by their own initiative, creativity, and the support of the leadership in the organization. QWL, when successful, can make the entire organization more participative as managers become accustomed to involving employees in decisions affecting them and as the QWL concept is viewed as a tool for accomplishing business goals.

QCs would probably work well in organizational decline, redirection, and start-up where innovative ideas are needed, but the focus must be on increasing productivity and reducing costs as much as possible. QWL programs would probably work well under growth, merger, and start-up conditions where the goal is to produce open communication and high employee involvement.

Implementing Employee Involvement Programs. Consider the following example. A company implemented an employee involvement program as a result of a union-management agreement. The program was implemented by forming local union-management committees that could address any work or environmental problems they wanted, from the color of the walls to how the work is designed. Each LWC differed in the issues it tackled and how much progress it made. Employee commitment to, and management support for, the program varied from location to location.

The employee involvement program was difficult to implement. Although it had a succinct set of goals, the goals themselves were very general and ambiguous. The structure was preestablished in that the union-management agreement specified how LWCs were to be formed. Management and union facilitators were often used to train LWC members in the purpose of the program and its activities. The facilitators taught the groups brainstorming, problem solving, and conflict resolution techniques. The facilitators also attended group meetings and helped the groups progress. Often, groups got bogged down in fairly mundane issues, such as the comfort of employees' chairs. Some groups felt that productivity issues were not legitimate because those were the responsibility of management. Other groups felt that they should focus primarily on productivity and worry much less about environmental concerns. Establishing employee involvement groups requires a considerable investment not only in money but also in the time and energy of the participants. Involvement of the LWCs increases work demands with uncertain returns.

The employee involvement program was a joint union and management effort. Bargaining established the goals and set the structure for the program, but how it operated depended on the users. Therefore, there was significant opportunity for users to modify the process. A supervisor may have treated his or her workgroup as an LWC, meeting periodically to discuss and hopefully solve various problems. In other cases, committees included representatives from different workgroups. Some regions of the company trained facilitators to work with the groups. As time progressed, the formal structure detailed in the union-management agreement became less important, and new ways of implementing the spirit of employee involvement emerged in some parts of the company.

The Impact of Change on the Business

The impact of change refers to the extent to which individuals, groups, and the organization as a whole are altered in some way. Elements of an organization are linked together. A problem with the employee involvement program in the example was that the program was incongruous with the prevailing culture. QWL was imposed on a culture that was generally autocratic. Top management was not used to involving lower-level managers in decision making. In addition, managers were not used to involving nonmanagement personnel in decision making. Lines of authority were important and hard to ignore. The program required substantial involvement of many people. From the employees' standpoint, the program was externally driven (that is, it was driven by union officials and top management). Though the potential for user-generated applications was high, the program was difficult to implement when the management style was basically nonparticipative and authoritarian.

The employee involvement program in the example was a management innovation that had been tried in various forms in a number of organizations over the years as the idea of participative management became popular and was found to be effective. The stimulus in the organization was a recognition on the part of both union and management that employees had the resources to improve the corporation's productivity and to facilitate the introduction of new technology.

The design of the employee involvement program specified who could participate in LWCs. Initially, the design was highly structured. Nonmanagement employees who were union members would be the core of each committee. A committee could consist of a natural workgroup or representatives from different workgroups depending on the availability of employees and the proximity of workgroups in an area. The design required a union steward to be present, and it allowed the involvement of a first-level manager. Union or management facilitators could participate in the group meetings. Another aspect of the design was establishing steering committees of higher-level union officials and middle- and top-level managers. The committees' role was to monitor and support the progress of the LWCs.

I stated above that the goals for the employee involvement program were very general, but the design for forming LWCs was structured. Over time, variations in the structure emerged and were encouraged by union officials and headquarters management. Employee involvement groups emerged under different names, such as "quality circles" and "common interest forums." Some groups arose spontaneously without official union representation or group facilitation. Because each workforce committee chose its own topics for discussion and established its own schedule, there was variation in how much the different groups accomplished and the types of products they tackled. Some groups found it difficult to get off the ground, with committee members resisting joint work with management to improve productivity. Other groups persistently focused on environmental problems, some of which were easy to resolve and some of which were difficult. Still other groups focused on issues of work design and productivity improvement, such as visits to customers to increase employees' understanding of customer needs. The employee involvement program still faced the barrier of adversarial relationships that had not evaporated despite joint union-management initiation of the program (although the number of grievances decreased).

Any organizational change is likely to be fragile. Each local employee involvement committee was a unique process. People dropped out and new ones came in. Even experienced groups lost ground if members changed or efforts were not successful.

The employee involvement program was needed especially in units that were more uncertain, for example, where there were production problems and it was unclear exactly how they could be overcome. However, uncertainty made the employee involvement program more difficult to operate. In some cases, LWCs were unsure exactly what types of problems they should handle. Some felt they should stick to environmental issues, while others felt more meaty productivity problems should be addressed.

The skills and abilities of the people on the LWCs were crucial to the success of the employee involvement program. Group facilitators worked with LWCs on content and group process. They also worked with upper management to integrate the program's efforts with corporate policies and actions to gain further support.

Interventions have their price. For example, a QWL program process aimed at enhancing employee commitment increases the likelihood that the process will be modified by the participants. One of the biggest problems in the employee involvement program was that middle managers resisted the initiatives of the LWCs, feeling that the committees usurped their authority. Thus, another price of the program was conflict.

The outcomes of the employee involvement program depended on the activities of the LWCs. In some cases, there was a pervasive impact on individuals, groups, and tasks. In other cases, there was very little impact. The outcomes of the employee involvement program were not highly visible. An LWC may work on a project that is highly successful and then get bogged down in deciding what to do next, or the participants simply get burned out. Employee involvement requires high emotional commitment. Employees are likely to have strong opinions as to whether or not participation in decisions is an appropriate activity for a union member and, more specifically, what types of projects the LWCs should undertake.

The employee involvement program required improvement. The goals of the program and the process of carrying it out needed to be clarified. Top management needed to demonstrate commitment to it in a visible way. Other interventions were needed to change the culture of the corporation at all levels to bring about a more participative, open environment and to improve union-management relationships. Emphasis had to be given to following through with the projects and recommendations of the LWCs to demonstrate the value of their work.

Program Decline and Failure

Many observers of QC and QWL programs have found that decline and failure are frequent. Eventually, groups meet less often because other work is more pressing or because the groups become less productive and the resources committed to the program dwindle (Lawler and Mohrmann, 1985). Resisters to the program become more vocal as they realize there is less support. The combination of resistance from middle managers, decline in enthusiasm, and resource limitations from budget cuts may contribute to a program's downfall.

Lack of commitment is another reason for productivity program decline. As the outset, people at all organizational levels need to be committed to the program. Voluntary participation and publicly expressed support for the program are likely to enhance commitment (Goodman, 1982). In some cases middle managers are not involved in the program, which may be initiated by top management and union officials and implemented at lower organizational levels. Consequently, middle managers are not given the opportunity to commit themselves to the QWL effort. However, when top management announces the program, middle managers cannot say no. Middle managers see little value in a program that appears to usurp their authority and that threatens their job security.

Commitment to a QWL program often declines over time because the situation changes. Initially, the environment may be supportive, with managers who are concerned about improving productivity, a chief executive officer who wants to demonstrate a democratic style of management, or a cooperative union-management climate. But the situation may change when the economy picks up, the CEO leaves or devotes attention to other concerns, or difficult bargaining issues emerge.

QCs may run out of steam when they exhaust quick fixes that demonstrate the group's ability to solve problems or generate ideas for productivity enhancement. Retraining may be necessary for group members to learn more technical skills or group process skills, yet there may be little support for the training if the group's output has slackened.

Another problem is that the reward process may not reinforce the group effort. For instance, the organization's performance appraisal and compensation system may call for ranking individuals and giving bonuses to the top performers. Obviously, this discourages cooperative group efforts. Or a gain-sharing plan may be established so that the group members benefit financially from the group's efforts, but the amount awarded to each individual may be trivial, especially in light of how much the group saved the company.

Typically, considerable effort is given to starting a QC or QWL program. However, the enthusiasm and hype during the program's inauguration is likely to weaken as expectations are not met and the realization of the support and commitment necessary to sustain the program sets in. One idea is to plan for program maintenance at the front end (Goodman, 1982). Another idea is to establish a long-term training curriculum and schedule, or a long trial-and-measurement period. Also, setting realistic expectations for goal accomplishment is another way to avoid letdown when immediate gains are not achieved. In addition, programs are likely to be more successful when they are spread throughout the organization, and not just limited to isolated units that must work in other groups not using the program, or in groups that do not take the program seriously.

The above examples of experimental participative programs show the importance of leaders modeling a participative style. The example of implementing a QWL program showed the characteristics of such change efforts (for example, the clarity of the goals and opportunities for user modification, the impact of QWL on the business, ways of facilitating the change, and change outcomes). Reasons for QWL program decline and failure were discussed (for example, running out of ideas for short-term productivity improvement), along with conditions for successful QWL programs (for example, strong union and management support).

Dimensions of QWL Programs and Their Evolution

This section reviews characteristics of QWL efforts and how these efforts evolve. The structure, process, and content of QWL programs are outlined and then used to distinguish between first-, second-, and third-generation QWL. Finally, I describe a way to track QWL progress.

Structure. Structure is the form of the QWL program in terms of the number of local groups, their size, composition, and coordination. Structure also refers to the fit between the program and the politics, policies, and general climate of the organization. It also includes the extent to which the program is adapted to meet local needs. How the program is controlled centrally is another element of structure. For instance, regional or corporate headquarters staff organizations may monitor and attempt to control the line QWL efforts, such as the training program offered to support QWL, the issues addressed by the local groups, and how the groups are evaluated. How many people are involved in the effort is another structural characteristic. Some work participation efforts involve only a small number of representatives, whereas others involve many employees, managers, and union officials.

Process. Elements of QWL process are decision making, facilitation, training and education, and union-management relationships. Decision making refers to how much authority the QWL groups have to act on their own. Decision-making process also refers to how the group makes decisions—for example, by vote or discussion until consensus is reached.

Facilitation is the assistance the group receives from a person trained in group dynamics. One or more group members may facilitate their own group. In fact, as group members receive training in such areas as problem identification, problem solving, conflict resolution, and decision making, the group may not need a special facilitator. Facilitators are often employees who are given training and temporary assignments to work with QCs or QWL groups, or they may be professionals in the field of organizational development who are hired either as temporary consultants or as full-time employees. There are advantages to training employees as facilitators. They have credibility with the groups as being one of their own. Also, when they return to their jobs, they hopefully continue to use their skills as they interact with workgroup members.

Facilitator and group member training focuses on group dynamics. This training may also be technical in nature, helping group members to learn more about new technologies. Another type of education is simply conveying information about the state of the organization—how well the organization is doing in the industry. Group members may visit customers to better understand how the group's product or service is being used and what the customer's needs are. Workshops on business topics such as finance and marketing may be offered to give employees insight into how their expenses and their contributions to productivity and quality affect the bottom line. The primary goal in this training is to make group members more responsive to the goals of the organization and to the needs of the clients.

Another aspect of the group process is the tenor of union-management relationships in the firm. Obviously, QWL tries to promote—and depends upon—a cooperative environment; traditional union-management relationships are adversarial. These conflicting pressures influence the success of QWL.

For instance, in 1980 when AT&T agreed with the three unions representing its employees to establish QWL, many local QWL efforts were initiated. However, the strike of 1983 (the year prior to the Bell System divestiture) had a devastating effect on some local QWL efforts. The trust that had been established between union and management during the first two years of QWL eroded as union members began to worry about job security and as management prepared to reorganize and cut costs to make the corporation more competitive. Importantly, commitment to the QWL program was renewed by top management and union officials at the conclusion of the 1983 bargaining session. Unfortunately, damage at local levels often took considerable time to overcome. A similar process unfolded with the 1986 AT&T strike, which created another cycle of progress, decline, and progress.

Content. QWL content refers to what the groups work on. As stated earlier, QCs usually limit their activities to productivity concerns. Anything is fair game for QWL groups, such as debating whether to eliminate smoking in work areas, holding a lottery to raise funds for a new break area, or planning the department's Christmas party. Environmental concerns are often easier to deal with. Some groups take the QWL label literally and confine their efforts to worklife (that is, environmental) concerns. Other groups begin with environmental concerns and progress to productivity issues.

The Successful Evolution
of Employee Involvement Programs

In some companies, a new phase of QWL is evolving, one that tries new structures and attempts to integrate QWL more thoroughly with the daily operations of the business. Consider the efforts of GM and the UAW (Maccoby, 1986). The original Tarrytown plant model of participative management utilized a committee structure in a bureaucratic environment—a first-generation model. A second generation of QWL was embodied in the Pontiac Fiero plant, which placed supervisors in the nontraditional role of facilitator and put workers into direct contact with customers, but still utilized an assembly line. The new Saturn plant may be an emerging example of third-generation QWL, with innovations such as the abolishment of the assembly line and union stewards serving as counselors elected by the team.

Table 3 describes first-, second-, and third-generation QWL programs in terms of the structure, process, and content of the programs. Each of these is reviewed below.

First Generation QWL. First-generation QWL efforts are viewed as programs—essentially appendices to the organization's structure. To use Chapter Five's terminology, they are incremental organizational changes, although some champions of QWL within the organization would probably like them to become frame breaking. There is generally a mismatch, and conflict often arises between the organization's by-the-books, regimented, bureaucratic structure and the intended free-flowing, participative spirit of QWL. Of course, a QWL intervention would not be needed to begin with if the organization's culture were open and participative.

First-generation QWL is likely to be imposed by top management, often from corporate headquarters, because there is a belief that the organizational management needs to be changed if the corporation is to survive and thrive. Or union officials and top management may agree about the value of working together. However, QWL efforts are instituted at the local level. Thus, there may be a conflict between what corporate headquarters says it wants to see and what the line organizations believe is valuable. Also, when the organization's structure and general philosophy are bureaucratic and management does not change its style, QWL is in for trouble. For example, the company's compensation system may reward individual efforts, thus creating a competitive atmosphere as opposed to a spirit of cooperation.

First-generation QWL involves a selected group of employees. Groups are formed with appointed or elected representatives from different workgroups. The representatives may have different types of jobs because they come from competing work units. Consequently, they may have little in common ex-

Table 3. First-, Second-, and Third-Generation QWL Programs.

	First Generation	Second Generation	Third Generation
Structure			
Integration	QWL outside of/parallel to regular organizational structure; perceived as a program	Some integration of QWL with regular organizational structure	QWL inseparable from regular organizational structure; organizational structure becomes flatter
Adaptation	QWL structure externally imposed by centralized experts/authority	QWL structure shows some adaptations and local variations	Each local QWL structure unique to the particular working environment
Centralization	QWL structure centralized	QWL structure partly centralized, partly decentralized	QWL structure decentralized
Involvement	QWL structure involves only selected employees	QWL structure involves many or most employees	QWL structure involves all employees
Process			
Decision Making	Decision making is management prerogative; QWL provides input to management decisions	Ranges from QWL responsibility for some decisions at discretion of managers to managers being removed from day-to-day work decisions	Roles of management, non-management and union redefined; decisions now made by those closest to impact; organization managed jointly at all levels
Facilitation	Facilitation provided by centralized, external resources	Facilitation moved under decentralized, local control	Each employee acquires skills of facilitator; takes on role as needed

Training and Education	Need for training and education determined and provided by centralized, external sources; focus on orientation for all; skills for facilitators	Groups identify own training needs and arrange as needed; focus on skills needed for QWL process, for all participants	Training locally determined; expands to include any process or work-related skill needed; all acquire skills in QWL process and organization management including financial, etc.
Union-Management Relationship	Formal union-management relationship adversarial; much time spent building up informal communication, respect, trust	Union-management relationship takes on more collaborative, cooperative tone; both sides move back and forth between collaborative and adversarial roles as needed	Collaborative union-management relationship formalized, or roles redefined as traditional distinctions between management and nonmanagement become blurred
Content Issues	Issues peripheral to the business; tend to focus on the environmental	Expanded range of issues moves beyond environmental to encompass employee, union, planning, policy, business, and day-to-day work issues; constraints are contract and company policy	No distinction between "QWL issues" and other issues; all ideas considered; contract and company policy built on QWL foundation

Note: I want to thank Linda Streit and Rosemary O'Connor for their work on this table.

cept perhaps the building in which they work. Hence, the emphasis is on environmental issues, as stated earlier in this chapter.

Regarding process, first-generation QWL groups are limited in their decision-making authority and they often complain about lack of support from management. The groups may make decisions about fairly trivial matters or they may work hard on more substantive issues, such as establishing a system for selecting vacation times or a system for training new employees, only to find that their decision is undermined by a conflicting corporate policy or by lack of resources.

Facilitation of first-generation groups often comes from outside the local group. Full-time facilitators may be appointed; these are usually former line managers or nonmanagement employees who are chosen because they have the necessary interpersonal and organizational skills. They receive special training and then set to work providing start-up training for new QWL groups. They also facilitate group meetings. The type of training needed is determined regionally or at corporate headquarters. The major goal is to be sure the facilitators have the required knowledge and skills and that the participants receive the proper orientation.

The relationship between the union and management remains primarily adversarial in first-generation QWL. Considerable time is spent building up informal communication, respect, and trust. QWL often results in fewer grievances (Dalton and Tudor, 1984). In particular, it reduces the number of trivial grievances that are time consuming but rarely have solid grounds, such as complaints about a boss's directives.

Finally, first-generation QWL issues are generally peripheral to the business, focusing on environmental concerns. When the QWL participants represent different local groups, the color of the walls and similar issues may be all they have in common. Also, such environmental concerns are safe issues for discussion. Local union officials will not claim these concerns are management's prerogative, and there is less danger that the groups will be discussing traditional bargained-for issues, such as the amount of overtime or financial incentives. Moreover, environmental concerns result in tangible, visible products that give the group members a feeling of success.

Second-Generation QWL. Second-generation QWL begins with a merger of participative management with the organization's structure. Managers and union officials work together to discuss work problems and business goals. Natural workteams meet to discuss their QWL efforts. Thus, participative management is no longer an alien force imposed on a bureaucratic structure. The philosophy of QWL is now meshed with the day-to-day operations of the business (Miles and Rosenberg, 1982).

Second-generation QWL shows local adaptation. Sticking to a rigid set of rules about who can be part of a QWL team is no longer viewed as necessary. Because natural teams are involved, second-generation QWL affects most if not all employees, not just selective representatives. Regional or corporate steering committees still guide the QWL efforts by monitoring progress, selecting facilitators, and providing orientation and training.

The process of second-generation QWL gives more decision-making discretion to employees. In some cases, managers retain their authority and make decisions with input from their workgroups. In other cases, managers delegate authority to their workgroups.

Facilitation of second-generation groups tends to be decentralized. Each local area appoints its own facilitators, identifies its own training needs, and arranges for the training. This may mean contracting with a local consultant to generate and provide the training the group feels is necessary, as opposed to accepting the standard training developed by the corporate headquarters. Also, the goal is to train all participants. In fact, training in problem solving and conflict resolution may be precursors for effective second-generation QWL. In one case, middle managers and local union presidents and vice-presidents began attending joint problem-solving training at the suggestion of a senior manager. This improved union-management relationships and fostered a climate of trust that lead to increased QWL efforts within the natural workgroups.

Second-generation QWL groups move beyond environmental concerns to discuss productivity. The company policies
or the union contract may impose constraints on which topics
are permissible. Yet there is substantial adaptation and flexibility. For instance, the group may develop a flexible work schedule (flextime). As long as contractual issues of overtime and pay
do not intervene, the group may agree on a way for employees
to have flexibility in their work schedules to accomodate doc-
tor's appointments and other personal errands.

Third-Generation QWL. The structure of third-generation QWL
is merged with, and indistinguishable from, the structure of the
business. In general, people have more discretion because the
organizational structure is flatter and managers have larger spans
of control. In such a structure, QWL will become a way of
doing business—a style of behavior—rather than a formal program. Its operation will be different in each work location and
all employees will be involved.

Autonomous or self-managing workgroups are one example of third-generation QWL where the groups operate on their
own with little or no interference from management. Third-
generation QWL is easier to achieve in a new plant start-up. An
example is the Volvo plant in Sweden where automobiles are
manufactured by teams whose members do all phases of production. In this scheme, the distinction between union and
management breaks down. Decisions are made by those most
affected by them. Also, the organization is managed by joint
union and management efforts at all levels—middle managers
working with local union officials, top managers working with
top union officials, as well as occupational and first-line managers working together on QWL teams.

Facilitation of third-generation QWL is the responsibility
of all participants. Everyone acquires group process skills. Also,
everyone is trained on a variety of work-related skills so members of the workteam can perform each others' jobs.

Overall, there is no distinction between third-generation
QWL issues and other concerns. Also contract issues do not limit

what the workgroup can deal with. Both the contract and corpo- rate policies rest on a QWL-participative management foundation.

The Need for Evaluation

QWL can mean turbulent times for an organization be- cause of the lack of clarity around what QWL is supposed to be and because of the resistance on the part of managers and occu- pational people who do not understand their role in the process. One way to foster a smoother transition and evolution is through continuous assessment and refinement of the process. Self-eval- uation is especially good because it is likely to increase commit- ment and participation. Perhaps assisted by the QWL facilitators, outside consultants, and/or a research staff, evaluation provides a record of growth, accomplishment, and standards of success- ful system integration, as well as directions for change and im- provement (Mazany and Humphrey, 1984).

Measuring the persistence of a QWL program tracks labor and management's awareness of the program, the related behav- ior (for example, the frequency of meetings), how people feel about the process and intervention techniques, and whether the organization's values support the new form of work organiza- tion (Goodman, 1982).

Assessing Attitudes Toward QWL. The personnel research group in a company's headquarters was asked by a regional QWL exec- utive board to help assess QWL activities in the region. The pur- pose of the assessment was to provide existing QWL groups with a "snapshot" of how they were doing and to give them a benchmark against which they could measure their efforts in the future.

The study consisted of two parts: First, a survey was sent to all departments in the region. The survey was sent to 2,500 employees; 950 responded, a response rate of 38 percent. Sec- ond, interviews were conducted with employees who were in- volved in QWL efforts in the region. Twenty-two individual interviews were conducted with ten managerial and twelve occupational employees to collect background data on the region's QWL efforts.

The survey data were analyzed to examine differences between employees who were involved in the QWL process and those who were not involved in the process. The data measured the perceived impact of QWL and general overall reactions to the QWL process.

Perceived Impact. Generally, employees who were involved in QWL viewed it more favorably and saw it as having a greater effect on a larger number of topics compared to those employees who were not involved in QWL. Fifty percent of the respondents who were involved in QWL either "agreed" or "strongly agreed" with the statement that "QWL has significantly contributed to sharing decision making among employees"; only 30 percent of the respondents who were not involved in QWL agreed. Similarly, 66 percent of the respondents who were involved in QWL felt that QWL had had a great effect on improving the work environment, as compared to only 42 percent of the respondents who were not involved in QWL.

General Perceptions. Both groups of respondents felt that there was a need for QWL; only 7 percent of each group responded that "there is no need for QWL; everything is fine." Almost half (49 percent) of the respondents who were involved in QWL felt that QWL projects had been successful, in contrast to only 19 percent of the respondents who were not involved in QWL. Similarly, 58 percent of the respondents who were involved in QWL felt that QWL projects were both meaningful and useful, as compared to only 30 percent of the respondents who were not involved in QWL.

In general, employees who were involved in QWL perceived more management and union support for QWL than did employees who were not involved in QWL.

Comprehensive Evaluations. The above example is excerpted from a more comprehensive evaluation of a local QWL effort. Complete questionnaire results, with separate analyses for different subgroups, were presented along with a summary of the issues derived from the interviews. The results and researchers' recommendations were presented to the regional steering committee.

Similar studies have been done for several other local QWL efforts. In one case, a steering committee asked for a questionnaire they could administer on an ongoing basis to track their progress and evolution. The questionnaire, provided in Exhibit 1, asks about the structure, process, and content, of the QWL effort, and each scale measures progress reflecting first-through third-generation QWL. (See Exhibit 1 in Appendix Two at the end of this chapter.) The higher the average score, the closer the unit is to third-generation QWL. The steering committee planned to administer, code, and analyze this diagnostic questionnaire themselves, repeating the evaluation at least annually.

Another example of a QWL evaluation was a study done for a company's national steering committee. The goal was to examine the emergence of second-generation QWL models in the company to provide examples to other groups within the company of the type of progress that could be achieved. The project was done jointly by researchers on the union's staff and the company's headquarters.

Two cases of second-generation QWL were identified, and the research team observed group meetings and interviewed the people involved at each site. Also, interviews were conducted with five local union vice-presidents and five middle managers at different locations to discuss their QWL experiences and vision for the future.

Some General Conclusions. Some of the latter study's conclusions and recommendations suggest ways of moving QWL efforts from first to second generation.

• The evolution of first-generation into second-generation QWL is not a smooth or continuous process.

The transition from first to second generation occurs in fits and starts. An effort may stay at one level for a long time before taking a great leap forward. New key participants entering the process sometimes cause it to regress and then recover ground before it can move forward.

Different components of QWL seem to evolve at different rates, and over time, individual components move into a second generational phase.

No examples of third-generation QWL efforts were studied. An important question is whether third-generation QWL evolves from second-generation QWL. Perhaps third-generation QWL requires new start-ups, with tailor-made organization structures, carefully selected employees, and no history of adversarial union-management relationships. Second-generation efforts need to be studied over time to watch for the emergence of third-generation characteristics.

• First-generation efforts typically stall unless encouraged to grow into second-generation models.

First-generation QWL activity will stall or plateau from frustration unless there is joint union-management encouragement to progress. Participants seem to lose their initial excitement after most environmental issues have been addressed. A distinction can be made between those first-generation efforts that flounder because conflicts cannot be dealt with and trust is not built between union and management, and those efforts that simply "run out of steam" because they have exhausted the possibilities at their present state of development. It is the latter that I refer to as "stalled" or "plateaued."

• Flexibility in adapting QWL structures and processes to fit the specific needs of the group is a key element in evolving toward a second-generation effort.

Workgroups vary widely in the type and similarity of work they do, in their geographic dispersion, as well as other factors. Issues such as how to achieve maximum participation and what unit of employees is the most effective as a basic QWL group (for example, natural workgroups, each work shift, or other units) are best resolved by each local group for itself through experimentation and perseverance. Efforts that evolve into second-generation QWL are not those that get it right the first time but groups that keep trying until they find the path that works for them.

Change Agent Roles

Moving a work unit toward third-generation QWL requires the commitment and energy of group leaders, group members, and facilitators. The cases showed that line managers may be key agents in fostering an employee involvement spirit and establishing the mechanisms, such as a common interest forum to encourage union-management cooperation. Local union leaders may also be key change agents by eliciting the support of their membership and by demonstrating cooperative behavior. Human resource professionals play an implementation role by helping to define the goals of QWL, providing training, evaluating the QWL effort and feeding back the results, and by publicizing and celebrating success efforts.

Some Recommendations

1. First-generation QWL efforts can be expected to stall before moving ahead into the second generation. Publicizing this information through the corporate QWL network may help to reassure stalled groups and encourage them to keep trying. Because stalled efforts seem to benefit from a catalyst, the company and union should announce to QWL participants all available conferences, seminars, meetings, videotapes, and training that might help groups to revitalize lagging efforts. The national steering committee should take an active role in organizing conferences, experience-sharing sessions, seminars, and other means by which QWL groups can be exposed to new ideas and examples of successful efforts and ways to gain top management and union support.

2. Local steering committees should be encouraged to experiment with new structures to extend the range of QWL involvement and participation to all employees in a way that fits their particular work setting. However, new structures need to be created within the QWL framework, that is, with joint participation by union and management and with the roles of each clearly defined. The national steering committee can encourage and set the tone for this by incorporating these ideas into QWL

orientation, education, and training materials, and by general publicity.

3. Steering committees can take advantage of existing organizational structures and processes in redesigning QWL to increase participation and better fit their work locations. For example, natural workteams (employees doing the same work at the same time in the same location) can be designated as QWL units or existing task forces and projects can be incorporated into the QWL effort with the oversight of a steering committee.

4. Ownership of QWL should be moved down to the local level. Local steering committees must have autonomy in determining their structure, goals, needs, and role in the process. Departmental or regional committees can be most effective as resource providers or "hands-off" coordinating groups.

5. Top level support for QWL can be made more visible by including QWL information in the orientation package for new supervisors; having union officials and management work together at all levels to address union and business goals and make these efforts known; and including a QWL component in a training package for all union leaders (stewards and local presidents).

6. A corporate steering committee can be an effective advocate for QWL by lobbying top levels of the company and the union. For example, committee members could meet individually and informally with members of high-level task forces to encourage and promote QWL as a vehicle for effectively implementing new technologies or redesigning organizations.

Summary

This chapter described various forms of employee involvement programs such as quality circles (QCs) and quality of worklife (QWL) efforts, with an in-depth example of how one employee involvement program was implemented. This chapter also described the structure, process, and content of a QWL effort and the evolution of QWL from the first through third generations. In general, QWL program evaluation conducted by human resource professionals is a way to monitor the progress of QWL and uncover areas for change and development. Identifying, clarifying, and dealing with the problems is a way to keep a floundering effort alive. The data can also be used to redirect or renew the effort and move it toward the second or possibly third generation. Evaluations should draw on multiple sources of information (both questionnaire-based quantitative data and interview-based qualitative data). Also, evaluations should be repeated over time to monitor the effort and use the data to suggest needed interventions for improvement. The chapter concluded with generally applicable conclusions and recommendations from QWL evaluation. Program evaluation methods will be discussed in Chapter Nine as one way human resource professionals can support organizational change agents.

Appendix One, below, offers several cases of QWL efforts showing the variety of forms, purposes, issues, and change agent roles. The cases describe the efforts of a few early adopters who were often frustrated by the resistance they encountered. They learned that QWL requires them to be educator, coach, facilitator, and crusader—certainly demanding and draining roles for a change agent.

The next chapter begins the section on the human resource function's support for change with a discussion of the role and design of the human resource/personnel department in a company.

Appendix One

Three QWL Examples

There are probably no pure examples of first-, second-, and third-generation QWL. The following cases describe QWL efforts that have elements of all three. The three cases are based on interviews with QWL participants in different locations. The first case is a local union president's description of a first-generation effort with some second-generation characteristics. The union president, John Baker (all names have been changed to maintain confidentiality), reviews how he and a middle manager worked together to establish a "common interest forum" to support local QWL activities. John also tells how the manager of another group in John's local was unsupportive, creating conflict and limiting QWL progress.

The second case is based on an interview with a group technician and union member, Jerry Wallace. In this example, natural workteams, calling themselves QCs, meet to discuss a host of issues, many centering on improving the work group's productivity. In addition, representatives from each workgroup meet periodically to review the progress of the QCs and raise issues common to all the workgroups in the office. This effort approaches the second generation in that it seeks to involve everyone in each natural workteam. Yet the effort is still viewed as something extra, attached to the work routine but not completely part of it. Though the groups occasionally deal with productivity concerns, some issues are off limits and others are fairly trivial.

The third case is of a middle-level manager, Max Thompson, who describes his effort to use QWL as a tool to set and accomplish business goals. A mid-level union-management committee is established to agree on business goals, communicate them to workteams, and get the workteams involved in meeting the goals. An issue in a second-generation QWL environment is how to maintain a formal role for the union, as specified in the union-management QWL agreement.

These cases were generated from an interview study of QWL efforts. Multiple interviews were conducted for each case, so different points of views were incorporated into a case where necessary although each case focuses on one of two individuals. The cases show a variety of QWL forms. Keep in mind that a given form is not a magic formula, despite the successes described here.

Case 1. John Baker, Local Union President: Descriptions of a Success and a Failure

This case focuses on John Baker, a local union president who has held this position for two years. As union president, he deals with two unit managers who provide a night-and-day contrast of approaches to QWL. In one department, which will be referred to as unit "A," QWL has cut down on disputes and grievances, kept lines of communication open, and helped avoid problems before they occur. The other department, referred to as unit "B," is another story. Here QWL has floundered. John described his attempt to get a steering committee established, but lines of communication broke down. Looking back, he now feels he should have insisted that they continue. He attributed the blame for the inability to establish a steering committee to the poor relationship he has with unit manager B.

John lamented that overall there is not enough visible high-level commitment to QWL. There is considerable rhetoric but no concrete support at the corporate and regional levels. He said that QWL can work at the local level when there is good communication between management and the union. However, even when such positive relationships exist, the danger is that the people will move on to other positions and progress will dissipate.

Unit A is a good example of a positive QWL experience. The unit manager and the union president agreed to form a unit-level common interest forum. This group consisted of the third-level manager who headed the unit, two second-level managers, the union president, two area representatives from the union (union stewards), and two facilitators (one from the company and one from the union). The facilitators acted as cochairs of the committee. Their mission was to tackle some issues never addressed except through grievances, such as timing of breaks and excessive overtime. The goal was to reach agreement on procedures before grievances occurred. They wanted to establish procedures early on in areas where they knew there were problems. In addition, the common interest forum would serve as a steering committee for QWL. The goal of the committee, and the reason they called it a common interest forum and not a steering committee, was that it would go beyond QWL to include labor relations issues such as those mentioned above. The interest forum met once a month during the past year.

John is convinced that the common interest forum helped the LWCs to operate more smoothly. Before the interest forum was started, the local teams did not have facilitators. Now the facilitators and the interest forum work hand-in-hand, demonstrating joint union-management cooperation. The facilitators help train new group members, explain the QWL process when a new group is forming, and get the group operating. Facilitators work with each LWC to establish whatever structure is needed. There is no one structure because each location is different.

John feels that the mere existence of the common interest forum shows the local committees that the company cares about the process. The interest forum is a resource group to help the local committee. For instance, it may help determine what training is needed at the local level, and it will contribute resources to develop packages to meet the training needs. An example of such a training program was a three-hour financial awareness seminar that was given to everyone in the unit and is now spreading to other units in the region. Though some employees felt it was not worthwhile because the information was not directly related to job performance, most employees thought it was helpful to understand the business. The seminar was a good example of how the union president and the unit manager could work together to provide meaningful training.

As another example, a problem arose with excessive overtime. The local committee felt that this problem was due to extended breaks and employees not being able to get the work done during normal hours. The interest forum talked about this as an issue and felt that other causes should be considered, such as how employees were assigned to projects.

The common interest forum routinely publishes its minutes and distributes them to all employees in the unit. This communicates what is happening and it builds an awareness of the value of the joint union-management effort. This full disclosure approach shows that neither side is selling out.

Turning to unit B, John felt that the unit's QWL progress has been limited to establishing the steering committee for QWL. The committee members can say that they have QWL, but there is no real support and quite a lot of frustration. The LWCs that operate in unit B do so without much contact with their union president.

Overall, the two examples show how to succeed and how

to fail. John is apprehensive about unit A's continued success. He feels it hinges on whether the unit manager who comes next is as supportive as the present unit manager. John hopes that the process will be fairly entrenched so that it will be difficult to pull it apart even if the next unit manager is not supportive of QWL.

John would like to see more communication and cooperation between union and management at the regional and corporate levels. He said that too often programs are dumped on the workforce and they resist them because they have no prior knowledge of them and have had no input into their development. Many problems could be avoided by getting the union and management officials talking.

In summary, John feels there has been some benefit from QWL, but there is a need for increased communication and trust among all employees. He is not overly optimistic about the future. The common interest forum is an idea that goes beyond QWL. This joint union-management cooperative activity could be of value at higher levels of the organization as well.

Case 2. Jerry Wallace, Technician:
Integrating QWL into the Natural Workteam

Jerry Wallace is a technician in a workteam that is one of six first-level groups under the second-level operations manager. Jerry said that QC activities and his chairmanship of his workgroup's QC began six months ago. The QC began by viewing videotapes of QCs in other companies. Jerry found these tapes to be inspiring. They showed how employee involvement and customer responsiveness had affected the business.

The QCs operate in meetings of the natural workgroups. The natural workgroups meet once a month for an hour or slightly more to discuss various issues. Then once a month, a representative from each of the workgroups attends a second-level group meeting. The first-level supervisors, as well as the second-level manager, attend that larger meeting. In the larger meeting, they review what each of the smaller groups has done. The larger meeting allows representatives from each of the groups to understand each other's issues and to report back to the smaller groups. Jerry said that he has been to all of the larger group and smaller group meetings since the effort began.

A key to keeping the groups productive, according to Jerry, is ensuring continuity. This is done by being sure that the groups meet every month even if there is not much to discuss. A problem that other groups have is that they skip meetings because there is no time to meet. Jerry believes that this is a mistake. He emphasized the importance of regular meetings. He also said that it is important for the chair to keep good notes. At a single meeting, as many as seventy small issues could arise.

When the QCs began in this operations area, all the people in the group were new. They discussed work problems as well as environmental concerns. Each month, they tried to solve one or two problems. They began the next meeting by sharing what had been accomplished. This got the meetings off to a good start. In the large office meeting, they might share as many as a hundred different issues. The second-level manager's secretary, Fran Gilbert, volunteered to take notes and schedule the large group meetings.

Jerry gave several examples of what his QC has accomplished. One of the first problems occurred in running wire over a frame. (Frames are metal structures holding the electrical equipment for the switches in a telephone company office.) In some places, there were gaps in the frame, resulting in the wire getting caught. They discussed several ideas to correct the problem and eventually one person in the group suggested using a window sealer over the frame. Jerry tried it himself when he was not busy. After that, they made it a practice to inspect the frame and apply sealer wherever necessary. Other problems the frame group dealt with included lighting in some dark areas, putting more ladders on the frame, and testing different tips of soldering irons because the tips were wearing out too quickly.

Jerry also mentioned that the QCs have dealt with aspects of the work environment such as having better chairs, choosing carpeting that will go in a new work area, and putting together a display case in the lobby of the building. The second-level QC has also started giving several awards. They got this idea from the videotapes. One award is a service champion prize, and Jerry showed me a plaque that included the four names of people who had received the award in the last six months. This goes to the technician who went out of his or her way to help customers on a circuit. The recipient gets the recognition of having his or her name on the plaque and also receives a small gift, such as a pewter cup. Jerry says that this helps office morale considerably.

One of the major factors keeping the frame group QC going has been Jerry's active chairmanship. He reiterated the importance of his keeping good notes on ideas and suggestions and reporting on them in the second-level QC meetings. He also emphasized the importance of his taking notes in the second-level QC meetings so he could report back to his fellow workers in the frame group.

Jerry felt that the way the QCs are organized encourages participation. Information from the larger group meeting eventually filters through the office. If a particular group is not involved because they do not meet or because their representative does not attend the second-level meeting, then they are left out. This draws them into the process. They begin feeling that if they are going to be in on what is happening, they have to have their own meetings and they have to send a representative to the second-level QC.

From the start of the QC effort, the groups dealt with both hard and easy problems. Fran is responsible for listing the accomplishments in the minutes of the meeting. These accomplishments are taken back to the individual groups so that everybody knows when there has been a success. Some problems may take months to work on, but as long as they are brought up in each meeting, people do not lose sight of them.

The activity of the QC carries over into work on the job. People volunteer to handle problems raised in the QC. For instance, Jerry decided he would work on the display case in the lobby because he had done that last year and he knew how to gain access to keys and other resources that were needed.

In conclusion, the QC activity as described by Jerry Wallace seemed to be an engaging process. Jerry said that there was no indication that the QC efforts were dropping off. If anything, they were finding more and more things to discuss. He seemed to be very involved himself, and he appeared to be an impetus for keeping the frame group QC alive. This shows the importance of the commitment of those involved. Jerry attributed the success of the QC effort to everyone, not just the second-level manager or Jerry's first-level boss. As long as the chairpeople schedule meetings for their groups and accurately report what is going on, the effort is likely to be successful. The group has dealt with substantive work issues that affect productivity as well as environmental issues. Finally, Jerry emphasized the importance of everyone's involvement in the activity, saying that it is not enough to have the involvement of just a few representatives.

Case 3. Max Thompson, Unit Manager:
QWL as a Tool for Accomplishing Business Goals

Max Thompson is a unit manager who has had extensive experience working with steering committees. He is a member of two state QWL committees. He views QWL as moving toward where it should be. By this he means that the goal is to have *all* employees involved in activities supporting the business goals. Accomplishing this is a learning experience and hard work. Ultimately, it is beneficial because people become more involved in their jobs.

For the past several years, Max has tried different approaches to QWL. This year he held a meeting of his immediate subordinates (second-level managers) and, from each of their groups, a first-line supervisor, a local union president, and a nonmanagement employee from each operations group. From this group, Max requested volunteers to become involved in QWL to help establish the unit's business goals. He wanted these people to go back to their offices to get "buy-in" to the goals and come up with ways to achieve them. By midyear, one local union president complained that though the natural workteams were actively working on business issues, this was not what he had in mind when he agreed to participate.

In fact, Max avoided calling these activities QWL, because QWL implied a certain structure that did not exist. Even though the process was jointly planned by union members and management, the union president feared that the union's role was being undermined. Max visited each office every quarter to review the progress with the supervisor and the union official. Max felt that something new was needed for the next year.

This "something new" came from a charge that Max gave to three QWL facilitators he brought in from the region's headquarters. He wanted them to generate a way to avoid the perception that the union's role was being undermined. The facilitators generated a four-phase process.

1. The three facilitators met with all second-level operations managers under Max with their union counterparts to review the QWL principles and get everyone involved in the process.

2. This was done first in one of Max's groups and then the other.

3. Each operations manager then held a similar meeting with the first-level supervisors and union representatives within their group. The operations manager explained the process and charged the supervisors and their union counterparts to hold meetings with each supervisor's group.

4. A meeting was held to review the business goals and ideas that were generated to help accomplish them during the year.

Max followed up this process by regular visits to each office. The process helped to alleviate the union's concern because when there was not a designated union representative in a natural team, the union selected someone as the representative.

What Max saw as new about this process was that the natural team approach ensured that everyone was ultimately involved. It started out with joint union-management cooperation at the unit level and then filtered down. Moreover, the union's role continued throughout the process.

In summary, the ingredients to the natural team approach include the involvement of every employee in each workgroup; union representation; training a focus on business goals; operations manager and first-level involvement; good facilitators; and steering committees to oversee the process. Also highlighted was the importance of having good facilitators.

Conclusion

Integrating QWL into an organization takes time. It requires changes in attitudes and behaviors, organizational processes and culture, and often the design of work itself. "A successful QWL system is a flexible, 'living' system continually redefined and modified to better the match between QWL and the organization, to meet the changing needs of the participants and to accommodate the growing sophistication of the participants" (Mazany and Humphrey, 1984, pp. 4–5).

Appendix Two

Exhibit 1. QWL Assessment.

This questionnaire has been designed to see what stage of development your QWL effort is in. It may also help to illustrate for you the growth of QWL efforts. Please read the descriptions along each scale and then choose the number that best describes where your QWL effort is right now. If you feel that your answer is between two descriptions, use an in-between number. A sample question is given below.

Sample:

How settled are you in your current job?

1	2	3	4	5	6	7
I am new to my job—I spend much time asking questions and learning my responsibilities			I am fairly proficient at my job—I seldom need help or guidance			I have become an expert in my job—I now spend time coaching and helping others

If, for example, you are relatively new but have successfully begun to sort out some of the confusion in having a new job, you might circle the number 2. If you are pretty good at some parts of your job, but have become an expert at other parts, you might circle the number 6.

If you do not know enough about your QWL effort to answer a specific question please skip it and go onto the next question.

(continued on next page)

Exhibit 1. QWL Assessment, Cont'd.

1. How is time allocated to QWL in your workgroup?

1	2	3	4	5	6	7
QWL meetings are not held regularly and are easily postponed or cancelled because of work pressures.			QWL meetings are scheduled and held periodically as needed on a regular basis.			QWL meetings are held "on the spot" to resolve problems as they arise.

2. What does QWL mean to your work group?

1	2	3	4	5	6	7
QWL is treated as "just another company program."			QWL is a tool through which we can try to manage the business in a participative way.			QWL is our management style—we run the business in a joint participative manner.

3. How closely is QWL tied to your regular work activities?

1	2	3	4	5	6	7
We see it as something apart from our regular work activities.			QWL is tied to our regular work activities through special issues, projects, etc.			QWL is a part of our everyday, work.

4. How is your QWL effort structured (by structured we mean the way your effort is set up or organized)?

1	2	3	4	5	6	7
Our QWL effort is set up as specified by the QWL training.[a]			Our QWL effort is basically similar to the specified structure with only some changes.			The structure of our QWL effort differs significantly from the specified structure.

5. To what degree has your QWL effort been modified since it was started to better serve the needs of your group?

1	2	3	4	5	6	7
We have never tried to vary the way we run our QWL effort.			We are in the process of "trial and error" in an effort to adapt QWL to suit our needs.			After much experimentation or design effort, we have found a QWL structure that works well for us.

(continued on next page)

Exhibit 1. QWL Assessment, Cont'd.

6. To what extent do you direct your own QWL effort?

1	2	3	4	5	6	7
Our QWL effort is primarily directed by nonlocal groups.b			Our QWL effort is, for the most part, self-directed but we get some direction from nonlocal groups.			Our QWL effort no longer gets any direction from nonlocal groups; they just provide resources (such as training or funds) when needed.

7. To what extent do you define and implement your own QWL effort?

1	2	3	4	5	6	7
We look outside of our QWL effort to nonlocal groups to define and implement our QWL process for us.			We look for information and help from nonlocal groups, but make the decision on how to implement QWL ourselves.			Our QWL participants decide for themselves what QWL means and how to implement it.

8. How many employees participate in your QWL effort?

1	2	3	4	5	6	7
Only a few employees participate in our QWL effort.			Many employees participate in our QWL effort.			All employees participate in our QWL effort.

9. How many employees want to get involved in your QWL effort?

1	2	3	4	5	6	7
Very few employees want to be involved in QWL activities.			Many employees want to be involved in QWL activities.			All employees want to be involved in QWL activities.

10. What opportunities are available for involvement in your QWL effort?

1	2	3	4	5	6	7
There is little opportunity for QWL involvement beyond a small, select group of employees.			There is some opportunity; however, there is not enough QWL activity to include all volunteers.			Opportunity for involvement exists for everyone through their day-to-day activities.

(continued on next page)

Exhibit 1. QWL Assessment, Cont'd.

11. How is QWL involved in decision making?

1	2	3	4	5	6	7
Our QWL effort provides input to our management decisions, but final decisions are a management prerogative.		Limited decision-making power is given to our QWL effort. Managers decide which decisions can be made by QWL.				Decisions are made by the person or group closest to or most knowledgeable about the issue, whether management or nonmanagement.

12. How are decisions made when large-scale change is necessary (for example, reorganizations or the implementation of new technology to support business/human goals)?

1	2	3	4	5	6	7
Our management makes the decision and our QWL group is simply advised of it.		Our management recognizes the need for change and gets input from our QWL effort.				Change is planned and implemented jointly by employees, union, and management.

13. How is facilitation for your QWL effort provided? (If you do not have facilitation, please skip to question 14.)

1	2	3	4	5	6	7
Facilitators for our QWL effort are from nonlocal groups.			Facilitators for our QWL effort are select employees from within our QWL effort.			Each employee within our QWL effort has acquired facilitator skills and contributes to the facilitation of our QWL effort.

14. Who has ownership of your QWL effort?

1	2	3	4	5	6	7
Employees here do not feel much ownership. The QWL effort seems to belong to nonlocal groups or a few local individuals.			Many employees feel ownership of our QWL effort.			All employees here feel ownership of our QWL effort.

15. Who provides QWL training within your QWL effort?

1	2	3	4	5	6	7
QWL training is provided by nonlocal groups.			QWL training is provided by key local individuals (previously trained).			Our training is provided by any previously trained participant.

(continued on next page)

Exhibit 1. QWL Assessment, Cont'd.

16. Who received QWL training within your QWL effort?

1	2	3	4	5	6	7
Only key people (for example, facilitators or steering committee members) receive QWL training.			All active QWL participants receive QWL training.			All employees receive QWL training.

17. What does QWL training consist of within your QWL effort?

1	2	3	4	5	6	7
QWL training focuses on facilitator skills.			QWL training focuses on all skills needed for the QWL process, for example, problem solving and teamwork.			QWL training includes all business skills needed—organizational and financial management.

18. What type of relationship exists between your union and management representatives?

1	2	3	4	5	6	7
Our union-management relationship is basically adversarial.			Union and management work both collaboratively (on QWL issues) and adversarially (on grievances) as needed.			New collaborative relationships have been formally agreed to.

19. Within your QWL effort, what do your union and management representatives work on?

1	2	3	4	5	6	7
Union and management are trying to work together to build informal channels of communication, respect, and trust.			Union and management have built up enough communications, respect, and trust to work together to resolve issues of local concern.			Union and management work collaboratively to define employee and business goals, do strategic planning, and implement plans.

20. What kinds of issues does your QWL effort work on?

1	2	3	4	5	6	7
Our QWL issues are peripheral to the business and tend to focus on the environment.			There is a range of issues in our QWL effort beyond the environment. They encompass employee concerns, union planning and policy, business, and day-to-day work issues.			In our QWL effort, there is no distinction between "QWL issues" and other issues; any issue can be handled.

(continued on next page)

Exhibit 1. QWL Assessment, Cont'd.

21. What types of constraints limit the issues your QWL effort can work on?

1	2	3	4	5	6	7
Constraints on the types of issues our QWL effort deals with are imposed by the way our effort is set up; the fact we are new at this; the members of our QWL teams are from different workgroups and have little in common; many issues are off limits, and so on.			Issues we work on are no longer limited by our inexperience; our lack of commonality; or our local management. We are now constrained by company policy and our union contract.			Our contract and company policies are now built on a QWL foundation—all ideas are considered.

Note: This questionnaire was developed principally by Linda Streit and Rosemary O'Connor.

[a]This training specified that QWL will be structured in the following way: it will be a five- to nine-member team making up the local workforce committee (LWC). The LWC will consist of one steward, one first-line manager, and volunteers from the workgroup.

[b]By nonlocal groups we mean regional, state, or departmental steering committees or headquarters groups.

7

Designing and Positioning the Human Resource Function

So far this book has examined forces for organizational change, change agent roles, ways to implement incremental and frame-breaking change, and technological innovation and employee involvement as directions for change. The next three chapters consider several human resource interventions to enhance change. These include the design of the personnel department and its intended interface with the rest of the organization (Chapter Seven), human resource forecasting and planning (Chapter Eight), and program evaluation and survey feedback methods (Chapter Nine).

Human resource professionals should be aware of how the structure of their department influences the organization. This chapter describes planning the reorganization of a company's personnel department. The chapter demonstrates how the design of the personnel department reflects the philosophy of human resource management in the corporation—specifically, how much control line managers and line department staffs should have over the selection, development, and evaluation of their employees. As such, the chapter deals with the human resource professional's role in the evolution of the organization and the process of accomplishing change.

This chapter also shows the role of the middle manager in implementing needed changes directed by the leaders of the business. The examples of redesigning a human resource department and a training unit demonstrate how task forces can involve middle managers in making recommendations for restructuring. The examples show the advantages and disadvantages of such a participative approach to organizational design. The examples focus on an internal staff department that services other departments in the company, but the issues are similar to a line department responding to a new environment while servicing external customers.

Personnel Department Clients

Organizations form personnel departments for several reasons (Tsui and Milkovich, 1987). One perspective on this holds that personnel departments are formed in response to organizational growth or the need to perform activities that require expertise. Another reason is that personnel departments arise to help the organization respond to the external environment—to deal with legislation, regulation, unions, and other interest-group activities pertaining to labor relations, equal employment, health, security, and safety. A third perspective is that the personnel department serves a strategic function by ensuring that the firm's human resources "fit" its business requirements and help accomplish the organization's objectives.

These different functions are evident when one considers the multiple constituencies served by the personnel departments. The personnel department interacts with its constituencies for resource exchanges. Managers and employees depend on the personnel department for products such as training programs, employee handbooks, or benefit forms, and for services such as information, advice, applicant referrals, or career counseling. Operating line executives rely on the department for advice or information. The line executives also provide the personnel department with important resources such as financial and/or political support. Human resource executives at the corporate or business level set performance standards. They may also impose specific demands, such as requesting information or data from the operating personnel departments (Tsui and Milkovich, 1987, pp. 521–522).

Given these different constituency or client relationships, the structure of the personnel department (that is, degree of centralization) must be designed to serve these multiple, and possibly conflicting, interests.

Forces Demanding New Structure

The structure of an organization includes the number and types of positions, whom the people in the positions report to, the number of organizational levels, and the size of the workgroups. The number of levels in a hierarchy is dependent on the desired span of control (the number of people reporting to one individual) and the amount of responsibility given to an individual in terms of the importance of a project, the extent to which performance must be monitored, the structure of the tasks to be performed, and the resources under the individual's control. Higher-level jobs are generally less structured, have more reporting people, and entail control over more financial resources than lower-level jobs.

There are many alternatives for structuring an organizational unit. It could be structured around functions to be performed, with separate workgroups and departments for each major function. It could be structured geographically, so that all the functions needed to service a particular geographic region are combined in one department. It could be structured according to the client or market served—for instance, all the functions needed to service a particular type of customer or industry may be grouped together. Also, the structure could be a combination of the above, with units structured to serve specific functions reporting indirectly to headquarters specialists in those functions. The organization's structure may change over time as client needs change, as functions become more specialized, and/ or as the direction or focus of the organization changes. Also, the organization may change as new product lines are adopted, unfamiliar processes are implemented, and management styles change (for example, attempting to increase worker involvement through self-managing workteams).

The structure of the organization should match the needs of the company to carry out its mission. The organizational leaders determine the mission and design of the firm to fit their philosophy and style of management and their beliefs about how best to carry out the firm's mission. How well the organization functions is largely determined by its structure. Structure specifies formal lines of communications, patterns of interaction, sources of policy, and production processes.

Organizations that have cumbersome, bureaucratic structures with many levels of control find themselves unable to respond quickly enough to changing business conditions. Moreover, financial constraints have required organizations to reduce their size to save money. This necessitates developing new, effective working relationships with fewer resources and fewer rules and regulations.

A Personnel Department Reorganization

A newly appointed vice-president of personnel, who had mostly marketing and operations background, was charged with designing a single department to service two recently merged firms, which will be called Alpha and Beta. Economies of scale would be possible, saving people and dollars. But merging the two existing personnel departments would not be a simple task for several reasons. Surplus employees would have to find new jobs in the company or they would be laid off. Turf battles would ensue, with managers striving to keep their groups intact —or at the very least to keep them in existence.

Another complicating factor was that there were distinct differences in philosophies of providing personnel services to clients. Some managers, primarily from Beta Corporation, believed that the personnel department should be the conscience of the organization. It created rules to be followed in order to ensure equitable opportunities for all employees and to guarantee uniform treatment of people as they moved from department to department.

The opposite view was expressed by Alpha Corporation managers—there should be as few rules as possible. Every manager is a human resource manager, according to this view. The personnel department's role is not to monitor or to be a law enforcement agency, except for the few issues that are actually a matter of law (for example, equal employment opportunity). In most cases (for example, performance appraisal, compensation, tuition assistance, and career development), the personnel department's role is to develop general policies and guidelines. The personnel department adds value by facilitating program development in client departments and by encouraging client departments to share ideas. The personnel department should allow managers the freedom to act as much as possible. For instance, managers in each department are ultimately responsible for using the department's available compensation dollars as they see fit, deciding how many people should receive bonuses, how these bonuses are distributed, or whether bonuses are given at the end of the year or during the year to award accomplishments. Local managers are also responsible for who receives tuition to attend degree programs related to business needs. In addition, local managers are responsible for completing performance appraisals and giving feedback to subordinates on their performance. The personnel department can provide guidelines for accomplishing these goals, but it is not accountable for making them happen.

The vice-president began addressing these issues by calling a meeting of middle and top managers in the personnel departments that would merge. The meeting also included line department representatives who had personnel responsibilities in those departments. The three-day meeting uncovered the differences described above, especially identifying what personnel functions should be imposed with rigid rules and what functions the managers could exercise as they saw fit. There was also considerable discussion about what functions should be controlled by the personnel department and what functions should be handled by personnel staff within each line department. Generally, the participants felt that the functions that required uniformity and equity should be the personnel department's responsibilities.

Functions that did not require uniformity and equity and that had to be sensitive to clients' specific needs could best be handled by the departments themselves. Career development programs are examples of the latter; executive development and staffing policies and procedures are examples of the former. Some functions could be relegated to the personnel department because they could be done more cheaply by a central organization (an example is running a central employment office in each region of the country).

The meeting ended by identifying the functions that should be given special attention during the coming months because of the changes in the company. These functions included force management, job grading, compensation, and career development. Task forces were established to explore each area. Another task force was to interview the more than one hundred company officers in the organizations serviced by the personnel department to obtain a picture of client concerns. This would be input for designing the new personnel department structure.

Several weeks after the meeting, the vice-president investigated what sort of help was available to redesign the personnel organization. He found he could hire an outside consulting firm that specialized in organizational design. He could also draw on organizational development experts within his own department. He chose the latter. Moreover, he decided to form a task force of middle-level Alpha and Beta personnel department managers, supported by several internal organization development specialists. The purpose of the task force was to recommend the directions for the department merger and redesign. Twenty managers were appointed to the task force. They represented all parts of the department, which included about 1,600 people located in all regions of the country. The task force had one month to explore organizational alternatives and to make a recommendation. The task force was cochaired by a manager from Alpha and one from Beta.

The only requirement the vice-president imposed was that the new organizational design should meet five general criteria. It should be *flexible*—recognizing the need to be adaptive to meet future, as-yet-unpredictable changes in the business. It needed to be *cost effective*. It also needed to be *client focused*, meaning that the personnel policies and procedures should meet client needs in a timely way. The personnel department had to be *easy to do business with*, that is, it had to avoid being a barrier to client objectives. In addition, it had to do everything possible to *enhance client success*. This meant that the programs, such as personnel testing and selection, interdepartmental movement of people, and compensation guidelines had to help the client organization do the best job possible.

Thus, the personnel vice-president was establishing the general philosophy to guide the behavior of managers in the department. The organizational structure needed to reflect this philosophy. Involving mid-level managers in the design process helped these managers understand the objectives of the new department and begin thinking about what structure would make the philosophy workable. Of course, the personnel vice-president and directors under him were under no obligation to adopt the recommended design. They could take pieces of it, adopt it, or ignore it altogether.

The organizational design task force began with considerable input. Most of the personnel department directors, who may have felt bypassed by this process, wanted to address the task force to ensure that members were aware of the directors' viewpoints. The task force also examined previously done studies by outside consultants on how other companies organize their personnel departments and the number and types of personnel functions they had. The client perspective was available from the officer interviews previously commissioned by the vice-president. Moreover, task force representatives from Beta's personnel department had already experienced considerable downsizing. They had guided their client departments' force reduction efforts and they had also reduced their own force.

The task force began its work by listing personnel functions that were currently conducted. It examined how the departments were currently organized. The task force considered skill requirements, such as the need for personnel professionals and generalist managers in the department, and it considered the extent to which personnel functions needed to be handled centrally. It recognized that some clients and personnel department directors believed that personnel responsibilities should be decentralized as much as possible, with each department taking responsibility for its own personnel efforts. The task force considered informal relationships within the personnel department and between the department and its clients. These included procedures to identify candidates to fill job vacancies and ways to develop ideas for new career programs.

Overall, the task force considered ways to change the personnel department to reflect the changing needs of client departments. In addition, it recognized that clients differed in what they wanted and expected from the personnel department. Some client departments were ready to handle many of their own personnel functions. They had the staff and they had the need to develop unique programs. The marketing department was one example because they felt that they had specific needs—for example, sales compensation plans, criteria for identifying high-potential marketing managers, and career paths within marketing. Other client departments felt that all personnel functions should be handled by the personnel department.

Recognizing the different client needs, conflicting forces within the personnel department, and the likelihood of further change, the task force designed an evolutionary model that allowed the organization's structure to adapt to the changing business and that recognized the trend toward decentralization. Single, corporate-wide personnel programs would give way to client-specific programs or general programs tailored to meet client needs.

The presentation to the vice-president and his staff began with the vision for the three to five years ahead. The presentation then showed where the task force members thought the department would be one to three years ahead, and then where it should be in nine to twelve months. The specifics of the models in terms of boxes in an organization chart were less important than the general direction for change the task force wanted to convey. The presentation emphasized that this direction could not be achieved overnight.

The ideal image for the future was termed the "long-term

decentralized model." It included a lean, centralized personnel department and small personnel units in each line department. An important element of this visionary model was the *client manager role*. Client managers would coordinate the personnel functions necessary to help accomplish major tasks, such as designing organizational structure, downsizing its force, or establishing career paths and associated selection and development standards. Such projects required multiple personnel functions. Rather than expect a client to call on multiple personnel specialists (not all of whom would necessarily understand the client's objectives), the client manager would coordinate these specialists, bringing them in as needed and ensuring that they help the process rather than impose barriers.

In a sense, every personnel manager was a client manager helping clients with personnel needs. In these terms, the client manager concept was a role, not a position. However, the task force felt that temporary client managers could be appointed to assist a client full-time with a specific activity. These would be headquarters personnel jobs because the major projects were usually carried out by client department's personnel headquarters staff. However, the personnel directors in the regions were also viewed as client managers. The regional personnel directors were responsible for delivering personnel services to the regional line vice-presidents. As such, the regional personnel directors and their staffs carried out the personnel programs developed at headquarters, and they designed unique services to meet local client needs (for example, special career development programs). The regional directors were also client managers in that they were facilitators, coordinators, negotiators, and a source of one-stop shopping for personnel services in the regions.

The long-term model specified functions to be handled by the headquarters personnel staff. This staff would be as small as possible. In addition, there would be a new group reporting to the personnel vice-president. This was termed "executive support and analysis." The group would be responsible for working with client organizations on their human resource plans. It would also conduct evaluations of personnel programs, such as new experimental compensation plans and ongoing QWL efforts.

The group would be responsible for the annual employee attitude survey—essentially a barometer of how well the clients were doing in maintaining employee morale and commitment. The new unit would also keep tabs on professional developments in human resource management, government laws and regulations pertaining to personnel, and what other corporations were doing in the personnel arena. The unit would include a staff of internal organization development experts to help clients on management effectiveness issues, such as the need for improving team cohesiveness. In addition, the unit would do routine work such as the personnel department budget and expense tracking and force analysis.

The hallmarks of this long-term organizational design were that it would allow the personnel department to be client focused, easy to do business with, and quick to respond to client needs. As needed, temporary groups would be formed to service a client, perhaps bringing in employees from the client organization to do the work. However, there were several drawbacks to this long-term approach. These included the potential duplication of staff in each line department and the difficulty of mandating uniformity when it was required.

The midway approach, which the task force felt could be achieved within three years, was termed a "team-matrix model." The term team-matrix meant that department managers would have to work closely together as required by projects even though they would report to separate groups within the department. This model was similar to the long-term view except that it had more people in the personnel department and fewer personnel people in the line departments. The personnel department staff was split into several groups, including a delivery operation, a policy and development group, and a group of client managers and their staffs. Whereas the long-term view had all the personnel functions under a single director, this midway view had several directors for various functions. Line departments would depend more on this personnel department than they would in the future when they did more of their own personnel work. This personnel department would have to take care to avoid dictating efforts and establishing rigid structure.

The model that the task force felt could be achieved most quickly was termed the "merged-downsized model." This had a similar structure to the one that currently existed in the two personnel departments being merged. There were several personnel directors at headquarters as well as in the field, all delivering services. The merged-downsized model assumed that the personnel department would do the bulk of the personnel work and that the line departments would not have their own personnel staffs unless they wanted them. Basically, the major goal of this model was to reduce the duplication of functions that would exist within the personnel department because of the merger. Client managers might be appointed. The task force recognized that when the company downsized the department, it would also have to bring in people from other departments on rotational assignments. These people would provide a valuable client perspective to personnel jobs that were basically managerial in nature and did not require in-depth training as a personnel specialist. Approximately 50 percent of the people in the new department would be a core of personnel professionals. The others would be on rotational assignments. Achieving this mix would require laying off people, since many of the current people in the department were seasoned personnel professionals who would not be marketable to line departments.

This more immediate recommended model would provide continuous service to clients while allowing them to decide how much they wanted to do for themselves. It offered a chance to experiment with a client manager role at the risk of adding another layer of management between the client and personnel functions.

Evaluation Criteria

The task force established a set of outputs which, if accomplished, would indicate that the personnel department was successful. The merged department would be successful if it was actively involved in the business planning process of the corporation. That is, human resource planning would be an integral part of each line department's business plan, recognizing that the quality and morale of the employees would be the key to the company's competitive advantage. Employee attitude surveys would be one indication of success in this area.

Success would also be evident from the use of the department's services or whether clients hired outside personnel consultants because the department was not sensitive to client needs. Wherever possible the department would charge back its services to client departments—for example, charging them for the cost of training programs and organization development consulting they utilized. The department would ensure that personnel services were competitive with the outside market and in fact were better because of a unique corporate perspective and understanding. The department would conduct ongoing reviews of personnel services to refine its products and services and ensure client responsiveness.

In addition, the personnel department would be successful when it was viewed by others in the company as a vital, important, and desirable department to work in. However, the personnel department was not solely accountable for human resource management. This was every manager's responsibility. As such, the department would be successful when its client departments were successful in effectively using their human resources, engendering high morale and organizational commitment. The department would be successful the more the leaders of the business adopted human resource management as integral to their other activities. To encourage this, part of compensation for top managers in the company would have to be tied directly to their success in developing and managing their people.

Socializing the Design

As the task force developed its recommendations, the members explained their ideas to their colleagues and to clients. This provided useful input for revising the models. The task force also had to deal with conflicts between top management over who should be responsible for what, how quickly things should change, and which managers should be responsible for what sorts of activities. For instance, one debate raged over whether each regional personnel delivery organization should be headed by a fifth-level manager (termed director) or a fourth-level manager. Alpha Corporation had fourth-level managers heading the field personnel organizations, and Beta had fifth-level managers in comparable positions. In an effort to hold down the number of higher-level managers, the Alpha people felt that fourth-level managers worked well in these positions and there was no reason to change, even though they would be responsible for more clients when the personnel departments merged. The Beta side felt that directors were necessary because of their interface with regional vice-presidents (sixth-level managers).

There were other level discrepancies between the two merged organizations. One side seemed to have third-level managers doing the work done by second-level managers on the other side. How much of this was actual level inflation and how much was perception was unclear.

Task Force Culmination

The personnel vice-president and his top management staff began implementing the new organization in the two months after the task force recommendations were presented. The design they adopted was similar to the merged-downsized model with some variations in the grouping of functions. The client manager role was established as a headquarters position, and four client managers were appointed. The executive analysis and support function was formed, as envisioned in the long-term model. Employees were moved from other parts of the department to staff this new group. Regional personnel directors were appointed instead of fourth-level managers. (The vice-president took some unexpected heat from some clients who were used to dealing with the fourth-level managers, and the vice-president attributed these complaints to inadequate communication to client groups about why this decision was made.)

Just as the reorganization was under way, it was halted. A corporate-wide effort was begun to reduce all overhead expenses, which included the public relations, legal, and personnel departments. In order to save salary dollars and other expenses, further extensive consolidation would be required. Each line department would have its own personnel people doing work specific to their own departments. Those functions that required uniformity would be centralized. Essentially, this seemed to mean that the firm would quickly evolve to a model very similar to the long-term decentralized view. It would maintain regional delivery units to provide common personnel services to the departments in the field. Other companies provided these services through a line department in a region, but the size and diversity of departments within each geographical area of the merged Alpha and Beta companies required regional personnel offices. Other changes entailed abandoning the client manager function after only about six months of operation. The position was unnecessary because each line organization would have its own personnel people to interpret and implement personnel department policy.

The appointments at top management in the new consolidated personnel department included directors from the Alpha and Beta personnel departments and some new people transferred into personnel from line departments. This diversity in the top management team helped ensure a fair process as people were chosen for the new organization and the force downsizing plan was implemented to identify people who were needed and those who were not needed in the new organization.

Implications for Change Management

The organizational design task force involved many managers throughout the department. Ideas were discussed openly and communicated to others. Though the final decisions were made by the top managers, having the task force probably led to a higher degree of understanding of what was happening and more debate over philosophy and mission than would have happened otherwise. Clients were involved in the process as well, although less than was desirable. The department experimented with ways to serve clients—for example, with the client manager function. It also explored criteria needed to evaluate success, and ways to measure those criteria.

The actual reorganization that followed the task force's recommendations was implemented separately in each director group in the department. The way one particular director handled the process is an example of a leader educating the management team by modeling consensus decision making.

Recall that the task force had been convened to design a merged personnel department. The task force envisioned that delivering personnel services would become more decentralized over time as the line departments were able to do more of their own human resources work. This would reduce the number of personnel people needed to be dedicated solely to personnel work. It also would give line departments more freedom to act by allowing them to develop programs that fit their unique needs. A reduced corporate personnel staff would develop generic programs when needed and monitor functions, such as equal employment opportunity, that compelled active and equitable treatment across departments.

Before the new design could be implemented, staff reductions were required. A personnel director, who had recently been transferred to the job from a marketing position, had definite ideas about how to conduct the downsizing and operate the personnel unit under his supervision.

The director had several major objectives. Human resource functions needed to contribute to the firm's competitive advantage in the marketplace. This meant, for example, that employee development programs needed to focus on skills required by the line departments to accomplish their business objectives. Rather than design human resource programs in the abstract (that is, focusing solely on what management theorists and organizational psychologists say is important), program development needed to start with line manager's business plans (that is, analyses of the type of people the line department wanted to attract, retain, and motivate). Therefore, making human resources a competitive advantage required being client responsive. It is also required educating clients on the value of people in accomplishing business strategies.

Another of the director's objectives was to manage the personnel unit by consensus. All managers in the group would need to agree on major decisions before actions were taken.

This meant frequent meetings so that everyone understood and agreed on the group's mission and its actions. The opinions of higher-level managers in the department would carry the same weight as those of lower-level managers.

The director avoided creating a typical hierarchical organizational structure with specific job assignments. He began by selecting the people he wanted for the team, based on his knowledge of their abilities and insights into business needs. He then held several meetings of the new team to discuss their business values, establish principles for how the group members would work together, and consider how the unit would contribute to the corporation's business goals. Relevant values identified by the group included integrity, courage, and respect. Operating principles included sharing responsibility, encouraging individual growth and development, communicating clearly, pooling diverse talent, and practicing what one preached. The discussion of the unit's functions considered what projects should be continued because of their contribution to the company's business strategies. Several major new efforts were identified, including a comprehensive examination of staffing processes, career planning and development programs, and the development of human resource strategy to guide line departments in establishing their human resource objectives.

The director wanted the members of his team to choose assignments that matched their career goals and interests. As discussion of the group's mission and projects unfolded, people committed themselves to particular projects. Each person eventually had a major project and several other minor projects. The project leaders were generally higher-level managers who reported to the director. This self-selection, matrix arrangement meant that most team members had several bosses. The director would ultimately be responsible for appraising each team member (among fifty management employees), with input from others who had worked with the individual. The arrangement allowed flexibility in organization design to match departmental needs. Projects changed over time and the resources required for a project changed, too.

An advantage of the matrix structure at the inception of

the organization was that managers were not split into groups that separated activities. Rather, there was the need for integration of functions, including high-potential manager development programs, career planning programs, appraisal plans, human resource forecasting and planning, and so on. A broad project might incorporate elements of all these functions. For instance, one client-related project team worked with the client department's personnel staff to develop a long-term view of the department's human resource needs and the implications of this view for succession planning, selection, training, performance standards, appraisals, rotational assignments, promotional opportunities, and retirements. The project helped the client department realize the strategic value of human resources for accomplishing its business objectives. It helped to identify what good human resource management meant and the steps needed to accomplish the human resource objectives.

Admittedly, the director's team was impatient and frustrated by the uncertainty of the start-up process. Other parts of the personnel department were angry over what they perceived as inaction and lack of direction. It took time for the team to grasp the meaning of a matrix design, the process of creating one's own job by committing oneself to assignments, the art of consensus management, and the scrutiny of projects to see that they enhanced competitive advantage. Although the process was difficult, most if not all team members agreed that the outcome was worth striving for. Hopefully, it would mean that the various departments were working on the right things for the corporation and were creating the feeling that everyone was contributing to his or her personal growth as well as to the bottom line of the company.

Similar to the corporate leaders discussed in Chapter Three, the director had a vision for the optimal process and outcome of his group. Gaining the cooperation of the team required teaching the process by example and involving as many team members as possible in the start-up phase. Numerous team meetings and conference calls were held to discuss objectives. Team members often shared with each other how they felt. Breakthroughs—important insights that seem to move the group

forward—were reinforced with agreement and sometimes ap-
plause. The director occasionally asked team members to lead
parts of team meetings, giving others an opportunity to model
leadership behavior in a participative environment and giving
everyone a chance to observe the learning in progress. Using action learning, referred to in Chapter Four, the team worked on
major, complex business issues.

Overall, there was considerable uncertainty and anxiety
as the reorganization unfolded. The reorganization task force
was convened in the beginning of June, and the final reorganization was not complete until the following March. In the process, the personnel department managers became more aware of
client needs and of the relationship between the structure and
function of the personnel department and the size, structure,
and goals of client departments. Moreover, future changes
would probably be needed as the company changed—for example, by moving into new ventures. This could entail further
reorganization and downsizing of the personnel department
to provide the needed client services. The message for those
who would stay with the company was that the future would
be challenging, but also uncertain and a struggle as the company continued to define, refine, and implement its business
strategies.

Providing Training Services: Another Example of Organization Redesign

As the personnel department reorganization evolved, another related reorganization was in the works at Alpha/Beta.
This entailed the consolidation of two units, each providing
similar management training (courses in leadership, decision
making, and group dynamics). The reorganization also entailed
merging training support groups, such as groups responsible for
preparing people to deliver technical training courses. One training organization was the centralized support group providing
services to most of the combined corporation. The other training organization provided services only to Alpha. When Alpha
was about to merge with Beta, the leadership of the two training organizations felt that consolidation would make sense.

This merger had been considered earlier but had been stopped because Alpha executives felt that the company needed its own training organization to deliver management training in line with its philosophy of management—a philosophy supported by a model that specified desirable management outputs, competencies, and training courses to help people develop these competencies. This model had been communicated to all managers as Alpha's human resource policy, and as such, the model generated employee identification with the company.

The training consolidation at the time of the Alpha/Beta merger made sense because essentially a new company was forming. Emphasis was being placed on a single corporate business direction, and one training organization was in line with that emerging corporate philosophy. Moreover, there was no sense in having two training organizations with slightly different curricula servicing different departments or different parts of the same department. Money could be saved by avoiding duplicate course development and administration.

A training consolidation task force was formed, and the personnel vice-president and training organization vice-president agreed on criteria to be met in implementing the change. They felt that the consolidated organization needed to demonstrate its responsiveness to client needs. Courses would have to be tailored to meet specific client objectives; they could not offer a single curriculum for all managers regardless of department. In addition, the training organization had to provide usage-sensitive pricing—meaning that the clients would pay based on use as opposed to paying a fixed share of the training expense regardless of participation by people in the department.

All this seemed logical and straightforward. However, politics and emotions made the consolidation planning a long, drawn-out process. There was a concern that though the current training units would remain where they were geographically, the training resources would no longer be at the disposal of the client departments. Put another way, some people in the personnel department did not trust the central training organization to be responsive to client needs. In addition, there were personality clashes between some managers in the two organizations. These managers had worked together previously and knew they would have trouble getting along. In addition, one personnel department executive (the director referred to earlier in this chapter) wanted to delay the consolidation until he was satisfied that there was not a better way to provide training. For example, the personnel department could take over development and delivery of all management training courses rather than merge them into a separate training unit. The director also wanted to be sure that there was consensus among all parties that consolidation was the right thing to do.

The issues were debated for three-and-a-half months until the events were such that the personnel vice-president essentially ordered the task force to implement the planned consolidation. There was no way to demonstrate the client responsiveness of the consolidated training organization before the consolidation took place and the new organization was operational. Also, there was no way to develop a totally usage-sensitive billing system that could be implemented at the point of consolidation. Managers joked about an organization announcement that would have merely two words, "Trust us!"

Here again was a demonstration of resistance to change. Everyone involved had a rationalization for their point of view. Conflicting values and differing personal preferences intertwined with a need to do what was right for the business. In the end, consensus seemed impossible, and the decision to go ahead with the consolidation was imposed. This did not eliminate the grumbling, but at least everyone knew where they stood after months of uncertainty.

Change Agent Roles in Organization Design

Mid-level managers may act as change agents with top-level support to involve departmental representatives in organizational redesign. The change agent's role is facilitating collaboration and analysis of alternative structures. Different group members are likely to champion a particular idea because it supports their vested interest. In this sense, each group member is a change agent defending a point of view. The group coordinator must deal with conflict by prompting communication and negotiation. This is a tough role, especially when group members view themselves as experts in organizational process, as was the case in the examples cited.

Recommended Actions

Change agents attempting to involve employees in organization design need a keen understanding of the different constituency viewpoints. Everyone is concerned about how the change will affect "me." The change agent may generate a more objective view by focusing the group on the implications of alternative designs, encouraging participants to express a vision of what things may be like under different scenarios. Also, helping the group members to take an evolutionary view may diffuse immediate personal interests and focus attention on long-term implications for the organization. Moreover, attention should be focused on interfaces with other departments and how these departments view the unit being redesigned. This should emphasize the common interests of group members to work together to enhance their reputation and contribute to their long-term success.

Summary

The cases in this chapter demonstrate how the design of a personnel department can influence how human resources are managed in the organization. In the case of the personnel department reorganization, the goal of the task force was to find a way to encourage line managers to be aware of employees' contribution to the firm's success. This would be accomplished by increasing line managers' responsibility for human resource management as much as possible. Moving toward a decentralized personnel department was felt by the task force to be a way to enhance line departments' freedom to act in the hiring, training, career pathing, and evaluation of its employees. Central control and monitoring would be exercised by the personnel department to comply with legal requirements. Also, the personnel department would develop generic programs that could be shared by line departments, often adapting the programs to a department's specifications. The central personnel department would be an internal consultant providing professional expertise to line departments in their efforts to initiate their own human resource activities. The central personnel department would also promote corporate-wide interest across line departments—for example, in running leadership development and executive succession programs for high-potential managers viewed as corporate resources.

The chapter also showed how the leader's style of management can influence employees' acceptance of new organizational design. In the case described, the department director encouraged each manager in the department to investigate and select his or her own new position.

In general, task forces engender debate and provide opportunity for conflict. The personnel department reorganization task force knew that its vision for the department probably would not materialize as planned. New players would enter the field at top management and other company changes would occur. Nevertheless, the task force hotly debated issues and tried to produce a meaningful and realistic organizational design. Certainly, the task force was a way for everyone to understand the issues. As the personnel department reorganized and the training consolidation unfolded, an awareness of the needs of the business became clearer and everyone had a better understanding of each other. Essentially, time and energy were invested in jointly studying the problem, exploring alternatives, and analyzing needs. The process was frustrating and laborious but also a learning experience.

I am not arguing here that task forces are the best way to design and implement changes in organizational structure. Rather, my goal was to highlight what can be learned from observing major organizational change processes. The cases show that change is as much emotional as intellectual. They also show that trying to achieve consensus is a difficult process, but one that may be worthwhile because it generates mutual understanding about changes with which everyone will have to live.

8

Human Resource Forecasting and Planning

 An important role for the change agent is to be demonstrator and defender of a change effort. Of course, the change agent wants the change to be successful, and may need encouragement from consultants to evaluate a program's success objectively. Also, the change agent may need facts to direct and modify the change effort.

Business objectives are accomplished through people. People establish directions for organizational change, and they implement the change. They can be change facilitators or change barriers. Business strategies are carried out in large part through human resource policies and programs for attracting, developing, motivating, and retaining the employees needed by the organization and by redeploying or dismissing the employees who are not needed. The leader of an organization establishes the extent of support for employee motivation and development. The leader creates the vision, communicates it to employees, and enlists their support. Lower-level managers establish mechanisms for implementing the vision.

Setting a direction for an organization requires knowledge about available resources and how the resources can be applied to corporate goals. This chapter focuses on human resource forecasting and planning as a change intervention. Effective planning requires analyzing alternative futures, some of which are desired and others of which are not. This involves considering future events that are likely to affect the organization, judging the probability that these events will occur, and estimating the degree to which they can be controlled. Critical issues are high-impact, high-probability events that are difficult to control. Corporations also have to be concerned with high-impact/low-probability events that are difficult to control. Even though such events may not be likely to occur, their impact should still be considered. Anticipating critical events can help the organization take advantage of positive outcomes and avoid negative outcomes.

The accuracy with which events are forecast is actually less important than whether the organization's leaders consider the multiple possibilities that are associated with accomplishing their business objectives. The intention of planning is not to set a rigid course for the future but to be flexible in response to environmental trends and to control events and take actions to create the future. Plans must move the organization toward business goals and ensure that the organization is in a position to grow and develop beyond a specific future date. This is a requirement for successful corporate evolution as defined in Chapter Two. This is also the source of an organization's competitive advantage.

Human Resource Forecasting and Planning

The goal of human resource forecasting and planning is to understand relationships among societal trends (sociopolitical, economic, demographic, and individual needs and values), technological developments, and business strategies. The outcomes are the actions the organization must take to attract, develop, and retain the talent needed to achieve business goals. There must be a focus on what the organization needs and on what individuals need and how these two sets of needs can be accomplished jointly. The organization must determine what knowledge, skills, and abilities will be required as new functions emerge, other functions continue, and still others decline or disappear.

Human resource forecasting and planning tries to answer the following questions: How will technological, social, economic, demographic, and political developments affect business directions, products, and global partnerships? How will these processes drive the human resource function? How will human resources contribute to accomplishing organizational goals and environmental events? What do people want from work and the company? How can individual career goals and organizational goals for growth and renewal be accomplished simultaneously?

Here are some additional strategic questions that address the numbers and types of people who will be available to work for the organization in the future.

• What major demographic changes (specifically, workforce changes) will take place in five to ten years—locally, regionally, nationally, and internationally?

• What are the characteristics of the company's current workforce (for example, numbers, age, gender, race, education, marital status, children, life goals, life-styles)? How will these characteristics change over time (due both to changes in current employees as they learn, have new experiences, and develop new needs, and to turnover in the organization)?

• What is happening in the sociopolitical environment (pending government legislation, judicial rulings, interest groups, lobbies, and labor movement trends) that affects the company's resource objectives?

• What does the company do now and in the future to ensure its human resource needs will be met?

Human resource forecasting and planning must be integrated into overall business planning in order to make optimal use of new intelligence concerning the marketplace and technology. A meaningful business strategy can be developed by taking into account demographic, global, labor, legal, and regulatory trends. Strategies for attracting, retaining, and developing people can be tied closely to the business plans. The idea is to make employees a force that contributes to the company's competitive advantage. The success of human resource forecasting and planning can be enhanced by tying human resource issues into the business planning process—that is, developing clear human resource strategies to support the overall business strategy. The organization needs to understand the current workforce (its skill and demographic profile) and the external environment today and in the future. The organization should anticipate force shortages and surpluses and implement appropriate human resource systems. Shortages suggest the need for recruitment, selection, and training systems. Surpluses suggest the need for redeployment and retraining as well as layoff strategies. The outcome is that the organization has the best people to develop and market products and services ahead of its competition.

There are at least three elements to human resource forecasting and planning: external analysis of current and anticipated events (environmental scanning), internal analysis of force needs, and linking this information to business plans. Each of these is described in more depth below.

Environmental Scanning

Environmental scanning is tracking a variety of trends, considering their implications for the company, asking questions about these trends, and suggesting needed actions. The trend information may be obtained from a variety of sources, such as the U.S. Bureau of the Census and the Department of Labor. Newspapers and other news services are additional sources (for example, the Bureau of National Affairs' *Daily Labor Report*). Some organizations join consortiums to conduct environmental scans and share the information.

For example, one recent environmental scan covered facts about the aging workforce (for example, in 1985, 37 percent of the current workforce was between thirty-four and fifty-four years of age; 51 percent of the workforce will be in this age group by the year 2000); the "baby bust" generation (for example, the labor force will grow slowly—1.47 percent growth in the 1980s and 1.3 percent growth in the 1990s with a scarcity of entry-level workers); and increased diversity in the workforce (for example, the growth in the workforce will be primarily due to women, minorities, and immigrants, with these groups composing 85 percent of new labor force entrants by the year 2000) [U.S. Bureau of Labor Statistics, 1985]. Implications include the need to review the adequacy of retirement programs, the need to review skills of people who may retire, the need for phased retirement programs to retain skills of older workers (for example, pension bonuses for working longer or part-time schedules for older workers), the need for imaginative recruiting strategies, and the need to ensure the advancement of women and minorities through innovative succession programs.

Such information and implications can be used to build scenarios for the future—that is, examples that place the organization in different environmental situations and suggest possible actions and their effects. Information about the environment should also be communicated to employees to help them plan their futures in terms of available training, new career opportunities, advancement possibilities, retirement (especially early retirement), and understanding what they can do to enhance their contribution to corporate goals.

Internal Analysis

This sort of analysis entails asking strategic questions about the organization's current workforce and obtaining the data to answer these questions. For instance, consider the following questions and the data that might be collected to answer them.

1. Are we attracting the employees we need?
Evidence to consider:
*   Number of hires
*   Selection ratios (hires/applicants)
*   Education levels
*   Minorities, immigrants, and women hired

2.   Who is leaving?
Evidence to consider:
- Rate of turnover
- Reasons why people are leaving
- The performance rank of people who are leaving
- Age, race, and sex of people who are leaving

3.   Are employees motivated? Are they fully utilized?
Evidence to consider:
- The relationship between performance and compensation
- Training days per employee
- Number of employees retrained and redeployed relative to the number of surplus employees
- Wages and salaries
- Benefits (Are they responsive to employees' needs?)
- Health care
- High-potential employee development
- Level of employee morale
- Promotions (and other job moves)
- How the company compares to competitors on the above indexes

4.   Do we know current and future skill needs?
Evidence to consider:
- Employees by function, level, age, sex, race, and location
- Analyses of current and future skill levels
- Analyses of expected skill shortages and surpluses

These variables are not always easy to obtain. Personnel data bases are expensive to initiate and maintain because they require continuous updating of complex information. Also, departments that operate independently may not see the need to collect the same information about employees. A company may not know why people are leaving because there is no systematic means of conducting exit interviews. Payroll data may supply information about wage increases as an indicator of efforts to motivate employees, but there may be no systematic recording of performance information to analyze whether top performers received higher bonuses than lower performers.

Some data are readily accessible, however. For instance, employee age will probably be on the payroll data base. Age and length of service can be used to determine retirement eligibility in the future and the probability of different numbers of people retiring during the next five or more years. One such departmental analysis revealed that during the next ten years as many as 70 percent of the current employees would reach the age when they would be eligible for retirement, whereas in another department only 30 percent of current employees would be eligible for retirement.

Data on employees' race and sex are usually recorded on personnel data bases because of equal opportunity requirements the corporation must meet. Other related data might be collected, such as the number of single women with children or the number of dual-career couples. Such information would suggest the importance of child-care support. It would also suggest the type of relocation plan the organization should have when it wants to transfer an employee (for example, offering to find a job for the working spouse, or not penalizing employees for turning down a transfer).

Line managers should be encouraged to think about current and emerging critical jobs and skills. A system to regularly collect such information as part of the business planning process will help managers think about the implications of their capital investment and organization change decisions for ensuring that human resources are available when they are needed. Most managers would not consider making an investment decision without examining needed resources, and these should include human resources. The following are six elements of a systematic jobs-and-skills analysis.

1. Identify and define the critical job functions in the organization or unit. "Critical" means major classifications of highly populated jobs or key decision-making or expert positions.

2. Specify the current number of employees by hierarchical level and function.

3. List major skill requirements by level and function.

4. Project the numbers of people required five years from now by level and function. (The time horizon will depend

on the rapidity of change and the uncertainty of the future. If major organizational changes are anticipated within a certain time frame, then that should be the focal point of the forecast. The more ambiguous the future is, the more difficulty managers will have making these estimates and the more they will resist the process.) Include estimates of turnover and retirement in the analysis.

5. Provide a rationale for major increases or decreases in people due to anticipated organizational or skill changes (for example, new operations, plant closings, new technology). Where more people will be needed, indicate possible sources ("feeder pools"). Where different skills will be needed, indicate how these may be acquired (retraining, hiring).

6. List major skill requirements by level and function as anticipated for five years from now. Indicate skills needed today that will not be required in five years and skills needed five years from now that are not needed today.

Linking Human Resource Plans to Business Plans

Business plans and human resource plans generally have the same components. There is an analysis of internal resources relative to corporate directions (for example, resources for desired capital expenditures, research and development, and the like). There is also an analysis of environmental trends, usually focusing on markets, suppliers, competitors, and government regulations. Human resource actions may be integrated into business plans by describing how human resource programs need to be adjusted to accomplish the overall business objectives by taking into account employee needs.

Too often, human resource policies and programs are developed in a vacuum apart from the needs of the corporation. A career planning workshop may be developed because career planning is in vogue. The program encourages employees to analyze their strengths, weaknesses, and career interests, but there might be no information about current and anticipated career opportunities in the organization.

Human resource plans should be an extension of the organization's business plans. The human resource component of the business plan should be developed by people who understand both the needs of the business and human resource dynamics in the organization. Human resource specialists need to be educated in the nature of the business, and line managers and business group planners need to understand the role of management in developing people. This may be accomplished through job rotations between departments, conferences to share information about current departmental activities, and meetings to create dialogues within the organization about human resource issues.

One way to highlight the tie between business objectives and human resource strategy is to generate scenarios of possible future events. A scenario is "a documented narrative of anticipated conditions that the organization expects to deal with at some time in the future" (Manzini and Gridley, 1986, p. 94). Scenarios encourage the organization to generate strategies to deal with these contingencies. A scenario combines analysis of environmental trends, organizational objectives, and human resource demand and availability. Scenarios are valuable for long-range thinking about possible discontinuities or innovations that cannot be predicted. They are not just variations around a midpoint or "most likely" case, but are structurally different views of the future (Mandel, 1982). Scenarios describe aspects of the environment that help in making meaningful choices. Also, they should be comprehensive—for example, they should cover demographic patterns, social and life-style factors, economic conditions, political and regulatory forces, technological forces, and international conditions.

The following are a few points that might be included in a positive scenario:

- A relatively stable and benign international environment
- Strong economic growth
- Continued growth of a global marketplace (10 percent average annual increase in world trade, declining tariff barriers, exchange rate stability)
- The baby bust has resulted in a declining domestic labor market
- Highly skilled and educated people in high demand

Here are some points that might be included in a negative scenario.

- Foreign competition increases dramatically
- Tariff barriers continue to undermine U.S. trade growth
- Foreign companies in U.S. employ low-skill or unskilled workers, keeping high-skill work abroad
- Standard of living declines in the United States
- Race and sex discrimination persist in U.S. organizations despite the fact that 80 percent of available new entrants to the workforce are women and minorities
- The trend toward deregulation in the early to mid 1980s is reversed, with increased government constraints over business and employment

Each one of these points would be fleshed out in a full scenario. In addition, numerous other points could be added to cover the areas of politics, technology, competitors, supply of goods, employee attitudes, the cost of benefit programs, demands for alternate work schedules, and so on.

From the standpoint of human resources, scenarios suggest the need for corporate policy changes (for example, regarding hiring, promotion, compensation, retirement, and layoffs); mandated government requirements (for example, in the equal employment and health and safety areas); union relationships; new employee relations issues; changing employee values; and labor force indicators (age, sex, education mix).

The test of good scenarios is whether they influence intelligent action. They should frame the issues and develop the capability to respond intellectually. This is most likely when the scenarios are worded in language leaders and managers can understand—for example, "Your job depends on it" (Peter Schwartz, personal communication, July 1987).

The Roles of an Organization's Corporate Headquarters and Business Units in Human Resource Planning

Companies vary in their degree of centralization. In some cases, corporate headquarters is essentially a holding company for unrelated businesses. In other cases, corporate headquarters provides centralized services merely to take advantage of economies of scale. And in still other examples, corporate headquarters presides over directing a set of functional departments that are highly integrated and need to work together smoothly to meet customer needs.

Managers may debate the importance of central control versus allowing units as much freedom to act as possible (see Chapter 7). The extent to which a corporate headquarters is responsible for human resource planning (as opposed to each business unit being responsible for its own human resource planning) will depend both on the philosophy of top management and the needs of the organization. In general, both business unit managers and corporate headquarters human resource specialists should have input to the human resource planning process. The corporate headquarters human resource staff should be responsible for generic policies and procedures. They produce an environmental scan and interpret the scan in relation to corporate strategies and issues. The business units should use this information as the units' activities and results are reviewed. Also, the business units should be responsible for a specific human resource plan and for understanding alternative courses of action that may be necessary if the situation changes.

Each business unit should be able to answer the following questions.

- What human resource plans are now in place?
- What business developments are anticipated?
- How might they influence human resource needs?
- What support is needed from corporate headquarters personnel department for personnel selection, executive succession, development, and the like?
- How does the business plan translate into employee roles and behaviors?
- What kinds of people are needed to achieve the business strategies? (education, management style, competency, values)?
- What needs to be done to identify these people?
- What types of people are available in the workforce?
- How should these people be recruited?

- What companies are trying to recruit the same people we are?
- How do we develop our employees once they are hired?
- How do we motivate employees?

Corporate headquarters should provide the support for answering these questions. The corporate headquarters staff should suggest likely events and raise the possibility of "wild cards"—unpredictable yet imaginable hypothetical events.

Toward an "Ideal" Human Resource Planning System

Manzini and Gridley (1986) outlined the following specifications to make human resource planning effective.

1. Integrate human resource planning with corporate or business planning, avoiding any semblance of a "stand-alone" personnel system with goals or criteria irrelevant to organizational needs.

2. Integrate human resource programs and policies with one another—to "get our act together" in the human resource department so that all activities operate synergistically in pursuit of organizational goals.

3. Provide a "what-if" planning capacity, and retain the flexibility needed to accommodate changing priorities, new environmental conditions, the impacts of technology, and other inevitable changes affecting the organization and its human resources.

4. Provide planning data not only for human resource programs but for the business as a whole, enabling comprehensive data collection and analyses relating human resource data to organizational objectives—whatever they may be.

5. Include qualitative factors as well as numbers and bottom-line results, such as the organization's core mission and the appraisal system's ability to identify and shape the leaders of tomorrow.

6. Consider the goals and aspirations of employees—particularly in career planning—as well as organizational objectives for pragmatic reasons that recognize the vital importance of merging individual commitment with corporate goals.

Establishing Human Resource Forecasting and Planning as a Vehicle for Change

So far, this chapter has addressed the importance of human resource forecasting and planning to identify appropriate human resource strategies in support of business objectives. The leader or manager who is trying to implement change must formulate and carry out plans to take into account employee needs as well as their contribution to the organization. The rest of this chapter describes a corporate effort to initiate a human resource forecasting and planning function. The example suggests ideas for human resource professionals to develop or expand human resource forecasting and planning in their organizations. (I want to thank John Fernandez for the opportunity to work on this function. I also want to acknowledge the contributions of Emily Bassman, Linda Shanosky, and Nathalie Lomax. Their joint efforts made this an exciting time and a meaningful learning experience.)

As a new business strategy began to form in our company, top officers started to recognize the importance of people to the company's future success. The company's competitive edge would lie not just in its technology but in the behaviors of the employee team. The corporation realized that employees would play a vital role in understanding customers' needs and integrating the efforts within the company to respond to these needs. Human resource forecasting and planning would focus on the changing demands of the company, the required skills and experience base of its employees, and the environmental trends that would determine whether the right people were available to meet business requirements.

The following account covers only the first nine months of a new department established to do human resource forecasting and planning. This was a time when we were adjusting to new roles, a new discipline, and the demands of making people a strategic resource for the business. It felt like a frame-breaking change to us. It was a learning process and simultaneously an educational process that established a dialogue with personnel department officers and business group leaders. The following activities were not planned at the outset but evolved as new ideas were suggested. The experience demonstrates both the value of forecasting and planning as part of an organizational change effort and how a department establishes its worth to the organization.

Defining the Function. We had been through enough reorganizations to know that the first task of a new group is to define its mission, outline the function, and establish responsibilities for different positions in the group, including identifying how many people would be needed and what they would do. We put this material together in a binder labeled "Human Resource Forecasting and Planning—Preliminary Strategies." Some of the material presented earlier in this chapter was included in the binder, specifically, the mission and purpose of human resource forecasting and planning, the responsibilities of corporate headquarters and the business units, and the examples of possible applications. We circulated this binder to our colleagues in the personnel department and in the business units, held a number of interviews to discuss the function, and developed ideas for needed actions. This was the beginning of the education process (both in terms of our own learning and educating others), and it positioned us to provide needed data for business planning.

Retirement Eligibility Analysis. One of our first projects was obtaining data for our vice-president on the numbers of people in different departments who would be eligible to retire during the next ten years. The results were startling for several departments, with as many as 70 percent of the employees eligible for retirement during the next ten years. This suggested the need to beef up recruiting strategies and/or provide incentives for some people to work longer (for example, continue to contribute to the individual's pension plan beyond age 65). We also identified questions that needed to be answered before such actions could be taken: for example, will those who reach retirement age have the skills we need? If not, perhaps we should encourage early retirement (prior to age fifty-five) by, for example, offering special financial incentives.

Environmental Scan. The need for an environmental scan arose in two ways. We had access to an environmental scanning report produced by a consultant. This was a compendium of dozens of trends and their implications. Also, we were asked by a senior executive to help him prepare for a videotape interview he was asked to do. He would be asked questions about the workplace of the future. For instance, the interviewer wanted to know what changes the company saw in the composition of tomorrow's workforce. What changes did we see in people's life-styles, personal values, and work values? What changes would there be in the nature of the work in the 1990s? What needed to be done to make the U.S. workforce more productive and competitive? Was there a relationship between demographic changes in the workforce and productivity? How would technological changes affect the workforce?

Answers to these questions were formed from the environmental scanning report, newspaper articles, and numerous other sources. This was the start of a much larger effort to provide a detailed environmental scan of issues we felt were pertinent to the company. An executive summary of the trends was circulated to top executives. This proved to be very popular, and material from the summary began to crop up in executive speeches. We felt we were building an awareness of the importance of external trends to accomplishing business objectives. The longer environmental scanning report was sent to managers on request. Kept in loose-leaf form, we continued to update the report as we obtained more information.

Outside Experts and Company Visits. We drew on several outside experts to obtain opinions about our mission and function. We joined the Human Resource Planning Society and attended workshops sponsored by that organization. Perhaps the most valuable learning activity was visiting other companies that were known for their careful human resource planning and that faced major human resource issues similar to ours. During each visit, we acquired one or two valuable nuggets of information or insights that we might not have had otherwise. For instance, a large bank showed us the importance of asking strategic ques-

tions about the workforce, such as whether the highest perform-
ing people received the highest financial rewards.

A visit to an automobile manufacturer showed the value
of a method for analyzing skill levels, experience, and educational backgrounds of current employees. The skills analyses,
which identified force shortages and surpluses, were tailored to
the type of functions in the unit. Forms were created to survey
employees about skills relevant to their particular part of the
business as well as general skills transferable across the organization. This was a consultative approach to human resource
forecasting and planning in that the personnel department staff
worked with departments that called them in.

We also learned from the visit to the automobile company that a human resource staff could avoid wasting time and
money generating force reports that were not needed by the departments. The firm purchased an easy-to-use personnel data
software package and trained the human resource staff in each
business unit to use the software to analyze the company's
existing personnel data base. In this way, the business units created the reports they needed. Thus, rather than crunching data,
the human resource staff could consider issues and analyze
them relative to the corporation as a whole and become a corporate-wide resource with information for top management and
the business units. The business units could produce reports
when they were required in a form that is most useful to them.

A visit to a major consumer products company showed us
how to use personnel data for force projections using statistical
models. The human resource staff helped operations departments hire the right number of people to avoid layoffs as new
technology was introduced.

Visits to a pharmaceutical firm and to a large electronics
company provided examples of highly detailed, human resource
planning systems that were integrated with business plans.
These procedures were complete with time lines and interview
guides. We also learned about related functions, such as planning for executive succession.

Learning about how other companies experienced change
was especially helpful. One firm had changed from a centrally

controlled organization with a strong central business planning function to a decentralized structure that held its business units accountable for their own human resource planning.

Another company was still struggling to achieve a balance between central control and local responsibility for strategic issues. The visit showed us how a corporate headquarters can help the business units conduct their own force analyses and incorporate the results of these analyses and environmental scans into their business plans.

Holding Human Resource Planning Conferences. As another way to educate our colleagues in the company, we held a one-day conference with several speakers on environmental scanning and ways to relate human resource planning to business planning. A manager from the large electronics firm referred to above talked about his company's strategic business and human resource planning processes. A manager within our own company talked about what his department did in an initial human resource planning effort. Our environmental scanning consultant reviewed a variety of trends particularly focused on changing demographics of the workforce and their implications for human resource policies. An economist from a major university faculty discussed the United States' changing economic future. Finally, a deputy secretary of the U.S. Department of Commerce discussed this country's competitive position in a global marketplace and the implications for productivity improvement, retraining, educational system support from government and corporations, and other needed efforts.

The conference was open to personnel department and business group managers responsible for business planning and human resource functions. Interest in attending the conference was much greater than we anticipated it would be. (We guessed there would be forty people at most and over a hundred people attended.) The conference was a way to quickly inform managers about the scope of the issues and the role the managers played in human resource forecasting and planning. The conference was videotaped, and the tape was edited for further communication of the ideas. Given the success of this conference, we began to plan topics for future conferences and workshops, such as forecasting methods, technological implementation, and women in the workforce.

Scenario Building. About the time of the conference, we were asked by our senior vice-president to work on a team to develop scenarios for the company in 1992 and what human resource strategies would help us get there. One scenario, written in the form of a magazine article, described the successes of a Hispanic woman service technician in meeting customer requirements. Innovative human resource strategies were described as contributing to her success, such as having had a six-month rotational assignment working on a customer's staff as a way to understand the customer's business. This and other scenarios, some not so positive, were used by the senior vice-president and others in their speeches.

The process of generating the scenarios required input from people who were knowledgeable about business direction. The outcome of the process was a set of actions the human resources department needed to take in support of our business strategy. We recognized that because some elements of our business strategy were fixed, some elements of our human resources programs and policies would be fixed. In other cases, however, because the implementation of the strategies could occur in different ways, human resource programs and policies needed to be adapted to accommodate different business initiatives. The document we produced described how this would occur and gave a number of examples.

Forecasting Critical Jobs and Skills. As part of scenario development, we interviewed key leaders in the company to obtain their views on the impact new business directions and changing technology might have on critical jobs for the next five years— especially if these critical jobs emerged and the needed skills did not already exist in the company. The outcome of these interviews suggested the need to form strategies to ensure that the people with the right skills would be available when they were needed. For instance, the finding that a certain type of engineer would be crucial five years from now coupled with the knowledge that the workforce would be declining in numbers suggested the need for financial support to students (for example, intern programs or scholarships to entice young people into the field and into the company). Another outcome of the interviews was that they sensitized managers in the business units about the need to think about critical jobs for the future and what would have to be done to ensure that the right people were available at the right time.

Integrating Human Resource Plans into the Business Planning/ Budgeting Cycle. Another step we took was to inject human resource planning into the regular business planning cycle. When the finance department asked each business unit for estimates of resource expenditures on R&D and capital improvement, it also asked for forecasts of numbers of people needed in different functions. Projections of hiring, retirements, and changes in employees' function were requested. Business planning submissions were encouraged to include a human resource component that described how human resource activities contributed to the business strategy in the unit. We hoped this would become more pervasive throughout the company as our educational process continued.

Generating Competitive Analogues. Our human resource forecasting and planning function became a resource for competitive knowledge on human resource issues. One of our major business groups was examining the development needs of its employees relative to changes in the business. The leaders of the business felt that employees from occupational levels through middle management needed education in the area of technological development, quality enhancement, customer relations, and managing and developing subordinates. As the business group managers planned their professional development, they asked us to do a competitive analysis of training in other companies. We wanted to know how much money and employee time other organizations, particularly our competitors, spent on different types of training and how they decided to invest their training dollars.

We obtained the information through contacts at professional training associations, from other companies (not our competitors), as well as from our own internal centralized training unit, which had access to competitive analysis studies that had already been conducted. In addition, we commissioned a consulting firm in Washington (which specialized in tracking business and labor trends) to survey the literature and to conduct a telephone study of firms that had similar problems to ours.

Another project examined the numbers and types of temporary employees working for our company and the extent to which other companies relied on temporary employees. The same consulting firm as used in the training study contacted other firms. The data were used to formulate a corporate policy about temporary personnel (how long they could stay with us, how to set rates of pay, and so on).

Internal Analysis Consulting. A further activity was working with several regional departments in the company to help them analyze their skill sets. In one case, a department felt that retirement rates during the next few years would be high given the age of the workforce. The department wanted to know the skills of the people who might be retiring and the skills of younger managers so they could formulate personnel selection and training strategies and possibly design incentives to keep people working longer if needed.

Specifically, our task was to investigate the aging workforce five years from now from the standpoint of the number employees eligible for retirement and the skills that would be lost as these people left the business. Also, the goal was to examine the promotable pool from the standpoint of the number of people who had the characteristics needed to be promoted.

The need for the aging-workforce analyses arose because top management felt that the workforce was aging rapidly and that there would be a large number of retirements. Though eventually there may be a need for some downsizing because of technological advancements, there was the possibility that too many people would leave too quickly if an incentive were offered to obtain volunteers for early retirement. In addition, there was the need to implement these technological advancements, a process that would require significantly more people, at least for several years. Environmental trends about labor force availability had to be considered.

The need for the promotability analyses arose because top management felt the people they were promoting were not as qualified for promotion as they should be, although they were technically proficient at their current level. The feeling was that there were not enough qualified people available in the company. Methods for conducting these analyses included examination of demographic characteristics of the workforce from the personnel data base and interviews with managers and crafts workers about criteria for promotion and current skill levels. In addition, scenarios were generated with a set of assumptions about what the department would be like five years from now in term of new technology, anticipated growth or decline, and equal opportunity employment goals for minorities and women. The intent was to develop hiring and staffing plans given what we learned about the current organization.

Other Planned Activities. At the time of this writing, other activities are planned. These include preparing a regular "people report" with data to answer such questions as the following: Are we attracting the employees we need? Who is leaving the business? Are employees motivated to perform their best? Do we know current and future skill needs? Some data, such as the number of hires, would be recorded monthly; other data, such as employee attitude survey results, would be reported annually. This would be an extension of the normal force tracking process that reported numbers of people by department and level every month. The data would be used by the company's officers and personnel department managers to evaluate the success of our human resource policies and programs.

Another planned activity was a series of interviews with business group leaders on how human resource systems help them to accomplish their goals. The interviews would present the leaders with a list of environmental trends and discuss which trends are most relevant to the leaders' organization. The dialogue would focus on the likely effects of these trends and the needed actions.

Change Agent Roles. The personnel manager or corporate strategist who undertakes human resource forecasting and planning becomes a change agent. The questions raised in the process of forecasting and planning prod executives and line managers to action, perhaps initiating new training programs or locating a new plant where there is a plentiful labor supply. The process also highlights the importance of people to meeting organizational objectives, perhaps leading to greater investment in career development or programs to help supervisors reinforce and support their subordinates' career motivation. Moreover, the process helps the organization consider different future directions so that managers will be prepared to handle change.

Summary

This chapter has reviewed the importance of human resource forecasting and planning to the management of planned change. Given the changes occurring in our business and the likelihood of further reorganization, we wanted to make an impact in a short time. The hope was that human resource forecasting would be done, and that it would be integrated into the company's business plans.

How to do this was a learning process for us. As quickly as we learned, we needed to educate others in the company. We conducted internal and external analyses. We drew on experts and other companies' experiences. We produced reports and held conferences. Our goal was to generate an awareness of the issues, not actually to do the planning ourselves.

Based on these experiences, I would recommend the following to other organizations establishing or reorganizing their human resource planning function.

- Add value to the company by being a resource for information others do not have.
- Interpret what the information means for the business—do

not just report interesting "gee-whiz" facts. Present examples of how the information can be used.
- Create a dialogue, not a one-way stream of information.
- Be timely. Interject human resource forecasting and planning activities into the normal business planning cycle so the information can be used.
- Reach the right people within the personnel department and within the business units.

9

Tracking and Evaluating Human Resource Change Programs

One role of the human resource professional is to help the change agent answer the question, "How am I doing?" Sometimes this requires encouraging or cajoling the change agent into evaluating the success of the change. The human resource professional's emphasis is on the effects of change on people in the organization and ways to improve the effectiveness of an intervention as it progresses. This chapter focuses on methods for tracking and evaluating change efforts with examples of personnel research, survey administration, and feedback. The information in the chapter can be used by human resource professionals to educate organizational leaders and managers on the importance of evaluating change and simple ways to do it. The chapter is also a reminder to human resource professionals about available qualitative and quantitative measures and meaningful and practical research designs. The examples of personnel research projects show the range of evaluation programs that can be sponsored by leaders and managers and conducted by human resource professionals in the organization, by external consultants, or by managers themselves.

Measurement

Measurement is an important concept in business. Financial indicators provide one picture of an organization's health. They allow a corporation's CEO and officers to evaluate the extent to which their business decisions are successful. They also provide a useful guide for decision making and a basis for forecasting future trends. Global indicators, such as return on investments, are a way to take the corporation's temperature. Other data include sources of revenues and costs, and the changes in these figures over time. Other indicators of organizational effectiveness do not directly reflect the company's financial bottom line, but they contribute to it. These include the quality and quantity of production, disruptions (accidents, strikes, and other costly disturbances), employee attitudes, and employee withdrawal (turnover and absenteeism) (Katzell and Guzzo, 1983).

Measures such as those mentioned above provide a report card of a manager's or a corporation's success. They can be a basis for rewarding top management. The axiom "employees inspect what their boss expects" highlights the idea that people attend to areas on which they are evaluated. The measurements an organization chooses, therefore, signal to employees what is important—that is, what deserves their attention and the allocation of the corporation's resources. For instance, rewarding managers for developing their people (for example, sending them to training programs, promoting them, providing equal opportunities for women and minorities, designing challenging jobs, and involving employees in making decisions affecting them) is one way to put teeth behind a corporate philosophy that values people.

Tracking and Diagnosis

Measurement is important for tracking and diagnosing problems. Periodic attention to employee attitude survey results is one way to pinpoint problems that may affect the employees' contribution to the business. Although morale is usually not highly related to productivity (that is, people may work hard whether or not they are satisfied with their jobs or the work environment), dissatisfaction may be a precursor to other costly problems, such as absenteeism and turnover. Input from employees is also a valuable way to track such factors as how top management is perceived, the reputation of the company as a place to work, how well local managers are doing to implement the company's objectives, and so on. IBM measures and rewards its managers partly on employee attitude data. The company has a strong, consistent philosophy that people are to be valued and respected and that employee development is important. Regular attitude survey data allow managers at higher levels to be sure that local operations are on track with this philosophy by indicating, for example, the extent to which employees feel there are opportunities for development. The data also provide direction to local managers to recalibrate their behaviors—for instance, to do more to encourage employee participation in decision making.

Evaluation Programs

Measurement is a way to test whether a program is working. If managers in fast-paced, competitive companies are expected to take risks, they need feedback on the extent to which these risks are likely to pay off. Early knowledge of the effects of an action makes it possible to change direction to avoid failure. This is not just a way to soften the extent of a risk; it provides a vehicle for ongoing experimentation. Taking a risk means trying out something new.

I once attended a meeting with a top executive from the marketing department and a top executive from the personnel department of a major corporation. The marketing department executive was explaining his view of a program to enhance the professionalism of the sales force. The executive's goal was to determine the skill requirements of each job in the department, establish expectations for learning the job, and then impose a method for judging each employee's level of mastery. The personnel executive asked how the marketing department would know when the program was successful. This question left the marketing executive at a momentary loss for words. He had a general goal in mind—improve the competence of the sales force. But what would the outputs be? After a pause, the marketing executive reflected that there would be several outcomes: improved reputation of the department in the industry, better sales figures, and reduced unit costs. However, he had not previously considered the need to evaluate his program.

In general, managers need an understanding of the value of program evaluation as a way to judge the success of alternative business directions. Knowledge of how to conduct an evaluation is also important. Even if managers turn to internal or external consultants for this activity, it is helpful for them to know what constitutes a meaningful evaluation—one that suits the purpose in providing usable information, not necessarily one that is rigorous in providing all the answers. In the area of program evaluation, managers should know when they need a Chevrolet and when they need a Cadillac, and it is often up to human resource professionals to guide them, especially when it comes to the effects of programs on the people in the organization.

Evaluating Evaluations

Before exploring different evaluation methods and research designs, the results of evaluations of managerial interventions offer insight into their value. Researchers at New York University recently reviewed ninety-eight studies on the effects on worker productivity of eleven types of psychologically based organizational change efforts (Guzzo, Jette, and Katzell, 1985). (The researchers defined intervention programs as the introduction of an experimental treatment or change.) Their review examined evaluations of realistic job previews to provide job applicants with accurate expectations; training instruction; appraisal and feedback methods; goal setting (with management by objectives as a special case); financial compensation programs; work redesign (job enrichment); decision-making techniques; supervisory techniques (for example, ways to increase subordinate participation in decisions); work rescheduling; and sociotechnical interventions (programs that consider the joint effects of new technology and social conditions). The research examined the effects of these programs on such productivity measures as the quality and quantity of output, turnover and absenteeism, and disruptions such as accidents and strikes.

The review found that, overall, these interventions significantly increased productivity. However, training and goal-setting interventions tended to have the most powerful effects. Large-scale sociotechnical interventions also showed greater-than-average effects on productivity. These effects were strongest on disruptions and weakest on employee withdrawal measures, with output measures in between. Changes in supervisory methods and work schedules had significant effects on withdrawal, whereas other programs did not. Combined programs resulted in more positive effects than separate programs, but not substantially larger. The interventions had a greater effect in smaller organizations than in larger organizations, and a greater effect in governmental organizations than in private for-profit firms. Sales and managerial workers benefited more from the interventions than blue-collar workers. Training was especially popular for managerial/professional workers; as stated above, this tended to have a comparatively large effect size.

The studies in the review used several different research designs. The smallest effect sizes occurred for the more rigorous designs (for example, designs with randomly selected people in the control group as opposed to designs with comparison groups of people who were specially selected for, or withheld from, the study). The largest effect sizes occurred when there were no comparison groups but when before-and-after measures were available for the group experiencing the intervention. As may be expected, the longer the interval between the intervention and the measurement, the less the effect.

The review also showed that overall, productivity programs do make a difference, but many factors contribute to their success in addition to the programs themselves. These factors include the organizational context, the research design, and the particular measure of productivity as well as what the program was intended to do. Individually, each study was valuable to the organization in which it was conducted. The study helped management decide whether to continue to experiment or implement the intervention in different parts of the organization. It also suggested ways to improve the intervention.

The finding that less rigorous research produces more significant effects suggests that multiple factors, not controlled in less rigorous research, may be unintentionally affecting the impact of the experiment. For instance, when random assignment to conditions is not used, the group chosen for the intervention may be the one needing it the most, or alternately the group chosen may be the most likely to succeed. Comparison or control groups may have been chosen because they were likely to fail.

Research Design Goals

The purpose of a research design is to evaluate the effects of a change or intervention while eliminating rival explanations —that is, eliminating other factors that could have influenced the results. There are two types of threats to a research design. One is the accuracy of the measures and the certainty that the study is testing what the researchers believe it is testing. This is called *internal validity*. There are several threats to internal validity and ways to overcome them (Cook and Campbell, 1976). The threats include inaccurate measurement, researcher bias, participant sensitivity to what is being measured, history (changes that would have occurred over time regardless of the intervention), and other intervening variables, such as the context in which the study is conducted. (See Cook and Campbell, 1976, for a variety of research designs to overcome threats to internal validity.)

A researcher's goal is to design a study that is tight enough to eliminate rival explanations. There are many ways to do this. One is accurate measurement. This requires ensuring the reliability of what is being measured over time and establishing that what the researcher thinks is measured is in fact what is being measured. For instance, absenteeism may be measured in terms of the number of days absent or in terms of the number of reasons for absence. Three weeks off for an operation, a single event, will probably not have the same meaning as fifteen days off during the course of a year for various personal reasons. The latter may indicate a performance problem or job dissatisfaction whereas the former may have nothing to do with work.

Attitude measures can be used effectively, but their problems should be recognized. They allow top managers to understand what the company's employees are feeling (for example, how they are reacting to a major corporate change or simply to what is happening in their local department at the time). Attitude measures also provide a conduit for employees to express their feelings. But, as noted earlier, attitudes are not usually the cause of behavior. For example, job satisfaction, an attitudinal variable, does not cause better job performance. It could be that people's attitudes are a reflection of their prior behavior. They may look back at what they have done and at their experiences and evaluate their attitudes in a way that is consistent with these behaviors and experiences. Also, ratings on one variable may influence ratings on another so that the order of asking questions may make a difference in results. The measurement scale may also make a difference, and variables may be correlated simply because a similar method is used. In general, people try to be internally consistent in their responses to a question so that one self-report measurement is likely to related to another simply because it is logical to the respondent (for example, experiences of job satisfaction are likely to be related to commitment to the organization). In addition, how questions are asked and the format for responding may influence ratings.

A good strategy is to use *multiple measures* rather than to rely on the accuracy of one technique. Observations, behavioral records, self-reports (through interventions or questionnaires), and performance measurements are variables that may be quantified. Qualitative information (that is, descriptions of what is going on) is also valuable and should be combined with quantitative data. Questionnaires are often used because they can be administered easily to many people. But because of the potential problems discussed above, the researcher may be misled by the results. Other data, perhaps in-depth interviews with a small number of people, may corroborate the quantitative results, provide clarifying information, and suggest new ideas and different factors that would not have been considered otherwise.

The assessment center process for measuring employees' potential to perform at higher organizational levels relies on multiple measurement. Employees participate in different exercises (business games, group discussions, simulations of business situations, and paper-and-pencil tests of ability and personality). Several observers write reports and make ratings. The data are then integrated by allowing each observer to review all the data, make judgments on different performance dimensions (decision making, leadership, and the like), discuss their judgments, and try to agree on their judgments.

The design of the research, in addition to the measures used, is a way to reduce threats to internal validity. The most rigorous research designs eliminate as many threats as possible, but often they are impractical or are sterile in that they alter the context so much that the situation studied does not reflect reality. Less vigorous "quasi-experimental" designs may be more practical, although their weaknesses in identifying the source of cause-effect relationships need to be recognized.

In addition to understanding that the degree of internal validity is a requirement of meaningful research, another important aspect of evaluation is whether the results transfer beyond the experimental situation. Will the same results hold in other departments or at other times? This is the issue of generalizability or *external validity.* Here, the subjects in the study and the setting for the study must be similar to the situation to which the researcher wants to generalize. For instance, a training program may work well in one department because the people need the training, but its value may not generalize to the entire organization.

The Scientific Method Versus Action Research: A Process Approach to Evaluation

An ideal evaluation applying the scientific method involves the prior specification of objectives and criterion measures, pre- and posttesting of experimental and control groups, randomly selected participants, and the use of statistics to determine causal links (Blacker and Brown, 1985). As stated earlier, less rigorous quasi-experimental designs are available, but they are limited in their ability to eliminate rival explanations for the results of a study. Nevertheless, information obtained from a quasi-experimental design is still useful. It may not be perfect, but it may supply enough evidence for reasoned judgment.

Another difficulty with using a scientific method to evaluate programs is that the goals of a management program are not necessarily concrete and objective. People may have different expectations for a program's success. Moreover, there is the difficulty of identifying and interrelating different programs, variations in the same program, or different ways the program can be implemented depending on the organizational environment.

The *process approach* to evaluation is often more realistic and long term than the scientific method. According to this view, the evaluation focuses on developing goals, identifying and trying different processes or applications of the program, and observing the incremental change rather than whether predetermined objectives were achieved. This action research model suggests the need for evaluation while a program is being implemented.

The action research–process approach to evaluation specifies the desirability of a close relationship between the researcher and those who are directly affected by the program. In addition, the program being tested will change over time. Rather than focusing on a predefined target, the process approach focuses on the process of change and on developing the competencies and motivation of people to handle the change. Involving the users of the program in its design is one way to increase the likelihood of its acceptance. Being willing to adapt the program to the users' needs is also necessary. Moreover, it is important to realize that different groups have different views about the purpose and intended outcome of the intervention (Blacker and Brown, 1985).

Returning to the case I referred to earlier about the competency model in the marketing department, the salespeople may see value in the program because it may increase their commissions. The top executive might be interested in it because it makes recruiting and keeping the best people easier. These are related goals, but they have different implications for the measurements used to evaluate them. The top executive is likely to be concerned about the intermediate goal of assessing the skills and qualifications of the people in the department, assuring their competence and reputation in the business community. The salespeople will maintain their focus on what to them is the bottom line.

Costing Services

Often managers shy away from evaluation because they claim there is no way to objectively measure the outcome. They mean that there is no easy way to measure a program's effect on the corporation's bottom line. The program is used because the manager judges it will have an indirect effect on the company's financial performance—perhaps a long-term impact. But because this cannot be evaluated using an easily obtainable metric, there seems to be no point in attempting an evaluation of the program. However, this view is not necessarily correct, even when the criteria for success appear soft (subjective and not easily obtainable). It is possible to evaluate a program using a metric that is easily comparable from one program to another. This metric is *unit cost*. Also, it is possible to evaluate the cost-benefit of a program even when it appears that only subjective evaluations are possible. In such a case, a subjective judgment of the dollar value of performance is obtained. The increased value of performance in dollar terms resulting from the program or intervention minus the cost of that program is then calculated. This is called *utility analysis*.

Establishing Unit Costs. A first step in utility analysis is to determine the unit cost of an activity, for example, the cost of sending one person through a particular training program, the cost of hiring a new employee, the cost of an organizational development consultant's time to run a team-building exercise, and so forth. Determining unit costs allows comparing the costs of different ways to supply the same service. Unit cost data can also be used to track cost-effectiveness over time, with the cost from one month compared to the same month a year ago or to the average of the preceding twelve months. (The cyclical nature of an activity may be one way to decide which comparative measurement to use. Cyclical activities, such as hiring during the spring graduation season, suggest the appropriate time for cost comparisons.)

Quality of Service. Although costs are important, a favorable cost advantage may be due to lower standards. One training program may be cheaper than another because the instructor is less experienced or the materials used were not developed with the same care. This suggests the importance of considering the outcome of the service or activity, not just its cost. The outcome may be subjective, such as better performance or more satisfied employees. However, such outcomes can also be translated into cost terms, such as the monetary value of a certain level of increased performance.

A utility analysis of an assessment center for sales managers asked a panel of supervisors to estimate the annual dollar value of sales for managers at the 50th percentile (the level of performance at which 50 percent of the managers are lower and 50 percent are higher). The supervisors were also asked to judge the value of performance at the 85th percentile (the point at which 85 percent of the sales managers are lower and 15 percent are higher). The 50th percentile was taken as the average sales volume, and the difference between the 50th and the 85th percentiles was taken as the average (or standard) deviation of sales managers' performance. In this case, the average yearly dollar value was $30,000 with a standard deviation of $9,500 (Cascio and Silbey, 1979).

In simple terms, utility is the increased dollar value of one procedure over another. The utility of the assessment center referred to above could be determined by multiplying the number of participants, the standard deviation of job performance in dollars, the correlation between assessment ratings and job performance, and the minimum job performance level of people passing the assessment center. The resulting value would then be subtracted from the cost of putting the people through the assessment center. This value would then be compared to the utility of other selection devices. (Cascio, 1982, provides an excellent overview of utility analysis with several good examples of how it can be applied to evaluate personnel selection and training programs.)

Evaluation as a Means of Accountability

Costing services for programs is valuable to managers in any functional area whether it be evaluating the costs of a new manufacturing process, a financial accounting process, a sales incentive plan, or an employee training program. In general, program evaluation is a way to hold employees accountable for their work. Utility analysis accounts for both the costs and benefits of work. It suggests ways to develop more cost-effective systems and to understand the contribution of a program to the organization. Utility analysis provides a common basis for comparing programs. Costing services is a way to track performance and provide feedback on individual and group performance. It can be used in choosing between programs and redesigning programs to make them more effective.

Sponsoring Research

So far, this chapter has examined research methods and designs that might be used by internal human resource professionals, consultants, or managers themselves. It is also worthwhile to consider the role of the sponsor of the research (for instance, a line manager who wants a change effort evaluated). The line manager's goal is to assess the success of the change, or its effect on employees. Actually, separating the design and implementation of the change from the evaluation makes sense. People who are accountable for the change may have trouble being unbiased or objective in evaluating the change. However, independent researchers should work with the line manager to thoroughly understand the purpose and nature of the change and to design an assessment that is meaningful to the organization in terms of the criteria for success and the reliability of the measurement. In this sense, the evaluation is not totally independent or blind. The sponsor is aware of the hypotheses and how they will be tested. In action research, the goal is to use the evaluation to maximize the success of the project.

The role of the research sponsor is, first of all, to recognize the need for an independent evaluation and to commission the study. As stated earlier, Chapter Three's guide for selecting consultants may help. Once the selection has been made, the following steps should be taken.

1. *Outline the scope of the study.* The extent to which data will be used to alter the change process as it occurs or the extent to which isolating the effects of specific variables (interventions) is important; data should not be communicated until the conclusion of the process.

The more important the need to isolate effects, the more rigorous and scientific the research design needs to be. This will affect how the intervention is implemented. For example, control groups mean withholding the intervention from some people at least temporarily. Random selection of people to groups or groups to conditions has implications for who is exposed to the intervention and when. A less rigorous, more action-oriented research design is likely when multiple variables are introduced at one time, and when control or comparison groups cannot be separated—everyone experiences the intervention at the same time, the change is long term in nature, outcome measures have multiple possible determinants, and measuring or controlling for all possible causes is not practical.

2. *Agree on roles.* In action research, the sponsor or change agent is a coresearcher with the experts who are responsible for the evaluation. In more scientific research, the relationship is less a partnership than a client or buyer-seller relationship where the researcher provides the agreed-on evaluation and may not report back until the evaluation is complete.

3. *Determine the criteria.* The researcher works with the change agent and perhaps with the people or groups to be affected by the intervention to identify outcomes. This refers to formulating a clear understanding of the purpose and intended

outcomes of the intervention and of the degree to which they can be attributed to the intervention.

Agree on measures of these outcomes. They may be objective (units that can be readily counted) or subjective (perceptual or attitudinal).

4. *Agree on the freedom the researcher has to conduct the study.* The researcher requires the authority to collect the data, and, in some cases, to contribute to how the intervention is implemented—especially if control groups, random selection, and newly designed data collections are involved.

5. *Anticipate possible breakdowns and develop contingency plans.* For instance, the sponsor may decide to alter the intervention midway into the process after a rigorous experimental design has been started. The sponsor may insist on seeing preliminary data before the study is complete, altering the initial agreement with the researcher. Or the intervention may be halted for some reason, leaving the researcher with unusable data. If the sponsor anticipates such changes or wants flexibility in the intervention design, administration, and evaluation, this should be clarified to the researcher as early into the project as possible so that the researcher can incorporate possible design alterations into the project.

6. *Agree on who owns the data.* The sponsor may want the data to be totally confidential and the researcher may want to report the results to the organization as a whole or perhaps to the professional community in a presentation or publication. Potential uses for the data after the study should be recognized and agreed on before the study begins.

7. *Agree on accountabilities and credit.* Separating the success or failure of an intervention from the evaluation itself may be difficult. The researcher may want some credit for the intervention itself in addition to the evaluation. This depends on the researcher's role in designing or influencing the intervention and the research. Usually the principal change agent or sponsor views the entire project as his or hers, and the researcher is one component of the project. In addition to agreeing on ownership and uses of the data, ownership and roles for the project itself should be clarified up front.

A written contract, as referred to in Chapter Three's suggestions for selecting consultants, is a good way to specify and clarify ownership issues.

8. *Facilitate the research as it is conducted.* The sponsor should be clear about, and should help set, the goals for the research and the timing of events.

The sponsor should clearly support data collection efforts, especially if they require cooperation from others (for example, asking people to fill out an attitude survey). This support should be visible (for example, letters of requests for data signed by the sponsor; memos or articles in a company newsletter describing the importance of cooperating or participating in the study).

9. *Clarify the extent to which participants (especially managers) will be held accountable for the success or failure of the intervention.* If the research is to be used as an appraisal tool, this could affect the participants' willingness to cooperate in providing accurate data. It may also affect how the researcher is perceived in the organization (for example, looked at with suspicion or respect). In addition, it may affect the sponsor or change agent's influence and respect.

If participants' performance is to be appraised partly on the results of the study, this should be stated before the project begins, with the reasons and the methods spelled out as much as possible.

The sponsor or change agent may be appraised on the degree of the intervention's success. The researcher should be aware of this and possibly work with the sponsor's management from the study's inception to clarify the scope of the study and accuracy of the results.

Examples of Program Evaluations

Leaders, managers, and human resource professionals who understand research design and methods and who can frame questions about standards for success are likely to probe for a deeper understanding of organizational phenomena and are likely to be open to testing new ideas. This section describes examples of program evaluation research conducted by an internal personnel department research group under my direction. The projects were conducted for clients in the personnel department and in line departments. The research examined the effects of company changes and programs on employees. The section shows the value of applied research to managers. (The author is indebted to the following colleagues for their contribution to the projects described here: Anthony DeNicola, Diva Dinovitzer, Nancy Hicks, Emilia Hill, Steve Holt, Joel Kleinman, Edward Mone, Rosemary O'Connor, Barbara O'Neal, and Linda Streit.)

Most corporations do not have in-house research experts to work with managers who want a program evaluation conducted. Such experts can be hired from management consulting firms, or obtained by hiring university faculty for special projects. Chapter Three's guide to choosing consultants for change efforts should also be helpful for selecting outside experts in program evaluation.

The following is a brief description of some of our research projects. These examples demonstrate relationships between the goals of the research, the methods used, and the ultimate application of the results. Also, though these projects were done by internal human resource professionals, the projects were generally started by line managers or top executives who were responsible for the programs; or they were started by us in support of personnel programs for which we were responsible.

Quality of Worklife Program Evaluations. Our goal here was to develop and administer qualitative and quantitative evaluations of the company's quality of worklife (QWL) program. This research was conducted separately for small client groups who were interested in tracking the success of their local QWL effort. We also conducted a study for the company's national steering committee. Methods included questionnaires and interviews. This research was described in Chapter Six.

Credit Management Center Pilot Evaluation. This research assessed job satisfaction of occupational employees in a new credit management center. The company was beginning to develop its own billing system and this required having customer credit services. New jobs were designed and tested. Our goal was to evaluate employees' reactions to the new work. Interviews and questionnaires were used to analyze employee perceptions after the employees had been on the job for six months.

Gain-Sharing Survey. We were commissioned to study the effects of instituting a profit-sharing program for a telemarketing group. The company already had a corporate profit-sharing award based on the financial performance of the entire company. In the new program, the group also would profit from the revenues generated by the group. One unit was chosen as an experimental group, and a second unit was chosen as a comparison. Preintervention surveys were administered. However, an intervening strike prevented the implementation of the gain-sharing system. Six months later, a new preintervention survey was administered in the experimental group. The comparison group had not agreed to participate. At this writing the gain-sharing system is being trialed, and interviews are being conducted to examine how well it is working.

Personnel Profile System Evaluation. A questionnaire was used to evaluate the use of a computerized system for generating personnel profiles for matching people to jobs. The results were used to eliminate unnecessary fields of information to save data storage space. The study also evaluated reactions to a new system that generated a résumé-style profile. A related study assessed employees' awareness and use of a newly implemented on-line computer job ad system.

Evaluating Training for New Technology Implementation. This study examined the effectiveness of communicating information about, and training managers to use, a new telecommunications system that would save over $90 million annually. Another part of this study was to evaluate sources of stress experienced by the people responsible for installing the new system and training employees in its use. The questionnaire results were fed back to the installation group to generate ways to lessen stress. The third part of the study examined the effects of the new system on users, with attention to how the implementation process could be improved at new locations.

The study of the training indicated that the information on the new system should be disseminated more widely and with more detail than was done the first time the system was implemented. Research on the pressure experienced by the installation group revealed that they saw their work as highly stressful.

The questionnaire survey was a way for employees to communicate to their bosses that the bosses often did not listen to their concerns; that they did not have proper training before being asked to perform a task; that the team did not work together well; that there were no written procedures about what was expected to do the job correctly; and that they were expected to accomplish a task in unrealistic time frames. These results were the basis for discussions with group members about how they could reduce their stress even though they had to continue working at an accelerated pace. Specifically, they developed ideas for more flexible work hours, more extensive training, and a better team spirit.

Developing a Model for Managing Technological Innovation and Change. Our goal in this research program was to understand the factors that contribute to the successful implementation of technological innovation and change, and to develop guidelines to facilitate such change. Several major studies were involved in this research program. One study used interviews to develop cases on how a computerized central monitoring system was introduced to track electronic switches that were geographically dispersed in a metropolitan area. The goal was to investigate sociotechnical issues, such as how the technological change affected reporting relationships, employees' feelings of status, and training requirements for technicians. The research showed how involving employees in the design and implementation process makes a difference in the acceptance of the technology. When users are involved prior to implementation, other ways for using technology are likely to be discovered, such as its value in giving technicians more rather than less flexibility in how they track and maintain the equipment.

A second study examined the effects of an office automation system, specifically electronic mail and electronic bulletin boards. Interviews and questionnaires showed how the system was used in different ways by managers at all organizational levels, and the results suggested directions for expanding the system. The central monitoring center and the electronic message system research resulted in the change model described in Chapter Five.

A third area of research tied to this change model was our work on the QWL program referred to above. We viewed this as a managerial innovation that supported the introduction of new technology. So our research informed us about ways to improve the QWL program itself as well as how to use it to involve employees in the implementation of technological innovations.

Retraining Program Evaluation. Designing methods to evaluate training programs was the focus of several of our studies. One project surveyed users and nonusers of management training. The results were used by a task force examining ways to reduce training costs and enhance efficiency. The study found that users' needs could be met better by sending trainers to client locations rather than sending students to the classrooms. As a result, the training centers were reduced from six to four at a considerable cost savings.

Other research was designed to evaluate a study-at-home program that allowed employees to obtain course material and study on their own. The courses focused on management and technical areas that were to prepare occupational workers for growing areas of the business, such as data systems. The research focused on assessing employee awareness of the program, participant reactions to the courses, and why some participants did not complete the courses. In addition, the research evaluated the impact of course completion on employees' careers.

Another project focused on evaluating a specific training course. An elaborate research design was formulated with pretests for ruling out the most serious threats to internal validity. There were plans for four comparison groups, pre- and post-tests, and random selection of subjects to conditions. Unfortunately, because the training organization was redesigned and new courses were instituted, the evaluation was never completed. However, the design was available as a model for future evaluations.

Survey Research. We designed and administered a variety of employee attitude surveys to help departments understand employees' feelings and track the effects of organizational change. These were survey feedback interventions, often conducted with an organizational effectiveness consultant. We provided the expertise on survey design, coding, data analysis, and report writing. Though the corporation had company-wide surveys with data available on major subgroups, such as a vice-president's organization, our smaller studies were tailored to the issues in the specific department.

Corporate Culture Assessment. After the AT&T divestiture in January 1984, a new company, AT&T Communications, was formed to provide long-distance telecommunications service. This new organization was a combination of three parts of the old Bell System: local operating companies that provided intrastate long-distance service; employees of the former AT&T Long Lines (the department that operated the interstate long-distance network); and the General Departments (staff departments in AT&T New Jersey corporate headquarters). One of our early research activities was a qualitative investigation of the issues arising from the merger of these previously separate organizations, each of which had a distinct corporate culture. This in-depth interview study was intended to supplement company-wide employee attitude survey data that were collected by a corporate headquarters group at the same time.

The qualitative study consisted of interviews with thirty-nine third- and fourth-level managers in four regions of the country. All departments in the company were represented in the sample. The managers selected were articulate and perceptive in identifying problems and concerns related to the after-math of the divestiture and the emergence of our new corporate culture. The findings gave us a better understanding of the change process. Responses focused on factors that both facili-tate and inhibit change. One of the most pervasive facilitating factors was the level of managers' awareness of our new corpo-rate values. The values of customer satisfaction, cost-conscious-ness, innovation, and prudent risk taking were recognized by everyone interviewed. The managers appreciated the need to effect rapid change at all organizational levels, and they seemed to be willing to implement these new values. Also, they realized that this would be an evolutionary process that would be emo-tionally difficult and that would require time.

The organizational transition was also characterized by countervailing forces that might inhibit change. One of the most significant factors cited was the sense of loss for the old com-pany and the anxiety associated with separation, as well as a personal loss of control. The former procedural guideposts and clarity of roles, relationships, and responsibilities were lost. As a result, managers felt uncertainty and apprehension about their careers. The perception of a generation gap within management was expressed as a split in values between the old and new man-agers. This split was viewed as a possible limiting factor to needed change.

Managers disagreed about the level of integration of peo-ple from different parts of the organization. Some respondents saw significant clashes; others saw no conflict. Clashes occurred in departments with mixes of people from different segments, as might be expected. Sources of conflict included different cri-teria for career advancement than were traditional in different parts of the company. Additional sources of conflict included disputes concerning territory, and different policies about costs, budgets, salaries, and personnel.

Other questions focused on the new values of risk taking, customer satisfaction, and cost-consciousness. The most contro-versial value was risk taking. Definitions varied from calculated, informed decisions to foolhardy actions suggesting a chance to fail and a loss of control. The study showed that though lip service was given to the term risk taking, the term was not well understood.

Associated with risk taking were changing perceptions of leadership and management style. Managers expected those in leadership roles to identify potential problems, be aware of events in the business, and quickly apply solutions. A proactive, goal-focused approach was favored over a reactive, discussion approach to resolve conflict. The trend toward delegation of responsibilities and participative management seemed to need further clarification and specificity.

The report of the study was sent to middle managers and above to serve as a basis for discussion as organizations were adapting to the change in the corporate environment. The report was a source of ideas about how the changes affected middle managers. It also helped middle managers understand the need for changing values and managerial style as the company began to operate in the increasingly competitive marketplace.

I do not want to overemphasize the impact of this research. It was one of many sources describing the change in corporate culture we were experiencing. Some of these sources were company newsletters. Others were external publications such as the *Wall Street Journal.* Our goal in the research was to have a systematic review of the issues that would help managers put the change into perspective and understand what was expected of them.

New Managers' Socialization Study. New managers are an important resource. They represent the infusion of fresh ideas into the organization. They are also the source of future leaders of the business. Socialization refers to the integration of these new managers into the organization. They need to understand the prevailing culture and be comfortable with their role as managers. The purpose of this study was twofold. First, we wanted to learn something about the relationships between new managers and their bosses—to examine the ways in which these relationships affect socialization. A second and more practical goal was to develop guidelines for integrating new managers into the company to enhance their chances for success and increase their satisfaction with their roles. The research consisted of focus groups (that is, group interviews) with new managers and then separate focus groups with their immediate supervisors. Thirty new managers were interviewed in groups of six or seven at a time. These included newcomers hired into management from outside the business and separate groups of managers newly promoted from occupational positions. Interview sessions were conducted as confidential discussions on subjects such as relationships with supervisors and co-workers. Expectations of new management roles, job assignments, and the work environment were also discussed relative to actual experiences.

All interview sessions were tape-recorded and then transcribed so that the common themes across groups could be identified. Transcription also provided quotations for the written report. All tapes were erased after transcription.

The research led to the following conclusions. Supervisors play a vital role in the socialization of new managers. They do this directly through the feedback, guidance, and the advice they give. They also do this through the expectations they communicate to subordinates and by their actions as role models.

Peers and subordinates also play a crucial role in socialization of new managers. Peers act as role models for appropriate behavior, as sounding boards for problems, and as sources of information about the company and the group culture and norms. Subordinates can be a source of information and can provide cues to the new manager as to how he or she is expected to behave.

We discovered a communications gap between supervisors and new managers. Frequently, points of view were not made explicit, and the boss and the new manager had different sets of assumptions. For example, behavior that a supervisor perceived as encouraging autonomy may have been perceived by the subordinate as indifference.

Overall, it seemed clear that new managers felt considerable stress as they learned their new roles. They were overloaded with information and responsibilities and faced ambiguity about role expectations. As the new managers learned the ropes, the stress seemed to be reduced.

This research was conducted along with a review of the

literature on socialization. Our study was fuel for the development of a number of programs, such as a two-and-a-half day new-manager orientation workshop; a new policy for identifying and developing high-potential young managers; a "manager as developer" workshop for supervisors; a guide describing resources in the company for career development; and work with client departments on employee development programs tailored to the needs of those departments. Thus, the research was exploratory but it set the stage for thinking about employee development and eventually for guiding development programs.

Exploring the Relationship Between Span of Control and Job Satisfaction. Our company was undergoing a series of efforts to trim down and reduce costs. In doing so, we were taking a closer look at organizational structure and workforce size. One way of restructuring to utilize personnel more effectively while decreasing costs is to increase spans of control (the number of people reporting to a supervisor). Considering the financial benefits that could result from increasing spans of control, it was important to assess the potential benefits and costs of such a change to job satisfaction. We felt that cost management must be weighed carefully against the business needs for employee development and organizational effectiveness. Increasing spans of control at the expense of job satisfaction could run counter to the goals of the business. So we conducted a study to examine the relationship between span of control and employee satisfaction. (This research was conducted by Linda Streit as her master's thesis at Rutgers University.)

Existing employee attitude survey data for over 7,000 employees were correlated with the size of the responding staff and the size of the respondents' peer group. This was an example of how existing data could be used to answer questions beyond the original reason for collecting the data.

The results showed no evidence that either component of span of control (that is, number of peers or number of subordinates) had any significant effect on managerial job satisfaction. However, occupational employees' job satisfaction declined as workgroup size increased. Relationships with co-workers were most positive and stress was lowest in small workgroups. There was evidence that occupational employees in smaller workgroups tended to have higher levels of participation in decisions and better relations with supervisors. Employees reporting greater participation and better supervisor relations indicated they were more satisfied with their jobs.

The results of the study indicated that increases in the spans of control at the second level of management and above would be unlikely to have measurable impact, either positive or negative, on managerial job satisfaction. However, increases in the spans of control for first-line managers could have negative effects on occupational employees' job satisfaction.

Guidelines for Survey Feedback: Employee-Guided Management

This chapter has already reviewed the problems and pitfalls of surveys as a research tool. However, many of the program evaluations described above used survey measurements, and one of the functions of the personnel research group was to conduct surveys for groups and feed back the information. This final section focuses on the survey feedback process as a valuable tool for human resource professionals.

Surveys capture employees' reactions to forces for change and organizational change strategies. Also, the process of collecting and using the information becomes a change intervention by raising issues and encouraging leaders and managers to listen and respond. Consider the following two cases.

A manager of an installation and maintenance division knew that the one-hundred-plus employees in her group were dissatisfied. The division was not working as a team. She heard one gripe after another about the lack of cooperation within the division. She was also hearing from her peers that her division was difficult to work with. Calling an organizational effectiveness consultant from the personnel department, the division manager conducted an attitude survey and worked with groups within the division to understand the results. The employees were initially skeptical and distrustful, but they found an openness and commitment from the division manager that they did not know existed before. The survey prompted honest discussion and the chance to work through problems, such as lack of opportunities for promotion and the enforcement of procedures that were no longer necessary.

In the other case, the chairman of the newly merged Alpha/Beta Corporation (name disguised) had presided over a complicated reorganization. The merger was a consolidation of departments. Where there were two marketing departments, there was now one. The same integration was needed for other departments as well, such as personnel and public relations. Eliminating redundancies and merging functions meant reducing the number of people. It also meant merging corporate cultures. One of the chairman's first concerns was the impact of the merger on employees. He wanted to know how the employees felt about the process and what the major concerns were. So he commissioned a corporate-wide attitude survey. Separate reports were generated for each vice-president's organization, and the chairman made it clear that the vice-presidents would be held accountable for improved results a year later. This meant that the vice-presidents had to use the survey results to understand employees' concerns and act on them.

These cases involve decisions or actions that affect employees' job security, skills, performance, and/or attitudes. Organizational development strategies promoting participative management encourage leaders to involve their employees in making decisions when the employees can make a contribution to the decision or when they are affected by the decision. Surveys, program evaluations, and structured involvement programs, such as QCs or QWL, are ways to obtain information from employees (see Chapter Six). However, it is not always evident how to use this information.

Appendix A (p. 255) outlines a process I call employee guided management (EGM). It is a set of guidelines for using information from employees to establish management strategies. It incorporates principles of participative management, participative decision making, performance feedback, and survey feedback to outline components for comprehensive programs of employee involvement. The process describes change agent roles in eliciting information, formulating and carrying out action strategies, and evaluating outcomes. The process is generally initiated by leaders and managers and is carried out with the assistance of survey design and analysis experts and organizational development consultants who help feed back the data to respondents for interpretation.

EGM is intended to be an ongoing process with the extent of its use depending on its need. For example, the process could run in cycles of six months. At the end of each cycle, a reassessment of the variables of concern is undertaken to guide future actions. New issues may be identified, establishing the focus for the next cycle.

Another element of EGM is the role of the consultant or facilitator. The provider of EGM must establish the purpose and offer alternative procedures for each component to fit the situation.

EGM is based on considerable research and theory in the area of survey feedback, and more generally, the value of feedback for guiding behavior. Appendix B (p. 267) reviews major findings from this literature as a basis for understanding why EGM works. This appendix shows how psychological theory and research are the foundation for survey feedback as a major human resource intervention and for the importance of evaluation as feedback on change in general.

Returning to the two cases described above, both survey collection efforts were initiated by the heads of the respective organizations. In the case of the Alpha/Beta merger, the company's chairman wanted a benchmark to begin evaluating the new organization. He also wanted to demonstrate his concern for employees. In the case of the division manager, a problem existed in the division, and she wanted to do something about it. In both cases, respondents participated voluntarily and anonymously. The environments were not necessarily open and filled with trust, but the surveys were a start in building this type of organizational climate. In the Alpha/Beta case, the events at the time were traumatic. Sweeping organizational changes and threats to job security could not be ignored. The survey was certainly not viewed as a way to fix these problems, but it was viewed as one way to measure progress. In the case of the division, the situation was under the control of the employees and the division manager. They could realistically expect to work through ways of solving their difficulties.

The information from the division survey was specific to the division. Without identifying respondents, it allowed each person to have input. The questions were focused on the working relationships in the group and on career opportunities. In the Alpha/Beta case, the information was more global and general. Though separate reports were available for each vice-president's organization, specific local issues at lower levels in the organization were not evident in the data. These could only be addressed if local groups took the initiative to examine the overall data and discuss what they meant to them. (Later corporate-wide surveys allowed data to be analyzed for lower-level groups.)

In both cases, employees were the source of information. Both cases used anonymous questionnaire procedures. Also, in both cases, employees were allowed to write in reactions in addition to responding to the multiple-choice items. Relatively few of the respondents to the corporate-wide survey took the opportunity to comment, whereas almost everyone in the division survey added a response, despite the potential for revealing one's identity with a specific comment.

The feedback process followed by the division manager was to discuss the results in small group sessions. This allowed probing beneath the surface and identifying possible solutions on issues such as working relationships, job transfers, and different work procedures. The feedback sessions were a form of team building. Although difficult initially, they showed that the division manager was serious about listening to her employees and working with them to improve conditions.

The Alpha/Beta corporate-wide survey, on the other hand, did not lend itself to this type of interaction. A few groups used the survey results as a take-off point for discussion, but this was not done throughout the organization. The data served as a temperature-taking device for large organization units, but not really as a way to bring people together to improve organizational conditions and working relationships. Any changes based on the data would have to be top-down—initiated by the vice-presidents in hopes of changing employee attitudes. The vice-presidents had the power to make changes, but there were so many factors going on at once in the company that any one change would not necessarily have the desired effect. Overall, the survey results were not as clearly under the control of management as was the case for the division-specific survey.

Summary

Measurement is a valuable tool for tracking, diagnosis, and holding people accountable for their actions. Program evaluation methods provide ways to compare different programs and processes affecting employees. The goal of program evaluation is to design the study and measurements in a way that will provide meaningful information. Threats to the integrity of the study (internal validity) must be avoided or at least recognized as potential limitations to the meaning of study results. Also, the study must reflect the situation to which the results are to be applied or generalized (external validity). Cost-benefit data and utility analysis use a common metric (dollars) to evaluate the usefulness of one program in comparison to another.

Leaders, managers, and human resource professionals should be aware of evaluation methods and should not be afraid to apply them even when measurement seems difficult. Rigorous evaluation methods are desirable, but less optimal procedures can also be useful. A simple evaluation process may be all that is needed to add insight or suggest ideas for improvement, even when alternative explanations for the results are possible. The combination of research results and reasoned judgment can be cost effective, time efficient, and useful. The roles of the researcher and sponsor should be clarified before engaging in the research. This includes agreeing on the scope of the research, relevant outcome measures, and issues of project and data ownership.

The research examples in this chapter were generally simple designs. Each project was focused on a specific problem or issue. Some of the research had a strategic focus in that it affected the entire corporation. The results had long-term value to the people who commissioned the study because the knowledge was valuable to future programs. This was true of the corporate culture assessment, the socialization study, and the span-of-control research. Other research projects had immediate applications to the local setting such as the studies of the department installing the new telecommunications system, of employee reactions to different personnel profile formats, and of employee reactions to the jobs in the credit management center.

The research methods were tailor-made questionnaires, interviews, group sessions, and combinations of these. The methods were chosen for the richness of information as well as expedience. The samples were generally small, but sufficient to supply useful information. Some of the research never reached fruition, such as the planned rigorous evaluation of the retraining program and the evaluation of the gain-sharing plan. There were other cases where we served as research consultants to help groups do their own research.

Much of the research was "one-shot." We did the study, fed back the data to the client, and perhaps helped the client use the information. The value of the research is in generating useful information for making decisions, suggesting a new direction for the department, or uncovering a good idea that might not have been thought of otherwise. In addition, the research contributed to the researchers' knowledge. Because we were also responsible for policy and program development in some areas, the research results were valuable in providing insight into corporate issues and employee concerns.

Finally, survey feedback and the employee-guided management process outlined in Appendix A help leaders and managers understand the value of information from employees and how the information should be structured to make it most useful. This generally requires involving employees, determining what information is relevant, and then using the information as a foundation for organizational growth and development.

The information collected and fed back does not have to be survey data, as in the two survey feedback examples. Group or individual interviews are other ways to collect information and possibly process it simultaneously. The important point is that leaders and managers guided by human resource professionals realize the potential value of measurement and evaluation and consider ways to act on the data to improve the situation for employees and the organization. The psychological foundation for the value of feedback is covered in Appendix B.

Human resource professionals should encourage line managers and leaders to evaluate the effects of major change efforts. The change agent must realize that the best defense for a program is the demonstration of its success. This requires establishing and measuring criteria for success in a way that clearly shows the effects of the program—that is, being able to attribute a change in measurement to the program, not to unintended or intervening events. That is where the methods described earlier in this chapter come in. The human resource manager can make a convincing argument for evaluation by tying it to the needs of the business to make maximum use of its resources, whether they be training dollars, employee time, a new technology, or interpersonal relationships. The human resource professional can ask cogent questions ("How do you know your program is working?" and "Are your employees working together effectively?") and then educate leaders and managers about ways to answer these questions.

10

Conclusion: Human Resource Levers for Change and Recommendations for Action

As was noted in the preface, human resource professionals have numerous levers for change at their disposal. They interpret external and internal trends and forecast needs so that steps can be taken now to ensure that future human resource needs are met. They partner with leaders and managers to generate, implement, and adopt innovations. They develop learning systems to communicate organizational values and to prepare people to handle change. They design programs to reinforce and develop employees' career motivation. They create interventions as catalysts for incremental and framebreaking change, and involve employees in the change process. They position the human resource function to influence organizational units, and to support and direct line managers. They evaluate programs and feed back results to help change agents calibrate their success and adjust their strategies.

Certainly, personnel functions not discussed here can be critical levers for change as well. These include appraisal methods, goal-setting procedures, and reward mechanisms. In general, human resource professionals need to understand how their actions contribute to an organization's operations and success.

Also, human resource professionals need to take actions to enhance the organization's responsiveness to its environment and to influence the environment to create a positive future for the organization and its members.

The field of human resources often focuses on tactical or transactional issues. Our field is replete with forms, procedures, and guidelines for how to manage people. Indeed, many line managers have come to view human resource professionals as monitors, controllers, and purveyors of red tape. Nevertheless, line managers also expect human resource professionals to provide the systems to get their jobs done, such as appraisal processes, compensation administration, and staffing. Sometimes the form or document becomes more important than its use. Human resource professionals must develop and maintain practical, easy-to-use systems. These transactional functions are necessary for an effective personnel function. However, they are not sufficient on their own.

Increasingly, human resource professionals are realizing they have a strategic or transformational function in the organization. This function is possible because many line managers recognize that the competencies and motivation of their employees constitute a competitive business advantage. A company's people differentiate the firm from its competitors. A firm cannot catch up with employee development as quickly as it can with technological advancement. Employee loyalty and commitment cannot be bought in the same way that other corporate assets are acquired. Many line managers recognize their responsibility to develop and manage their employees well, and they understand the value that human resource professionals can add to this process.

Organizations will change with or without the help of human resource professionals. Indeed, people issues are often the last to be considered in planning for organizational change. However, as several cases in this book demonstrated, people are a determining factor in the success of a change effort. Forecasting human resource needs and involving employees in making decisions are ways to enhance the change process. The book also showed the importance of positioning the human resource function to have a strategic influence on the organization. Human resource professionals must understand the strategic nature of their function and demonstrate its value to developing and accomplishing organizational goals.

I will describe a final case. I was recently involved in a team effort to formulate a corporate human resource strategy. (This was mentioned briefly in Chapter Eight as an example of scenario building and critical skills analysis.) The team members were headquarters personnel staff. As the work progressed, input was sought from a wider group of human resource and line managers, and eventually the plans were shared with the company's top officers. Our goal was to envision the corporation's business activities during the next five years and to form a human resource strategy that would achieve the corporation's goals during the planning period. We needed to think about the type of corporation we wanted to become in five years, given industry trends and corporate resources and objectives. We also needed to think about the human resource management activities that were necessary in the short term (for example, now and one year ahead). Moreover, we needed to draw on an analysis of environmental trends that addressed the availability of talent outside the company and the competition for that talent (topics discussed in Chapter Two).

This was an educational experience for the human resource professionals involved in the project. It focused attention on the strategic value of human resources as an extension of the firm's business plans and as a key resource for accomplishing those plans. But it was also a frustrating experience, especially at the beginning, because the task lacked structure. We had to create our own methods and continuously share our ideas with each other. As we progressed and felt more confident, we shared our ideas with others outside the group, within our department, and in other departments. There were seemingly endless meetings during which we debated broad strategic direction and fine-tuned words and phrases. Being clear and precise was critical if our planning documents were to have meaning and offer grounds for action. The shared experience of working in a team enhanced our commitment to the project, an experience similar to that of the organizational task force described in Chapter Seven.

Although this task force approach may not have been the easiest way to do human resource planning, it was a way to get us started at a time when the organization was clarifying its goals and the officers of the corporation were turning to the human resource department for help in enhancing employees' contributions. We knew this was a window of opportunity, but we also knew we did not have all the answers. Our task force was a way to educate ourselves and provide a foundation on which we could build.

The human resource function is changing in several major ways in many organizations. It is evolving from administrative overhead to a strategic, value-added position. Its traditional internal focus is changing to an external, often world, view that includes understanding how demographic, technological, business, and other trends influence the firm's ability to meet its human resource needs. It is changing from a here-and-now perspective to a future orientation, anticipating gaps in competence and planning actions to fill those gaps. Also, it is changing from attention to forms and procedures to attention to process —how well things are done—with emphasis on evaluating the success of human resource management and development efforts. Human resource professionals are learning how to facilitate and spearhead organizational changes. They are also learning how to involve employees in the process of change.

The multiple roles of human resource professionals discussed throughout the book suggest the following recommendations for action.

• Human resource professionals must be responsive to their clients within the organization. They need to understand the firm's principal functions and be able to interpret how human resource management can make a contribution to its goals. Moreover, they must position themselves in the organization in a way that allows line managers to benefit from human resource expertise.

• Professional development is important for human resource professionals just as it is for experts in other disciplines. Human resource professionals should keep current in their profession. Moreover, they should contribute new knowledge to the profession based on their evaluations. In doing so, they must distinguish between what can be shared with the outside world and what must remain confidential because of the firm's competitive position. (Indeed I am continuously mindful of this as I prepare publications such as this book.)

• Human resource professionals need to understand change processes and intervention points. They should analyze the human element in changes such as introducing new technology and altering organizational structures, and they should experiment with different points of intervention to plan for and implement change.

• As stated many times throughout the book, human resource professionals should develop a strategic view of their craft. This means that human resources must be integrally linked to organizational objectives. Human resource professionals must demonstrate the value of human resource management to accomplishing business goals and, in the process, educate line managers and executives about how to use the human resource function. In addition, human resource professionals need to teach line managers, executives, and themselves how to be organizational change agents.

• Finally, human resource professionals should adopt an expanded view of their function by understanding how it contributes to other organizational functions (for example, enhancing the success of marketing, engineering, and the like through employee selection and development). This expanded view should also include envisioning the future and calibrating their actions against both current and possible future outcomes. Consequently, human resource professionals must be flexible enough to alter programs and activities as evaluations suggest improvements and as the organization directs and redirects its course.

Overall, human resource professionals must be fully engaged in the business of their enterprise. They must be partners with line managers and executives in accomplishing organizational objectives. The goal of the human resource professional should be to contribute to corporate strategy, facilitate organizational change, enhance productivity, and increase the quality of worklife—outcomes that are important to both employees and the organization.

Appendix A:
Guidelines for
Employee-Guided
Management

This appendix outlines the Employee Guided Management (EGM) process described in Chapter Nine and introduced in London (1985b). EGM suggests ways to encourage employee involvement through principles of participation, performance feedback, and survey collection feedback. The thirty guidelines are divided into ten general components: conditions for effectiveness, objectives, type of information sought, source of information, data collection methods, feedback, using the information, monitoring strategies, outcomes, and the role of the consultant.

A. Conditions for Effectiveness

Several conditions are necessary for an effective EGM effort. Effectiveness is defined generally at this point as achieving positive outcomes.

1. EGM is more effective when those who are involved in the process design it and have control, responsibility, and authority over each component. The more elements of EGM a person is involved in, the more he or she is committed to it.

255

2. Those who participate should do so voluntarily. This may require anonymous responses from sources.

3. Once an employee is committed to the process, negative results are not grounds for discontinuing the process.

4. EGM works best in a democratic, open environment. At the same time, EGM helps to build and maintain such an environment.

5. EGM is more acceptable to a company's management the lower the costs and the higher the potential benefits. The costs and benefits can be expressed monetarily and psychologically. (An example of a psychological cost would be a top manager losing face because of negative attitude survey results.)

B. Objectives

Identifying the reasons for an EGM effort is crucial at its outset. This may seem obvious, but it is easy to ignore, or it may be taken for granted that the purpose has been established when in fact it has not. Another possibility is that EGM is established for the wrong reasons. For example, the goal may be to collect better indexes of task accomplishment when what is needed is better information about process issues involving interpersonal relationships and coordination. However, the focus of the EGM effort may change as underlying problems are uncovered. The initial information is really a stimulus for exploring issues during feedback sessions. Nevertheless, the initial purpose determines the type of information obtained, the source, and the meaningfulness of the information.

There are many different reasons for introducing EGM.

• "Temperature taking" (for example, measuring overall job satisfaction) and "diagnosis" (for example, examining characteristics of the job, company policies and procedures, and supervision).

• A short-term crisis intervention centered around a particular problem and a long-term intervention aimed at exploring and enhancing organizational health.

• A focus on interpersonal processes by collecting subjective data on workgroup relationships and a focus on job design elements via more objective indexes of job functions to enhance human resources utilization.

Feedback may have several different functions including uncertainty reduction; error correction; signaling the importance of various goals; comparing oneself and one's group to others; and enhancing motivation through rewards resulting from positive feedback or the reinforcing effects of feedback itself. These different functions provide other reasons for engaging in EGM.

6. The purpose for the EGM process should be clear and specific. The clearer and more specific the purpose for the process and the function of feedback, the more likely appropriate methods will be chosen, and the EGM process will be more effective.

Identifying the purpose of the process is tantamount to setting goals or objectives. This suggests the need for a realistic assessment of the purpose.

7. The initial objective should be realistic so that participants' expectations will be realistic.

The literature indicates the importance of the participants' control over the components of EGM and the salience of the objectives.

8. The target of the EGM process should be under the control of the participants. That is, the employees should have some say about the focus of the survey—that is, the issues addressed.
9. The issues of the EGM process should be important to the workgroup and the individuals involved. The target of EGM is likely to be more salient because it is the target. This suggests the importance of focusing on a meaningful target from the start.

C. Type of Information Sought

Information from employees varies in content (task versus process), subjectivity (for example, cognitive, affective, or behavioral), level of aggregation (individual versus group versus organization), frequency of occurrence, timeliness, and specificity.

10. The information collected should be specific and aggregated to a level that allows recipients to determine who is responsible and what can be done about it. The more general the information and the greater its applicability, the less recipients know how it applies to them and how to control it.

11. Survey data should be collected regularly and frequently. The more frequently information is collected, the more usable it is because it gives recipients more chances to react to it and correct errors. A workgroup leader may administer a twenty-item attitude barometer quarterly. A firm may administer a comprehensive company-wide survey annually.

12. The information collected should be descriptive of organizational conditions or individual behaviors.

Descriptive information may be based on subjective data (for example, ratings of job characteristics). However, it is reasonable to expect agreement on such data between individuals facing the same situation, where such agreement would not necessarily be expected from attitudes, judgments, or evaluations of the situations.

Attitudes, judgments, and evaluations are useful for "taking the temperature" of organizational conditions; descriptive (cognitive and behavioral) data are useful for diagnosis.

13. Data should focus on individuals and individual conditions (for example, individual behavior, performance, or attitudes) when work functions are independent. Group conditions should be measured when work functions are interdependent.

The choice of whether the focus of an EGM effort is on task or process information will determine many attributes of the data. The task refers to *what* was done, and process refers to *how* it was done. Task information is more likely to be objective, descriptive, specific, salient, and controllable, whereas process information is more likely to be subjective, affective, ambiguous as to meaning and relevance, and uncertain as to controllability.

14. The information collected should deal with task-oriented data rather than process-oriented data.

However, this is not to say that process is not important and should not be the focus of EGM. In fact, EGM is needed most when it comes to ambiguous issues that require employee involvement in understanding them and generating strategies to improve conditions.

An attribute of information related to its salience and specificity is its timeliness. Timeliness is more important the more specific the information. When the information is specific, as opposed to covering general issues such as overall satisfaction, the information should deal with issues that are of current concern. This in turn implies that the information should be fed back and reacted to as quickly as possible. Thus, the specificity of the information determines how quickly an EGM cycle should be conducted.

15. The information resulting from the survey should be specific and timely in order to generate a sense of urgency and the need for action.

Recall that Guideline 10 predicted that EGM is more effective when information is specific. Guidelines 10 and 15 together argue that EGM should be a dynamic, action-oriented process requiring immediate attention.

D. Source of Information

By definition, the source of information in EGM is the employee. The data may be objective information about employees, behavior, or performance, or they may be subjective information—that is, employees' perceptions and/or reactions to job and organizational conditions. As a stakeholder in the organizational process, employees affect and are affected by organizational programs and policies. As such, employees, as individuals or groups, may be both sources and recipients of the information. Alternately, information may be collected from one individual or one group of employees for use by another. Therefore, the source may be subordinates, peers, supervisors, and/or oneself.

Two groups of dimensions are relevant to the source of information. One is employees' motivation to give high-quality (that is, accurate and meaningful) information. The other is characteristics of the source that affect the reactions of the recipient to the information.

16. In order to increase employees' motivation to provide high-quality information,
- employees should participate voluntarily;
- the information request should be clear;
- the employees should have knowledge of the information requested;
- the climate of the organization or workgroup should be marked by open communication;
- employees should have reason to expect that positive actions will result from giving the information;
- in addition to providing information, employees should be involved in other elements of the EGM process (for example, be the recipients of the information and/or be involved in designing and implementing strategies based on the information);
- employees should depend on the recipient of the information for resources and support and/or should know that the recipient is dependent on them;
- the request for information should not be perceived as an invasion of privacy; and
- providing the information should not incur greater costs in time, effort, or money than the expected benefits.

17. The recipient should be perceived by employees as trustworthy and knowledgeable. The source and recipient should be similar (for example, in goals), have a favorable interpersonal relationship, and be in a position of

interdependence (as in a supervisor–work group relationship).

E. Data Collection Methods

Data collection methods include questionnaires, surveys, interviews, observations, and automatic monitoring devices, to name a few. More than one method is likely to be applicable for collecting information about a certain topic.

18.   More than one data collection method should be used and the different methods should agree in results.

Methods vary along a number of dimensions. These include the amount of data collected; the degree of depth of the information; whether data are collected from a sample or from all concerned (that is, a "census"); whether the results are qualitative (for example, narrative reports from interviews) or quantitative (for example, questionnaire results with close-ended responses); and the accuracy of the results. In some cases, the data are readily available. In other cases, a special data collection effort is necessary. This adds another dimension of concern —the possibility that the process of collecting the information affects the results.

A further consideration is how closely the method reflects the data of concern. To be more specific, in some cases the method yields a sign of what is important. This is the case with job satisfaction measures that presumably are a sign of some underlying cause (job characteristics, organizational policies, and so on) and which in turn affect other factors (for example, job behavior and performance). The danger is that the method may yield an index that becomes an end in itself.

19.   A method should yield accurate and salient information.

The method should match the purpose. For example, if the initial purpose of the EGM effort simply is to assess the overall level of job satisfaction, then an inexpensive questionnaire will do. After feedback and reflection on the results, more in-depth, objective data on work conditions may be required.

The complexity of the data collection method affects how responsive EGM is to the issues of concern. In general, the method should be designed to yield only as much data as needed.

20. Employees should delve below the surface to understand and ultimately control the phenomena in question. As such the EGM cycles increase in complexity and salience over time. Once adequate control is obtained, the complexity and salience of the issues decline.

21. The data should be collected, analyzed, and fed back as quickly as possible to maintain interest and a sense of immediacy.

These two guidelines imply that a balance must be achieved between how quickly the data can be prepared and the quality of the data.

F. Feedback

Of relevance here is who receives feedback, the form in which it is given, and the reactions to it.

22. Feedback should be given to individuals who are accountable for the data and who have control over factors affecting it.

Feedback may be given in a written report or in oral presentation. It may be given one-on-one (supervisor to subordinate), in small groups (natural work units), or in large groups. The term *feedback* implies that the recipients are passive. However, though the data should be as clear as possible, it is necessary for the recipients to interpret the information from their perspective and begin to use it.

23. Feedback should allow active participation of the recipients (for example, in the form of opportunities to ask questions and discuss the meaning of the results).

24. The favorability of the results and the self-confidence of the recipients affect the feedback method. Positive results make it necessary to focus on recipients' competence and personal control to avoid complacency, whereas negative

or average results, which are more likely to be denied or ignored, should begin with strong points and emphasize what rewards are likely to result by overcoming weaknesses. Confident, resilient recipients can confront negative results more rapidly than those with a poor self-image.

Earlier sections dealt with the types of information and the sources of information that are more likely to be accepted. I also discussed when group or individual feedback should be used (see Guidelines 10 through 17). This highlights the tie between the components of EGM such that the type and source of information affect the feedback methods.

G. Using the Information

EGM is likely to be more effective the more the participants are involved in all stages of the process. EGM works best when those who provide information receive feedback and are responsible for doing something about the results. A key issue in using the information is the participants' desire to respond.

25. In order to increase recipients' desire to respond to feedback,
    • the issues addressed by the information should be under the recipients' control;
    • the perceived costs of action should be low in relation to the potential benefits; and
    • the issues should be sufficiently salient and the benefits sufficiently high to make action worthwhile.

Much goes on between receiving feedback and using the information. Relevant processes include interpreting and integrating the data; generating and evaluating alternative actions; deciding on one or more courses of action; determining a way to monitor whether the actions are effective; and so forth. This places task demands on individuals and process demands on groups. Various organizational development techniques are available for reducing the time, effort, and monetary costs of these demands. Such methods include team building, laboratory training, and process consultation.

26. Organization development interventions within the EGM
     process should be tied to specific needs, be undertaken to
     accomplish specific goals, and have the cooperation of the
     participants.

     Just as the time between collecting the data and feedback
should be minimized (Guideline 21), the timing between feedback and taking action based on the feedback should be minimized.

27. EGM should minimize the delay between feedback and ac-
     tion. In general, EGM is more effective the shorter the
     time span between information collection, feedback, and
     use (see Guidelines 15 and 21).

H. Monitoring Strategies

     The purpose of monitoring the EGM process is to keep it
on track and redirect it if necessary. Monitoring and evaluating
increases the salience of the process and informs the participants about what elements are important. The monitors may be
consultants to the project, outside evaluators brought in for the
purpose, and/or the participants in the process.

28. EGM should be monitored and evaluated to answer the fol-
     lowing questions.
     • Has a clear purpose been identified and agreed to by
       the parties involved?
     • Is the information collected salient to the purpose, reli-
       able, and sufficient?
     • Is feedback given?
     • Are the action strategies developed based on the feed-
       back, and are they carried out?
     • Are the strategies effective?

     The first two questions require subjective judgment. The
goal should be to achieve consensus among those involved that a
clear picture has been identified and agreed to and that the information collected is salient. The third and fourth questions

are descriptive, asking whether feedback has in fact been given and whether action strategies have been developed. Answering these questions is basically a matter of reporting the occurrence of events. The fifth statement on effectiveness requires a statement of outcomes.

I. Outcomes

To a large extent, the desired outcomes should be evident when establishing the purposes of the EGM effort. In fact, these intended outcomes may be the precipitating factors for using EGM. That is, the reason for the effort is to bring about the outcomes. Effectiveness of EGM refers to generating positive outcomes. Earlier I stated that the information collected should describe organizational conditions and individual behaviors (Guideline 12). The outcomes of EGM are the changes in these variables over time.

More distant criteria may also be relevant. These may include employee behavior (withdrawal or level of participation), task performance, and adjustments in group structure. The possible functions of feedback reviewed above suggest other criteria including error correction, goal setting, and increased feelings of competence and control.

29. The criteria should be close to the variables of concern (closer conceptually and closer in time). The further the criteria are from concerns (remote conceptually and remote in time), the more they are likely to be affected by variables extraneous to the EGM process.

J. Role of the Consultant

The consultant may play an indispensable role in designing and conducting an EGM effort. Probably the most effective role is that of nondirective counselor. This role does not seek to influence by expressing a particular viewpoint but by clarifying and mirroring the views of the participants. As such, the consultant is a catalyst helping to overcome barriers.

30. Consultants should be nondirective in order to encourage the involvement of the sources and recipients of the information.

See Chapter Three's outline of consultant roles and ways to choose a consultant.

Appendix B:
Effectiveness of
Survey Feedback Programs

 Survey feedback is the process of feeding back attitude survey results to workgroups. Such efforts are usually one-shot events when the group meets to review and discuss survey results (Solomon, 1976; Gavin and Krois, 1983). Though the literature is replete with articles and books on how to conduct survey feedback (for example, Alderfer and Holbrook, 1973; Nadler, 1977; Bowers and Franklin, 1977), evaluations of the process have not always been positive. Often, the procedures are used in combination with other organizational development techniques, making it difficult to isolate the effects of survey feedback.

A number of positive outcomes may result from a survey feedback program (after Lawler, 1986).

1. Improvements in work methods and procedures may be suggested.
2. Attraction and retention of employees may improve if the data are used.
3. Output and quality may improve.

4. Decision making may improve as a result of better communication.
5. Group process and problem-solving skills may increase.

Potential negative effects may occur (also after Lawler, 1986):

1. Substantial training costs may be incurred.
2. Support personnel may increase if the organization runs its own program.
3. Unrealistic expectations for organizational change may occur, especially from implied promises. (For example, change may be implied merely by the survey questions—for instance, questions about personal development and growth.)
4. Middle managers may resist the process if they are evaluated on the results.
5. Lost time may occur if groups meet and the survey is completed at the workplace during work hours.

In a brief but excellent review of research on survey feedback interventions, Nadler (1976) concluded that survey feedback has positive effects in some situations and under certain conditions, and the process of collecting, analyzing, and using the data is an important determinant of the nature and extent of the effects. A crucial point is that processing feedback data seems to be more important than the content and collection of the data. Another important consideration is member participation in the process, particularly in the feedback stage, which is vital for the acceptance of the information. Nadler criticized the literature on grounds that there is almost no use of objective organizational data, with primary reliance on self-report from organizational members, and there is a lack of theory—especially a lack of models for the process of collecting and feeding back data (also see Salancik and Pfeffer, 1978). A computer search of the survey feedback literature revealed little evidence to suggest that the state of the art has changed in the eight years since Nadler's review appeared. (This point is also made by Terpstra, 1982.) Here I attempt to build a foundation for employee-guided management research and application, and for the importance of program evaluation in general as feedback to change agents on the success of their efforts. This foundation stems from the experimental research and theory on feedback.

In the past five years, there have been several major reviews of the value of feedback to individual and group performance. Each presents a theory and review of the literature on a different aspect of feedback. Ilgen, Fisher, and Taylor (1979) examined factors affecting how feedback is received by individuals. Such factors include the source of information, the nature of the message, and recipient characteristics. Nadler (1979) examined the effects of feedback on task group behavior. Ashford and Cummings (1983) showed how the recipient plays an active role in seeking feedback. Larson (1984) focused on the role of the source (specifically the supervisor) in giving performance feedback. These four articles provide insights into the dynamics of feedback processes that may be applied more generally to receiving and using information from different sources to guide and enhance a manager's actions. However, there is a need for an integration of the different perspectives in this literature. Each of the reviews is examined briefly below as a foundation for an integrated model of employee guided management.

Ilgen, Fisher, and Taylor (1979) explored the psychological processes affecting the contribution of feedback to effective role performance. The recipient's perception of feedback depends in part on characteristics of the source of feedback. Feedback serves to direct behavior and either to influence future performance goals (an incentive function) or to reward or punish (a reinforcement function). The source and message characteristics of feedback interact with how the recipient processes information. In this regard, Ilgen, Fisher, and Taylor examined how accurately feedback is perceived, its acceptance by the recipient, the willingness of the recipient to respond to the feedback, and the intended response. Information is likely to be perceived more accurately and be accepted when it comes soon after the behavior, when it is positive, when the feedback is frequent, and when the source of the feedback is viewed as having expertise, familiarity with the task, trustworthiness, and power (that is, control over valued outcomes). For feedback to be effective, the recipient must believe in his or her own competence to control the situation.

Nadler (1979) defined feedback as information about the actual performance or action of a system used to control the future actions of a system. He noted that research on feedback and group functioning is extremely fragmented and in need of integration. Feedback keeps goal-directed behavior on course, increases error detection, enhances individual learning, and increases motivation by demonstrating what behaviors contribute to successful performance. Feedback is more effective when it is specific. Though feedback to people individually is best at directing individual performance, group feedback is more effective when the group members depend on each other to complete the task, when group members have differentiated roles, when they are affiliation oriented, and when the nature of the information collected deals with group process (interpersonal relations or climate) aimed at helping the group work together more effectively. Evaluative feedback (positive or negative) helps group members form attributions about each other and about the group as a whole. The effects of group feedback depend on how it is used. For instance, feedback has a motivating effect if it increases the development of, and adherence to, group goals, and if the group receives help in using the feedback (for example, a good demonstration of how it should be used in problem solving). Group feedback may lead to affective outcomes, such as level of attraction to the group, and to cognitive outcomes, such as acceptance of group problems. It may also affect behavioral outcomes, such as task performance, membership behavior (for example, withdrawal and level of participation), and coping behavior.

Ashford and Cummings (1983) argued that it is necessary to understand feedback-seeking behavior to understand the feedback process. Individuals actively seek feedback while negotiating their organizational environments in pursuit of valued goals. The motivation to seek feedback stems from its potential functions of reducing uncertainty (by determining whether one's behavior is accurate and how it is evaluated), signaling the relative importance of various goals, creating the feeling of competence, allowing self-evaluation, and giving the person the chance to defend his or her ego. Ashford and Cummings point out that motivation to seek feedback is not entirely straightforward. For example, whereas feedback may be useful for correcting errors and reducing uncertainty, it may be dysfunctional if it threatens self-esteem. Indeed, low performers who need feedback most may be the most reluctant to seek it. Feedback may be obtained simply by monitoring the environment or by active inquiry. The strategy used to obtain feedback will depend on its costs in terms of effort, the possibility of losing face, and the amount and type of inferences required.

Larson (1984) considered factors influencing the source of feedback and how feedback is given, specifically with reference to supervisors giving performance feedback to subordinates. Regarding antecedents of feedback, a source should be more willing to give feedback information when the object of the feedback can control the results. More feedback is likely to be given when the results are positive, the source and recipient get along well, the information is salient (that is, perceived to be important), and the information discussed is tied to organizational rewards. The amount and quality of feedback will increase when the source of feedback is dependent on the recipient, the source is responsible for providing data, and when there are positive norms in the organization for giving feedback (for example, if there is a climate of open communication). Consequences of giving feedback are that it increases the salience of the information and the importance of the process. When feedback brings about a positive change, it may result in an increase in the amount of power and control felt by both the source and the recipient. Larson argued that two variables that are "prepotent" (that is necessary for effective feedback) are salience of the information and the recipient having control over the focus of the feedback.

REFERENCES

Alderfer, C. P., and Holbrook, J. "A New Design for Survey Feedback." *Education and Urban Society,* 1973, *5,* 437–464.

Ames, B. C. "Corporate Strategies for a Shrinking Market." *The Wall Street Journal,* Jan. 13, 1986, p. 26.

Anderson, G. "German Bosses Stress Consensus Decisions, Technical Know-How." *The Wall Street Journal,* Sept. 25, 1984, p. 1.

Ashford, S. J., and Cummings, L. L. "Feedback as an Individual Resource: Personal Strategies of Creating Information." *Organizational Behavior and Human Performance,* 1983, *32,* 320–398.

Bardwick, J. *The Plateauing Trap.* New York: AMACOM, 1986.

Bartunek, J. M., Gordon, J. R., and Weathersby, R. P. "Developing 'Complicated' Understanding in Administrators." *Academy of Management Review,* 1983, *8,* 273–284.

Beckhard, R. *Organizational Development: Strategies and Models.* Reading, Mass.: Addison-Wesley, 1969.

Beckhard, R., and Harris, R. T. *Organizational Transitions: Managing Complex Change.* Reading, Mass.: Addison-Wesley, 1977.

Beckhard, R., and Harris, R. T. *Organizational Transitions: Managing Complex Change.* (2nd ed.) Reading, Mass.: Addison-Wesley, 1987.

Bedeian, A. G. "Contemporary Challenges in the Study of Organizations." *Journal of Management,* 1986, *12,* 185–202.

Bellew, P. "Apple Computer Co-Founder Wozniak Will Leave Firm, Citing Disagreements." *The Wall Street Journal*, Feb. 7, 1985, p. 38.

Bennett, A. "Airline's Ills Point Out Weaknesses of Unorthodox Management Style." *The Wall Street Journal*, Aug. 11, 1986, p. 15.

Berg, E. N. "Can Troubled Trilogy Fulfill Its Dream?" *The New York Times*, July 8, 1984, pp. 1, 19.

Blacker, F., and Brown, C. "Evaluation and the Impact of Information Technologies on People in Organizations." *Human Relations*, 1985, *38*, 213–231.

Block, P. *The Empowered Manager*. San Francisco: Jossey-Bass, 1987.

Bowers, D. G., and Franklin, J. L. *Survey-Guided Development I: Data-Based Organizational Change*. La Jolla, Calif.: University Associates, 1977.

Boy Scouts of America. *Shaping Tomorrow*. Irving, Tex.: National Office, Boy Scouts of America, 1984.

Bulkeley, W. M. "Culture Shock: Two Computer Firms with Clashing Styles." *The Wall Street Journal*, July 6, 1987, pp. 1, 14.

Burck, C. G. "Will Success Spoil General Motors?" *Fortune*, Aug. 22, 1983, p. 100.

Burr, D. "People Express Grows Bigger Without Getting Fat." *The Wall Street Journal*, Jan. 7, 1985, p. 24.

Cascio, W. F. *Costing Human Resources*. New York: D. Van Nostrand, 1982.

Cascio, W. F., and Silbey, V. "Utility of the Assessment Center as a Selection Device." *Journal of Applied Psychology*, 1979, *64*, 107–118.

Cook, T. D., and Campbell, D. T. "The Design and Conduct of Quasi-Experiments and True Experiments in Field Settings." In M. D. Dunnette (ed.), *Handbook of Industrial and Organizational Psychology*. Skokie, Ill.: Rand McNally, 1976, pp. 223–326.

Dalton, D. R., and Tudor, W. D. "Unanticipated Consequences of Union–Management Cooperation: An Interrupted Time Series Analysis." *The Journal of Applied Behavioral Sciences*, 1984, *20*, 253–264.

Didsbury, H. F., Jr. (ed.). *The World of Work: Careers and Future.* Bethesda, Md.: World Future Society, 1983.

Digman, L. A. "How Well-Managed Organizations Develop Their Executives." *Organizational Dynamics,* Autumn 1978, pp. 63–80.

Easterbrook, G. "Have You Driven a Ford Lately?" *The Washington Monthly,* Oct. 1986.

Elkins, J. "Megatrends." Presentation at the New Jersey Institute for Management Studies, Parsippany, N.J., Jan. 23, 1985.

Ferris, G. R., Schellenberg, D. A., and Zammuto, R. F. "Human Resource Management Strategies in Declining Industries." *Human Resource Management,* 1984, *23,* 381–394.

Ferris, G. R., and Wagner, J. A., III. "Quality Circles in the United States: A Conceptual Reevaluation." *The Journal of Applied Behavioral Sciences,* 1985, *21,* 155–162.

Finkelstein, J., and Newman, D. "The Third Industrial Revolution: A Special Challenge to Managers." *Organizational Dynamics,* Summer 1984, pp. 53–65.

Foy, N. "Action Learning Comes to Industry." *Harvard Business Review,* Sept.–Oct. 1977, 158–168.

Gavin, J. F., and Krois, P. A. "Content and Process of Survey Feedback Sessions and Their Relation to Survey Responses: An Initial Study." *Group and Organization Studies,* 1983, *8,* 221–247.

Goodman, P. S. "Why Productivity Programs Fail: Reasons and Solutions." *National Productivity Review,* Autumn 1982, pp. 369–379.

Guzzo, R. A., Jette, R. D., and Katzell, R. A. "The Effects of Psychologically Based Intervention Programs on Worker Productivity: A Meta-Analysis." *Personnel Psychology,* 1985, *38,* 275–291.

Hall, D. T. "Project Work as an Antidote to Career Plateauing." *Human Resource Management,* 1985, *24,* 271–292.

Hammett, J. R. "The Changing Work Environment." *Employment Relations Today,* Autumn 1984, pp. 297–304.

Hampton, W. J., and Norman, J. R. "General Motors: What Went Wrong?" *Business Week,* Mar. 16, 1987, pp. 102–110.

Hannaway, J. "Managerial Behavior, Uncertainty, and Hierarchy: A Prelude to a Synthesis." *Human Relations*, 1985, *38* (11), 1085–1100.

Hayes, T. C. "Start-Up's Challenge: Rapid Growth." *The New York Times*, July 8, 1987, p. D6.

Henderson, C. "As AT&T Breaks up, a New Company Readies to Pick up the People." *Florida Trend*, Jan. 1984, pp. 79–82.

Hirschorn, L. *Beyond Mechanization: Work and Technology in a Post-Industrial Age.* Cambridge, Mass.: MIT Press, 1984.

Howard, A., and Bray, D. W. "Today's Young Managers: They Can Do It, but Will They?" *The Wharton Magazine*, 1981, *5* (4), 23–28.

Howard, R. *Brave New Workplace.* New York: Viking Penguin, 1986.

Huber, G. P. "The Nature and Design of Post-Industrial Organizations." *Management Science*, 1984, *30*, 928–951.

Huse, E. F. *Organization Development and Change.* St. Paul, Minn.: West, 1975.

Ilgen, D. R., Fisher, D. C., and Taylor, M. S. "Consequences of Individual Feedback on Behavior in Organizations." *Journal of Applied Psychology*, 1979, *64*, 349–371.

Isenberg, D. J. "The Tactics of Strategic Opportunism." *Harvard Business Review*, Mar.–Apr. 1987, pp. 92–97.

Kanter, R. M. *The Change Masters: Innovation for Productivity in the American Corporation.* New York: Simon & Schuster, 1983.

Katzell, R. A., and Guzzo, R. A. "Psychological Approaches to Productivity Improvement." *American Psychologist*, 1983, *38*, 468–472.

Kidder, T. *The Soul of a New Machine.* New York: Avon, 1981.

Kotter, J. P. *Power and Influence: Beyond Formal Authority.* New York: Macmillan, 1985.

Kreiling, J. "When the Chips Are Down, Play It Straight." *AT&T Journal*, July 1987, pp. 4–7.

Landen, D. L. *Beyond QC Circles.* 1982 Productivity Brief 12. Houston, Tex.: American Productivity Center, 1982.

Larson, J. R., Jr. "The Performance Feedback Process: A Preliminary Model." *Organizational Behavior and Human Performance*, 1984, *33*, 42–76.

Lawler, E. E., III. *High Involvement Management.* San Francisco: Jossey-Bass, 1986.

Lawler, E. E., III, and Mohrmann, S. "Quality Circles After the Fad." *Harvard Business Review,* Jan.–Feb. 1985, pp. 65–71.

Lehner, U. C. "With His Bid for EDS, GM's Smith Continues to Make Bold Changes." *The Wall Street Journal,* July 2, 1984, pp. 21, 24.

Lombardo, M. "Leadership Development." In M. London and E. M. Mone (eds.), *Career Growth and Human Resource Strategies.* Westport, Conn.: Quorum, forthcoming.

London, M. "Toward a Theory of Career Motivation." *Academy of Management Review,* 1983, *8* (4), 620–630.

London, M. *Developing Managers.* San Francisco: Jossey-Bass, 1985a.

London, M. "Employee-Guided Management: Steps for Involving Employees in Decisions and Actions." *Leadership and Organization Development Journal,* 1985b, *6,* 3–8.

London, M. "Organizational Support for Employees' Career Motivation." *Human Resource Planning,* forthcoming.

London, M., and MacDuffie, J. P. "Implementing Technological Innovations: Case Examples and Guidelines for Practice." *Personnel,* Nov. 1987, pp. 26–38.

London, M., and Mone, E. M. *Career Management and Survival in the Workplace.* San Francisco: Jossey-Bass, 1987.

London, M., and Stumpf, S. A. *Managing Careers.* Reading, Mass.: Addison-Wesley, 1982.

Lueck, T. "Why Jack Welch Is Changing GE." *The New York Times,* May 5, 1985, sec. 3, p. 1+.

McCall, M. W., Jr., and Lombardo, M. *Looking Glass, Inc.: An Organizational Simulation.* Technical Report No. 12. Greensboro, N.C.: Center for Creative Leadership, 1978.

Maccoby, M. "A New Way of Managing." *IEEE Spectrum,* June 1984, pp. 69–72.

Maccoby, M. "The New Generation of QWL." *QWL Resource Bulletin,* 1986, *3,* 1–3.

McGonagle, J. J., Jr. *Managing the Consultant: A Corporate Guide.* Radnor, Pa.: Chilton Books, 1981.

Mandel, T. F. *Scenarios and Corporate Strategy: Planning in Uncertain Times.* Stanford Research Institute, Research Report No. 669, Nov. 1982.

Manz, C. C., and Sims, H. P., Jr. "Leading Workers to Lead Themselves: The External Leadership of Self-Managing Work Teams." *Administrative Science Quarterly*, 1987, *32*, 106–128.

Manzini, A. O., and Gridley, J. D. *Integrating Human Resources and Strategic Business Planning.* New York: AMACOM, 1986.

Marks, M. L., and Mirvis, P. "Merger Syndrome: Stress and Uncertainty." *Mergers and Acquisitions,* Summer 1985, pp. 50–55.

Marlatt, G. A., and Gordon, J. R. "Determinants of Relapse: Implications for the Maintenance of Behavior Change." In P. O. Davidson and S. M. Davidson (eds.), *Behavioral Medicine: Changing Health Life Styles.* New York: Brunner/Mazel, 1980, pp. 410–452.

Martin, J. *Telematic Society: A Challenge for Tomorrow.* Englewood Cliffs, N.J.: Prentice-Hall, 1981.

Marx, R. D. "Relapse Prevention for Managerial Training: A Model for Maintenance of Behavior Change." *Academy of Management Review,* 1982, *7*, 433–441.

Mazany, T., and Humphrey, M. "The Role of Self-Evaluation in QWL System Maintenance." *The Work Life Review,* 1984, *3*, 3–10.

Miles, R., and Rosenberg, H. R. "The Human Resources Approach to Management: Second Generation Issues." *Organizational Dynamics,* Winter 1982, pp. 26–41.

Mirvis, P., and Marks, M. L. "Merger Syndrome: Management by Crisis." *Mergers and Acquisitions,* Jan.–Feb. 1986, pp. 70–76.

Mitroff, I. I. "Two Fables for Those Who Believe in Rationality." *Technological Forecasting and Social Change,* 1985, *28* (3), 195–202.

Mumford, A. "Action Learning." *The Journal of Management Development,* 1987, *6* (2), 3–4 (special issue).

Nadler, D. A. "Using Feedback for Organizational Change: Promises and Pitfalls." *Group and Organization Studies,* 1976, *1*, 177–186.

Nadler, D. A. *Feedback and Organization Development: Using Data Based Methods.* Reading, Mass.: Addison-Wesley, 1977.

Nadler, D. A. "The Effects of Feedback on Task Group Behavior: A Review of the Experimental Research." *Organizational Behavior and Human Performance*, 1979, *23*, 309–338.

Naisbitt, J. *The Year Ahead: 1985.* Washington, D.C.: The Naisbitt Group, 1984.

Ottaway, R. N. "The Change Agent: A Taxonomy in Relation to the Change Process." *Human Relations*, 1983, *36*, 361–392.

Ramsing, K. D., and Blair, J. D. "An Expression of Concern About Quality Circles." In K. H. Chung (ed.), *Academy of Management Proceedings* (42nd Annual Meeting). Wichita, Kans.: Academy of Management, 1982.

Reich, C. "The Innovator." *The New York Times Magazine,* Apr. 21, 1985, pp. 29+.

Reich, R. B. *The Next American Frontier.* New York: Time Books, 1983.

Rimer, S. "The Airline That Shook the Industry." *The New York Times Magazine,* Dec. 23, 1984, pp. 18+.

Roth, T. "Employee Involvement Gains Support." *The Wall Street Journal,* Dec. 12, 1986, p. 1.

Salancik, G. R., and Pfeffer, J. A. "A Social Information Processing Approach to Job Attitudes and Task Design." *Administrative Science Quarterly*, 1978, *23*, 224–253.

Schlender, B. R. "Calculated Move: Apple Tries to Achieve Stability but Remain Creative." *The Wall Street Journal,* July 16, 1987, pp. 1, 10.

Schuler, R. S., and MacMillan, I. C. "Gaining Competitive Advantage Through Human Resource Management Practices." *Human Resource Management*, 1984, *23*, 241–255.

Solomon, R. J. "An Examination of the Relationship Between a Survey Feedback Technique and the Work Environment." *Personnel Psychology*, 1976, *29*, 583–594.

Stumpf, S. A. "Business Simulations for Skill Diagnosis and Development." In M. London and E. M. Mone (eds.), *Career Growth and Human Resource Strategies.* Westport, Conn.: Quorum, forthcoming.

Sutton, R. I., Eisenhardt, K. M., and Jucker, J. V. "Managing Organizational Decline: Lessons from Atari." *Organizational Dynamics,* Spring 1986, pp. 17–29.

Terpstra, D. E. "Evaluating Selected Organization Development Interventions: The State of the Art." *Group and Organization Studies*, 1982, *7*, 402–417.

Tornatzky, L. G., and others. *The Process of Technological Innovation: Reviewing the Literature.* Washington, D.C.: National Science Foundation, 1983.

Tsui, A. S., and Milkovich, G. T. "Personnel Department Activities: Constituency Perspectives and Preferences." *Personnel Psychology*, 1987, *40* (3), 519–538.

Tushman, M. L., Newman, W. H., and Romanelli, E. "Human Resources Special Report." *The Career Center Bulletin*, 1985, *5* (2), 6–13.

U.S. Bureau of Labor Statistics. *Handbook of Labor Statistics.* Washington, D.C.: U.S. Bureau of Labor Statistics, 1985.

Weathersby, R. P. "Education for Adult Development: The Components of Qualitative Change." *New Directions for Higher Education*, 1980, *29*, 9–22.

Weick, K. *The Social Psychology of Organizing.* (2nd ed.) Reading, Mass.: Addison-Wesley, 1979.

Wexley, K. N., and Baldwin, T. T. "Management Development." *Journal of Management*, 1986, *12*, 277–274.

Wysocki, B., Jr. "The Chief's Personality Can Have a Big Impact—for Better or Worse." *The Wall Street Journal*, Sept. 10, 1984, pp. 1, 12.

Yankelovich, D., and Immerwahr, J. "The Emergence of Expressivism Will Revolutionize the Contract Between Workers and Employers." *Personnel Administrator*, Dec. 1983, p. 34.

Zonana, V. F. "Flying High: Montgomery Securities Uses Flash and Brass to Expand Its Business." *The Wall Street Journal*, Jan. 3, 1985, pp. 1, 8.

INDEX

281